ASSESSING LINGUISTIC ARGUMENTS

Edited by

JESSICA R. WIRTH
University of Wisconsin–Milwaukee

HEMISPHERE PUBLISHING CORPORATION

Washington   London

A HALSTED PRESS BOOK

JOHN WILEY & SONS

New York   London   Sydney   Toronto

Hemisphere Publishing Corporation
1025 Vermont Ave., N.W., Washington, D.C. 20005

Distributed solely by Halsted Press, a Division of John Wiley & Sons, Inc., New York

1 2 3 4 5 6 7 8 9 0   M I M I   7 8 3 2 1 0 9 8 7 6

Library of Congress Cataloging in Publication Data

Main entry under title:

Assessing linguistic arguments.

Papers from the 4th annual linguistic foundation symposium held at the University of Wisconsin–Milwaukee, May 9–10, 1975.
  Includes indexes.
  1. Linguistics—Methodology—Congresses.
I. Wirth, Jessica R.
P126.A8   410   76-25529
ISBN 0-470-98916-5
Printed in the United States of America

CONTENTS

PREFACE

The nature of linguistic argumentation was the theme of the fourth annual linguistic foundations symposium* at the University of Wisconsin-Milwaukee May 9-10, 1975. This volume includes the revised versions of the papers presented and discussed there, with the addition of three other papers relevant to the theme of the symposium: those by Myrna Gopnik, Michael Kac, and the introductory paper by Rudolf Botha.

The existence of several theoretical disputes in generative-transformational grammar (e.g., the controversies over the abstractness of underlying forms postulated in phonology and syntax) has given rise to questions regarding the correctness of

*The first three symposia dealt with delineating the domain of grammars, explanation in linguistics, and testing linguistic hypotheses. The papers from the symposium on delineating the domain of grammars are collected in the volume *Limiting the Domain of Grammar* (edited by D. Cohen, UWM Bookstore); the papers from the explanation and testing conferences appear in the volumes *Explaining Linguistic Phenomena* (edited by D. Cohen, Hemisphere Publishing Corporation, 1974) and *Testing Linguistic Hypotheses* (edited by D. Cohen and J. Wirth, Hemisphere Publishing Corporation, 1975).

the methodology and reasoning utilized in transformational linguistics. The symposium, accordingly, was addressed to an examination of argument types currently used in linguistics. It is hoped that careful examination of linguistic methodology will bring to light some of the bases for the current theoretical disputes and thereby help guide productive research in linguistics.

The papers in this volume may be studied through a perspective suggested by Chapter 1, in which Botha raises several questions that must be answered to evaluate analyses of linguistic argumentation. The remaining chapters contain discussions of linguistic argumentation that raise a number of fundamental questions in linguistic methodology and suggest some answers:

Chapter 2: Are general statements about the properties of underlying forms empirical generalizations? If not, are arguments that use such generalizations as crucial premises valid?

Chapter 3: What are the properties of those valid arguments whose conclusions require the postulation of abstract structures? Is transformational grammar a theory of language or a (meta)language for the representation of observation statements about natural language?

Chapter 4: Are the strong conclusions usually drawn from arguments like the "Hallean syllogism" really warranted? In particular, in the comparison of alternative theories of language, if it is demonstrated that one theory captures generalizations that an alternative theory does not, does such a demonstration suffice to show the falsity of the other theory? If not, what additional assumptions are necessary for such a conclusion to be justified?

Chapter 5: What is required for a particular grammatical hypothesis to have "independent motivation"? Can one appeal to "independent motivation," as usually used in the justification of particular grammatical hypotheses, to justify one theory of grammatical form over another?

Chapter 6:   Can the schools of "generative semantics" and "interpretive semantics" be distinguished as having distinct views of science? Do their methods of argumentation differ, and if so, do they differ in virtue of distinct views of science?

Chapter 7:   Is aesthetics the sole basis for the acceptance of one hypothesis over another?

Chapter 8:   Given that the generative-interpretive controversy is a debate over the form of grammars, what types of arguments are and are not capable of resolving the controversy?

Chapter 9:   Are the parameters selected as relevant to the explanation of language facts arbitrarily chosen? Is the particular choice of such parameters an empirical decision or not?

Chapter 10:   What type of argumentation is necessary to determine the proper characterization of dialectal and language differences?

These papers are published in the hope of stimulating additional fruitful research into the properties of arguments used in linguistics.

This volume should be of interest to linguists, psychologists, and philosophers of science, and any scholar concerned with methodology and reasoning in an empirical science.

ACKNOWLEDGMENTS

The symposium was funded by grants from the following sources:

1. The Graduate School of the University of Wisconsin-Milwaukee
2. The Office of the Dean, College of Letters and Science, the University of Wisconsin-Milwaukee
3. The Lectures Committee, the University of Wisconsin-Milwaukee
4. The Departments of Linguistics and Philosophy, the University of Wisconsin-Milwaukee

The UWM Linguistics Group gratefully acknowledges receipt of these grants.

Discussion at the symposium was enhanced by a panel of invited discussants, whose comments contributed to refinements of the papers for publication. I take this opportunity to thank the discussants for their participation in the conference: Daniel Dinnsen (Linguistics, Indiana University), Sidney Greenbaum (English, University of Wisconsin-Milwaukee), David Halitsky (Linguistics, New York University), Kathleen Houlihan (Linguistics, University of Minnesota), Larry Martin (Linguistics, University of Iowa), Kenneth Miner (Wisconsin Native American Languages Project, University of Wisconsin-Milwaukee), Linda Norman (Linguistics, Indiana University), Peter Schreiber (English, University of Wisconsin-Madison), Linda Wessels (Philosophy, University of Wisconsin-Milwaukee).

I would also like to express many thanks to Fred Eckman, James Clark, and Rachel Kapp for their help in organizing the symposium, to Robert Hanson and Marvin Loflin for their enthusiastic support, and to the rest of the symposium participants for engaging in stimulating debate.

1

On the analysis of linguistic argumentation

Rudolf P. Botha
University of Stellenbosch
Stellenbosch, South Africa

1. DOING A "NONNORMAL" SORT OF THING

This volume brings together a number of papers that present attempts by linguists to analyze, in a deliberate manner, the nature of linguistic argumentation. Now, to analyze the nature of linguistic argumentation in a deliberate manner is, in a sense, a "nonnormal" thing for linguists to do. To show in what sense, let me briefly indicate the "normal" sort of manner in which linguists are involved in linguistic science. Linguists are in the first place scholars who *do* linguistic science, who *perform* linguistic science. Only in a second (or further) place are linguists scholars who *think* about, *talk* about, and, maybe, *worry* about the nature of linguistic science. In a nutshell, then: "Normally," linguists are oriented toward uncovering the nature of human language, not the nature of linguistic science. And, to attempt to analyze in a deliberate manner the nature of linguistic argumentation is to attempt to uncover an aspect of

1

the nature of linguistic science. This is why deliberately analyzing the nature of linguistic argumentation may aptly be said to be a "nonnormal" sort of thing for linguists to do.

I come now to the first major question to be considered in the present chapter.

(1)   Why is it that a growing number of linguists—among them the contributors to the present volume—are doing the apparently "nonnormal" sort of thing of undertaking deliberate analyses of the nature of linguistic argumentation?[1]

The basis for an answer to this question is to be found in the current state of development of theoretical linguistics. This state may be characterized as that of suffering a "foundational crisis."[2] The fact that present-day theoretical linguistics is suffering a foundational crisis is reflected by the various fundamental sorts of disagreement among contemporary linguists. Let us consider some of these sorts of mutual disagreement as they exist among linguists all of whom, at a given stage, were working within the framework of a fairly homogeneous paradigm of transformational generative grammar. These linguists currently find themselves in mutual disagreement about questions such as what the goals of linguistic theories are, what the fundamental problems of linguistics are, what problematic data should be included within the scope of linguistic theories, what fundamental conceptual categories should be adopted for giving an account of the problematic data, what constitutes an acceptable solution to a linguistic problem, and so on.[3] These sorts of disagreement among linguists have caused the once fairly homogeneous paradigm of transformational generative grammar to fragmentize.[4] At the level of the general linguistic theory, this process of paradigm fragmentation over the past decade has yielded, in American linguistics alone, the following diversity of views:

(2)   a. In the domain of syntax–semantics: Such (partial) theories as two major variants of interpretive semantics, lexicalist syntax, various articulations of classical generative semantics, case grammar, humanistic linguistics,

     intuitive grammar, nonformal grammar, relational grammar, nondiscrete grammar, and Montague grammar.

b. In the domain of phonology: Such (partial) theories as the various variants of classical generative phonology—including, among others, abstract phonology, concrete phonology, "ordered" phonology, "nonordered" phonology—as well as markedness phonology and the various articulations of natural phonology.

Many of the (partial) theories listed in (2) have, of course, been rivals. In a given field of scientific inquiry, such a proliferation of rival (partial) theories is symptomatic of a foundational crisis.

It is now possible to develop an answer to the question why a growing number of linguists has started doing an apparently "nonnormal" sort of thing, that is, undertaking analyses of a deliberate sort of the nature of linguistic argumentation. It is in the face of foundational crises that scholars start doing sorts of things which appear to be "nonnormal." Kuhn (1970), in his capacity of historian of science, has advocated the following view:

> It is, I think, particularly in periods of acknowledged crises that scientists have turned to philosophical analysis as a device for unlocking the riddles of their field. Scientists have not generally needed or wanted to be philosophers. Indeed, normal science usually holds creative philosophy at arm's length, and probably for good reasons. To the extent that normal research work can be conducted by using the paradigm as a model, rules and assumptions need not be made explicit. In section V we noted that the full set of rules sought by philosophical analysis need not even exist. But this is not to say that the search for assumptions (even for non-existent ones) cannot be an effective way to weaken the grip of tradition upon the mind and to suggest the basis for a new one. It is no accident that the emergence of Newtonian physics in the seventeenth century and of relativity and quantum mechanics in the twentieth should have been both preceded and accompanied by fundamental philosophical analyses of the contemporary research tradition. (Kuhn, 1970, p. 88)

Notice that the analysis of a form of argumentation is not a sort of linguistic analysis. It is essentially a sort of philosophical analysis. With this fact in mind, we can now derive from these quoted remarks by Kuhn an answer to the question of (1) above. The answer is this: Linguists have turned to the deliberate analysis of the nature of linguistic argumentation as a device for isolating the causes of the crisis in their field, as a device for bringing order to their field, or, in Kuhn's words, "as a device for unlocking the riddles of their field."

Suppose that Kuhn is correct in this interpretation as to the role played by philosophical analysis in scientific inquiry. Then linguists are doing a sort of thing which is only apparently, and not really, "nonnormal." For, then, it is "normal" for scientists working in a period of crisis to undertake philosophical analyses. Thus, for linguists to do the "nonnormal" sort of thing of deliberately analyzing the nature of linguistic argumentation is really, in the present period of crisis, to do a "normal" sort of thing.

In connection with the "normal nonnormal" sort of thing which linguists are currently doing, an obvious second question arises:

(3) What does it entail to analyze the nature of linguistic argumentation?

Let us make the following, not overly controversial, assumption: The analysis of the nature of linguistic argumentation proceeds in terms of the analysis of individual linguistic arguments. Against the background of this assumption the general question of (3) may be broken down into the following five narrower questions:

(4) a. What are the specific aims set for analyses of linguistic arguments?
b. What are the nature and properties of analyses of linguistic arguments?
c. What are the conceptual instruments needed for carrying out analyses of linguistic arguments?
d. What are the standards of adequacy that analyses of linguistic arguments have to satisfy?
e. What are the reasons for which proposed analyses of linguistic arguments may fail to satisfy the standards alluded to in (4d) above?

In a chapter having the restricted scope of the present one, it is impossible to consider each of the questions of (4) in depth. Instead of dealing with each of these questions in a superficial manner, I will discuss the first one, (4a), in some depth. I will do this with two objectives in mind:

(5) a. to show what specific aims linguists have set for their analyses of linguistic arguments, and
     b. to indicate for each of the chapters included in the present volume which of these specific aims it pursues.

I hope that the discussion of these two general points will provide a perspective from which the chapters of the present volume may be studied. This perspective will, however, be incomplete. In order to provide a full perspective on these chapters, the questions of (4b–e) would have to be dealt with in a nonsuperficial manner as well.

Let us now consider seven of the aims that linguists have pursued in their analyses of linguistic arguments. It will become clear that the pursuit of only some of these aims has contributed directly to our understanding of the nature of linguistic argumentation.[5]

2. EVALUATING "SUBSTANTIVE" ARGUMENT FORMS

Unlike logicians such as Copi, linguists have not operated with a single, narrow concept "argument form." At least two, distinct, concepts "argument form" figure in linguists' analyses of linguistic arguments.[6] First, linguists have taken an argument form to be a "type" or "class" of arguments that is distinct, in a substantive linguistic sense, from other "types" or "classes" of arguments. Such a "substantive" argument form is taken to be a distinct entity in virtue of the fact that a particular sort of substantive linguistic claim is made in its conclusion, in its major premiss, or in (one of) its minor premisses. Second, linguists have taken an argument form to be a "type" or "class" of arguments that is distinct, in some philosophical sense, from other "types" or "classes" of arguments. Such a "philosophical" argument form is taken to be a distinct entity in virtue of the fact that one or more of its component parts have a special logical, epistemological, or methodological property.

In principle, a distinction may be drawn between three types of "substantive" argument forms. The first incorporates a special sort of substantive linguistic claim in its conclusion, the second in its major premiss, and the third in (one of) its minor premisses. Let us consider the first of these subtypes with reference to the following substantive linguistic claims discussed by Postal (1968, p. 81).

(6) a. "Segments are normally non-Implosive."
     b. "Vowels are normally non-Nasal."
     c. "Non-Grave (front) vowels are normally non-Rounded; non-Compact (not low); Grave (back) vowels are nor-mally Rounded."
     d. "Consonants are normally non-Glottalized."
     e. "Consonants are normally non-Pharyngealized."

These claims (6a–e) are all of the same substantive linguistic sort: They are claims about the relative naturalness of pho-nological segments. All individual linguistic arguments which, in their conclusion, make a claim of this substantive sort may be considered instances of the same "substantive" argument form: They are naturalness arguments. Analogously, all individual linguistic arguments which, in their conclusion, assert or deny the existence of a transformational relationship between two types of sentences are instances of the same "substantive" argument form: They are transformational arguments.[7] In short, every substantively distinct sort of conclusion proposition de-fines a distinct "substantive" argument form.

Second, consider now the arguments that Postal (1968, p. 81) presents for the two naturalness claims of (6a) and (b).

(7) a. "*Segments are normally non-Implosive.* Hence there are no languages with only Implosive segments, although languages with only non-Implosive segments are found everywhere."
     b. "*Vowels are normally non-Nasal.* Hence there are no

languages with only Nasal vowels, although languages with only oral vowels are common."

The two linguistic arguments (7a) and (b) contain the same substantive linguistic claim as their major premiss, that is, as their "inference-licence."[8] This major premiss may be reconstructed as follows:

(8) If languages that have a given segment are common, whereas no languages occur that use the "opposite" segment, then the former segment is more normal, that is, natural, than the latter.

According to Postal (1968, p. 169), the substantive linguistic claim is "an assertion about relative generality in distribution among the entire class of languages." All individual linguistic arguments that incorporate this sort of claim in the form of a major premiss constitute instances of a single "substantive" argument form: They are relative-frequency arguments.

Analogously, when used as major premisses in linguistic arguments, each of the following two linguistic claims defines a distinct "substantive" argument form:

(9) a. If two given sentences are paraphrases of one another, then it may be the case that they are transformationally related.
     b. If two given sentences exhibit the same cooccurrence restrictions, then it may be the case that they are transformationally related.

The "substantive" argument forms defined by (9a) and (b) are discussed by Bach (1974, pp. 166ff.) in some detail. The general point is clear: Every substantively distinct major premiss defines a distinct "substantive" argument form.

Third, we come now to the third type of "substantive" argument forms: that incorporating a special sort of substantive linguistic claim in (one of) its minor premisses. Consider the following three sorts of substantive linguistic claims:

(10) a. Whereas the sentence S_1 is grammatical/ambiguous, the sentence S_2 is ungrammatical/nonambiguous.
   b. Whereas in the earlier stage S_1 of the language L there occurred the linguistic forms $F_1, F_2, \ldots, F_n$, in the later stage S_2 there occurred the related but distinct linguistic forms $f_1, f_2, \ldots, f_n$.
   c. Whereas the dialect D_1 of the language L has the rule R, the dialect D_2 of L has the related but distinct rule r.

Linguistic arguments that incorporate, in the form of minor premisses, linguistic claims of the substantive sort of (10a) present intuitive evidence for their conclusions. Such arguments are instances of a distinct "substantive" argument form: intuitive arguments. Linguistic arguments that incorporate, in the form of minor premisses, linguistic claims of the substantive sort of (10b) present diachronic evidence for their conclusions. These arguments are instances of a distinct "substantive" argument form: diachronic arguments. Finally, linguistic arguments that incorporate, in the form of minor premisses, linguistic claims of the substantive sort of (10c) present dialectal evidence for their conclusions. These arguments instantiate a "substantive" form of argument that may be called dialectal arguments. The general point here is that every substantively distinct form of evidence, presented in the minor premisses of linguistic arguments, defines a distinct "substantive" argument form.

   Having clarified the notion "'substantive' argument form," it is now possible to state a first aim that linguists have set for their analyses of linguistic arguments:

(11) *the aim of identifying and evaluating "substantive" argu-ment forms used in linguistic inquiry.*

Schane's contribution to the present volume illustrates the manner in which the aim of (11) may be pursued. Let us consider two examples of the "substantive" argument forms analyzed by Schane. The first example incorporates, in the major premiss of its instances, the following linguistic claim:

   Of several competing [synchronic grammatical, R. P. B.] descriptions, the one which will explain most insightfully the direction in which language is *headed* is to be preferred. (Schane, 1976, p. 172)

The second example incorporates, in the major premiss of its instances, the following linguistic claim:

an abstract representation must be equivalent to one of its allomorphs (Schane, 1976, p. 176)

When analyzing the nature of linguistic arguments and linguistic argumentation linguists, in fact, more often than not deal with "substantive" argument forms. Let us consider a few typical examples of such analyses to be found in recent literature.

(12)   a. *"Substantive" argument forms defined in terms of a particular substantive sort of conclusion*: the analysis by Bach (1974, pp. 166ff.) of arguments all of which, in their conclusion, postulate a transformational relationship between sentences; the analyses by Botha (1968, sec. 3.5.3.2; 1971a, chap. 4; 1973, chap. 3) of arguments which, in their conclusion, make mentalistic linguistic claims.

b. *"Substantive" argument forms defined in terms of a particular substantive sort of major premiss*: the analysis by Bach of arguments incorporating as their major premisses such claims as (9a) and (b) above; the analysis by McCawley (1973; pp. 87–88) of syntactic arguments incorporating as their major premiss the claim that transformations apply "blindly"; the analysis by Partee (1971) of syntactic arguments incorporating, as their major premiss, the claim that transformations preserve meaning.

c. *"Substantive" argument forms defined in terms of a particular substantive sort of linguistic evidence presented in their minor premisses*: analyses by Bach (1974, sec. 7.71), Botha (1973, sec. 5.2), Derwing (1973, sec. 7.3), Labov (1972), and Leech (1968) of arguments presenting intuitive evidence for their conclusions; analyses by Botha (1971a, chap. 4; 1971b;

1973, chaps. 3, 4) of arguments presenting various sorts of external linguistic evidence for their conclusions—including diachronic evidence, dialectal evidence, idiolectal evidence, sociolinguistic evidence, and neuropsychological evidence.

These examples, of course, are not presented as an exhaustive list of analyses by linguists of "substantive" argument forms used in linguistic inquiry. Clearly, however, analyses of "substantive" argument forms can, if adequate, contribute in a direct manner to our understanding of a particular aspect of the nature of linguistic argumentation. Adequate analyses of these argument forms reveal the manner in which linguists' views about natural languages are integrated into the substantive fabric of linguistic argumentation. Moreover, analyses of this sort may show where this substantive fabric is weak and where it is not so weak.

3. EVALUATING "PHILOSOPHICAL" ARGUMENT FORMS

Recall that, for the purpose of the present discussion, a "philosophical" argument form is regarded as a distinct entity in the sense that it has a special philosophical property. This philosophical property may characterize either a given structural component of the argument form or the argument form as a whole.

A distinction may be drawn between three types of "philosophical" argument forms analyzed by linguists. "Philosophical" argument forms of the first type constitute distinct entities in virtue of the fact that their major premises are formulated in terms of such philosophical notions as "evidential independence," "independent motivation," "refutability," "explanatory power," "predictive success," "simplicity," "generality," and so on. "Philosophical" argument forms of the second type exist as separate entities in virtue of the fact that one or another epistemological property—for example, doubtful relevance, (non-)evidentness, (non-)probability—characterize one of their structural components. "Philosophical" argument forms of the third type are defined as distinct entities in terms of the logical relation—entailment, support, and so on—which they incorporate. "Philosophical" argument forms of this third type represent the argument forms of logic discussed in the Appendix to the present chapter.

This brings us to a second aim that linguists have pursued in analyzing linguistic arguments:

(13) *the aim of identifying and evaluating "philosophical" argument forms used in linguistic inquiry.*

Several analyses of linguistic arguments pursuing the aim of (13) appear in recent literature.

First, consider analyses dealing with "philosophical" argument forms of the first type mentioned above. In the present volume the chapters by Perloff and Wirth and by Sadock present analyses with the aim of (13). Perloff and Wirth analyze a "philosophical" argument form whose major premiss is formulated in terms of a notion of "independent motivation":

> In contemporary linguistics a style of argument has begun to play an increasingly important role. That style of argument claims that a proposal or hypothesis is independently motivated. Since different linguists use arguments from independent motivation in different ways, it seems to us to be of some importance to undertake an analysis of independent motivation, and to see how that style of argument is to be assessed. (Perloff and Wirth, 1976, p. 95)[9]

Sadock, in turn, analyzes a "philosophical" argument form in whose major premiss the notion "capturing/missing (significant) generalizations" plays a key role:

> The famous argument against autonomous phonemics given by Halle (1959) has become a model for generative grammatical methodology. Several attempts to copy it (including one by the present author) have been made, usually with the same intent: to demonstrate one linguistic model to be superior to another. Here I wish to examine that argument form on its philosophical merits. I will attempt to demonstrate that the conclusion that Halle came to was too strong, and that, in general, the conclusions which generative grammarians reach on the basis of arguing from the loss or capture of generalizations are too strong. (Sadock, 1976, p. 85)[10]

Botha, moreover, has attempted a substantial number of analyses of "philosophical" argument forms of the type under consideration. Thus, Botha (1973, chap. 6) presents analyses of "philosophical" argument forms that appeal in their major premisses to such distinctions and concepts as "*consistent with* vs. *explained by*," "*represent* vs. *explain*," "width of explanatory scope," "predictive success/failure," "prediction vs. explanation," "ad hocness/uniqueness," "absence of disconfirming evidence," "strength and interestingness," "strength and refutability," "*empirical* vs. *notational*," "restricted descriptive latitude," "conceptual redundancy," "conceptual homogeneity," "simplicity/economy/elegance," "heuristic fruitfulness," "absence of alternative theories," "counter-intuitiveness," and so on. The discussion by Zwicky (1970a) of the Free-Ride Principle is a further example of an analysis of a "philosophical" argument form used in linguistic inquiry.

Second, consider now analyses of "philosophical" argument forms of the second type provided for above. Kac's (1976) contribution to the present volume contains, among other things, an analysis of syntactic arguments that instantiate this second type of "philosophical" argument form. He analyzes and evaluates syntactic arguments whose conclusions are constructed in terms of "abstract constructs" which constitute "fictions" rather than "valid abstractions." In addition, Kac discusses syntactic arguments in whose conclusions "hypothetical constructs"—whether "valid" or "fictitious"—are allegedly confused with "observational representations."

Botha (1973) analyzes two such "philosophical" argument forms used in linguistic inquiry: external arguments and internal arguments. External arguments have the distinctive property that, whereas their minor premisses—the propositions presenting the evidence for the conclusion—are relevant to their conclusions logically, it is doubtful whether these minor premisses are relevant to their conclusions qualitatively as well. In the case of internal arguments, apparently, the minor premisses are both logically and qualitatively relevant to their conclusions. These two "philosophical" argument forms are systematically related to certain "substantive" argument forms used in linguistic inquiry. Thus, arguments that present diachronic evidence for a synchronic linguistic claim are typical instances of external arguments. And, arguments that present intuitive evidence for synchronic linguistic claims instantiate internal arguments.

Third, analyses of "philosophical" argument forms of the third type are mentioned in the Appendix to the present paper in connection with the distinction between the logical concepts "argument" and "argument form." Botha (1973) presents an analysis of several of these "philosophical" argument forms: confirmatory arguments, defined in terms of a logical relation of progressive reduction; explanatory arguments, defined in terms of a logical relation of regressive reduction; generalizing arguments, defined in terms of a logical relation of simple induction; and demonstrative arguments, defined in terms of a logical relation of deduction.

As is the case with analyses of "substantive" argument forms, analyses of "philosophical" argument forms can, if adequate, contribute in a direct manner to the understanding of the nature of linguistic argumentation. Analyses of the latter sort lay bare the logical, epistemological, and methodological concepts, distinctions, and principles that jointly constitute the philosophical backbone of linguistic argumentation.

The majority of analyses by linguists of argument forms used in linguistic inquiry may be classified as analyses either of "substantive" or of "philosophical" argument forms. In a few cases, however, this classification is not possible. In his contribution to the present volume, Dougherty (1976, sec. 4) draws a distinction between "the *theory-comparison* argument form" and "the *theory-exposition* argument form." These two "argument forms" cannot be viewed either as "substantive" or as "philosophical." In fact, it is not clear what the expression "argument form" means for Dougherty if it does not mean something like "research strategy."[11]

4. RECONSTRUCTING THE LOGIC OF JUSTIFICATION OF LINGUISTIC INQUIRY

The preference expressed by Chomsky (1972b) for the lexicalist position over the transformationalist position relates to, among other things, differences in productivity between gerundive and derived nominalization. In the course of presenting his motivation for this preference of his, Chomsky makes the following statements:

> Summarizing these observations, we see that the lexicalist hypothesis explains a variety of facts of the sort illustrated by examples (6) through (10) (in part, in conjunction with other assumptions about underlying structures, such as (12)). The transformationalist hypothesis is no doubt consistent with these facts, but it derives no support from them, since it would also be consistent with the discovery, were it a fact, that derived nominals exist in all cases in which we have gerundive nominals. Hence the facts that have been cited give strong empirical support to the lexicalist hypothesis and no support to the transformationalist hypothesis. Other things being equal, then, they would lead us to accept the lexicalist hypothesis, from which these facts follow.[12] (Chomsky, 1972b, p. 6)

The noncomplex statements that Chomsky makes in this excerpt may be presented in the following two lists:

(14)   Statements about the Transformational Hypothesis
   a. The transformationalist hypothesis is no doubt consistent with the facts.
   b. The transformationalist hypothesis derives no support from the facts.
   c. The transformationalist hypothesis would also be consistent with "other" facts.
   d. The facts give no support to the transformationalist hypothesis.

(15)   Statements about the Lexicalist Hypothesis
   a. The lexicalist hypothesis explains a variety of the facts.
   b. The facts give strong empirical support to the lexicalist hypothesis.
   c. The facts follow from the lexicalist hypothesis.
   d. The facts would lead us to accept the lexicalist hypothesis.

Two crucial questions arise in connection with Chomsky's statements as listed in (14) and (15).

(16)   a. What, precisely, is Chomsky asserting in each of these statements?

b. Are these assertions true or false?

In order to be able to answer these two questions, it is necessary to determine, among other things, the content that the following concepts have in generative grammar.

(17) a. "being consistent with"—see (14) (a) and (c)
      b. "deriving no support from"—see (14) (b)
      c. "giving no support to"—see (14) (d)
      d. "explaining X"—see (15) (a)
      e. "giving strong empirical support to"—see (15) (b)
      f. "following from"—see (15) (c)
      g. "leading to accept"—see (15) (d)

To determine the content of the concepts listed in (17) is no trivial matter. To see this, consider, for example, Chomsky's compound assertion—not listed in (14) or (15)—that the transformationalist hypothesis is *consistent with* the fact that the derived nominals of (8) in note 12 do not occur but that it would also be *consistent with* the fact, were it one, that these nominals do occur. Clearly, the fact that these derived nominals do not occur and the "fact" that they do occur are two mutually exclusive facts. How, then, is it possible for a hypothesis to be consistent with both of two mutually exclusive facts? What content must the concept "consistent with" have in order for Chomsky's statement under consideration not to be internally contradictory? It is striking that in the opinion of McCawley (1973, p. 5)—who defends a variant of the transformationalist hypothesis—the fact that the derived nominals in question do not occur *conflicts with* the transformationalist hypothesis.[13]

The concepts listed above in (17) denote closely interrelated aspects of the logic of justification of generative grammar. In order to determine the content of these—and related other—concepts, the nature and properties of this logic of justification must be clarified. This can be done by setting a third aim for analyses of linguistic arguments:

(18) *the aim of reconstructing the logic of justification of linguistic inquiry.*

The aim of (18) can be broken down into the narrower aims of determining what the component parts of this logic of justification are, of explicitly describing each of these component parts, of ascertaining and explicitly specifying the nature of the interrelatedness of the component parts, of determining why these component parts are interrelated in the manner in which they are, and of uncovering the limitations and potentialities of the component parts of this logic of justification. Botha (1973) has made an attempt to reconstruct an aspect of the logic of justification of transformational generative grammar. Through an analysis of a large number of linguistic arguments, he deals with the aspect of this logic of justification that may be reconstructed in terms of various nondemonstrative argument forms, associated conditions of evidence, and associated acceptability standards for linguistic hypotheses.[14]

How, now, is the aim of (18) of reconstructing the logic of justification of linguistic inquiry related to the aim of (13) of identifying and evaluating "philosophical" argument forms used in linguistic inquiry? Linguists—such as Perloff and Wirth, and Sadock—have pursued the latter aim by selecting for analysis isolated "philosophical" argument forms that are, in one sense or another, of "special interest" to them. In order to pursue the former aim one must proceed beyond the analysis of isolated "philosophical" argument forms. In particular it must be determined how the various isolated "philosophical" argument forms are interrelated and, moreover, how they are related to the other component parts—for example, evidence conditions and acceptability standards—of the logic of justification of linguistic inquiry. Like analyses aimed at isolating and evaluting the "philosophical" argument forms used in linguistic inquiry, analyses of linguistic arguments aimed at reconstructing the logic of justification of linguistic inquiry can, if adequate, contribute in a direct manner to our understanding of the nature of linguistic argumentation.

5. UNDERSTANDING THE USE OF PARTICULAR ARGUMENT FORMS

In order to arrive at a full understanding of the nature of linguistic argumentation, it is not sufficient to isolate and evaluate linguistic argument forms alone. A deeper question has to be considered as well: What are the nonincidental reasons why linguists use the argument forms which in fact they use? By keeping this question in mind when analyzing linguistic arguments, linguists in effect set a fourth aim for the analyses which they undertake:

(19) *the aim of clarifying the reasons why linguists use the argument forms which in fact they use.*

Consider, for example, linguists' use of diachronic arguments, that is, arguments presenting data about linguistic change(s) as evidence for synchronic linguistic claims. Why do linguists use arguments of this form? Kiparsky (1968) has suggested an answer to this question in the following terms:

> What we really need is a window on the form of linguistic competence that is not obscured by factors like performance, about which next to nothing is known. In linguistic change we have precisely such a window. (Kiparsky, 1968, p. 174)

That is, the reason why linguists, such as Kiparsky, use diachronic arguments lies in the inadequacy of their insight into the nature of the synchronic data that might have been used for, or against, claims about the form of linguistic competence.

In the literature, not many analyses of linguistic arguments that explicitly pursue the aim of (19) are to be found. Dougherty (1976), in his contribution to the present volume, pursues, among other things, an aim which seems to be related to that of (19). Thus he states that:

> I am interested in understanding the intellectual frame of a researcher's thoughts (about the status of linguistics as a science, the nature of explanation, the goals of research, etc.) as this frame is reflected in the actual organization and structure of his arguments. The actual frame of a researcher's thoughts determines the questions he asks, the answers he is willing to accept, and the detailed results he will enumerate. (Dougherty, 1976, p. 113)

It has been mentioned in Section 3 above that Dougherty draws a distinction between two "argument forms": "the *theory-*

comparison argument form" and "the *theory-expositon* argument form." Dougherty, moreover, draws a distinction between two views of the research of nature: "the typological view" and "the mechanical view." This distinction he then projects onto contemporary linguistics, obtaining in this way a "typological view of language" and a "mechanical view of language." On the basis of this projection Dougherty proceeds to assert that linguists' use of the "theory-comparison argument form" and of the "theory-exposition argument form" is a function of their adherence to "the mechanical view of language" and the "typological view of language," respectively.

Of rather a different sort is the discussion in Botha (1973, sec. 6.3) of the reasons why linguists use "philosophical" argument forms of the type whose major premiss is formulated in terms of such methodological notions as "explanatory power," "refutability," "conceptual homogeneity," "heuristic fruitfulness," and so on. Against a background of principled analyses of argument forms, conditions of evidence, and acceptability standards used in transformational grammar, Botha suggests that linguists use arguments of this "philosophical" form because of a given property that linguistic arguments of certain other forms have. In particular, it is asserted that the former type of "philosophical" argument form is used by linguists in the justification of linguistic hypotheses

> because of the nondemonstrative nature of the explanatory and confirmatory arguments used for purposes of such justification. (Botha, 1973, p. 298)

Because of the nondemonstrative nature of these argument forms, linguists use arguments of the "philosophical" form in question

> for purposes of "boosting" in a differential manner whatever justification is already available for their linguistic hypotheses, a differential manner intended to enable these grammarians to distinguish between those of their linguistic hypotheses which are "scientifically more meritorious" and those which are "scientifically less meritorious." (Botha, 1973, p. 298)

Evidently, analyses of linguistic arguments which pursue the aim of determining why linguists use the argument forms that they do in fact use may contribute greatly to the understanding of the nature of linguistic argumentation. Such analyses cannot be insightful, however, if they are undertaken in the absence of adequate logical analyses of the argument forms in question.

6. CLARIFYING THE STATUS OF THEORETICAL LINGUISTIC PRINCIPLES

A proper understanding of the theoretical principles of linguistics requires, among other things, that it be clear what the epistemological status of these principles is, and what methodological roles are played by these principles in linguistic inquiry. Since these theoretical principles are involved in the arguments used in linguistic inquiry, an obvious way of clarifying their epistemological status and methodological roles is to analyze these arguments. Such analyses of linguistic arguments, accordingly, pursue a fifth aim:

(20)   *the aim of clarifying the epistemological status and methodological roles of theoretical linguistic principles.*

It will be shown below how analyses pursuing the aim of (20) may contribute in an indirect manner to our understanding of the nature of linguistic argumentation.

Zwicky (1973) draws a distinction among three sorts of theoretical linguistic principles: "methodological principles" and "systematic principles," which latter, in turn, comprise "arguable propositions" and "organizing hypotheses." This distinction relates to the epistemological status and methodological roles of theoretical linguistic principles. Moreover, this distinction is reflected in the linguistic arguments in which these principles are involved. Let us consider Zwicky's category of "methodological principles" in order to see how the pursuit of the aim of (20) may contribute, in an indirect manner, to our understanding of the nature of linguistic argumentation.

Methodological principles," or "rules of thumb," for Zwicky (1973) are not assumptions capable of verification or falsification in any ordinary sense. Instead, their function is to suggest what the most likely state of affairs is in a given situation, in the absence of evidence of the usual sort. This being the case, the indication given by a methodological principle is always outweighed by pertinent evidence. (Zwicky, 1973, p. 468)

Zwicky's (1973, p. 468) following three examples of "methodological principles" clarify the above characterization:

(21) a. "The Majority Vote Principle" in comparative reconstruction: "if the majority of daughter languages agree in having a certain feature, then that feature is to be attributed to the protolanguage."
      b. "The Contrast Principle" in phonology: "if segments are in contrast, then they are underlyingly distinct."
      c. "The Surfacist Principle" in syntax: "*ceteris paribus,* the syntactic structure of a sentence is its surface constituent structure."

Note, incidentally, that Zwicky's "methodological principles" represent assumptions about the nature of natural language(s), not about the nature of linguistic science. Consequently, these "methodological principles" are in fact substantive in nature.

What, now, does Zwicky's characterization of the epistemological status and methodological role of "methodological principles" reveal about the nature of linguistic argumentation? As regards their methodological function, "methodological principles" provide for a particular argument form that may be used in linguistic inquiry. Arguments of this form—which incorporate these "methodological principles" as major premisses—are used to justify linguistic hypotheses in the absence of empirical evidence for these hypotheses. As regards their epistemological status, "methodological principles" are nonempirical, that is, in Zwicky's terms, they "are not capable of verification or falsification in any ordinary sense." This epistemological status of Zwicky's "methodological principles" directly affects the "power" or "strength" of the arguments in which they are incorporated as major premisses. Arguments of this form are "weaker" than those incorporating "evidence of the usual sort." That is, to put it in Zwicky's (1973, p. 470) terms, "the indication given by a methodological principle is always out-weighed by pertinent evidence."

The salient point here is that through the analysis of linguistic arguments with the aim of clarifying the epistemological status and methodological roles of theoretical principles, two related points about linguistic argumentation have been established. First, linguists use a special argument form that incorporates as a major premiss nonempirical, "methodological principles" such as (21a–c) for the purpose of justifying linguistic hypotheses in the absence of empirical evidence. Second, on account of the nonempirical nature of these "methodological principles," arguments of the form in question are relatively "weak." From the epistemological status and methodological roles of Zwicky's two other sorts of theoretical principles—"arguable propositions" and "organizing hypotheses"—conclusions of a similar sort may be drawn about the nature of linguistic argumentation.

Eckman's contribution to the present volume represents an attempt to establish, through analyses of linguistic arguments, the epistemological status of a certain class of linguistic principles:

> In what follows, I shall attempt to show that, in a number of cases, the laws and principles which linguists have stated, and the supporting evidence which has been provided, are devoid of empirical content in that they are not subject to falsification by observation of any things or events in the real world. (Eckman, 1976, pp. 35–36)

7. DISCREDITING AN ENTIRE APPROACH TO LINGUISTIC INQUIRY

Consider the following remarks offered by Chomsky (1964) on the methodological bases of taxonomic linguistics:

> Insofar as consistency and convertibility are taken as the only valid metacriteria, linguistic theory is concerned only with the level of observational adequacy. This theory makes no claim to truth; no evidence conflicts with it, just as none can be offered in its support. The only criticism that is relevant is that taxonomic phonemics, as indicated above, seems more of an inconvenience than a convenience, if embedded within a full grammatical description. This point of view takes a theory to be, essentially, nothing more than a summary of data. (Chomsky, 1964, p. 98)

These remarks form part of a negative appraisal of taxonomic linguistics by Chomsky. This negative appraisal involves, among other things, certain argument forms used in taxonomic linguistic inquiry: an argument form appealing, in its major premiss, to a notion of "consistency," and an argument form invoking, in its major premiss, a notion of "convertibility." Chomsky's negative appraisal of these argument forms illustrates a sixth aim that may be set for analyses of linguistic arguments:

(22) *the aim of, ultimately, bringing into discredit an entire approach to linguistic inquiry.*

To analyze linguistic arguments with the aim of (22) in mind is to use methodological analysis as a means of winning a battle of a substantive linguistic sort.

Dougherty's analyses of linguistic arguments pursue the aim of (22). Consider the manner in which he states the "main question" of his chapter in the present volume:

> At any given time, just as there will be many alternative theoretical mechanisms being proposed, there will be many different methodologies in use and many different methodologies proposed. Each instrument of research, whether it is in use already or whether it is newly proposed, must, through confrontation with empirical facts, be validated or refuted no less than the theoretical proposals which the instruments are used to justify. How these instruments, in particular the argument forms, can be isolated and identified, and further, how they can be evaluated for strength, will be the main questions of this investigation. (Dougherty, 1976, p. 112)

This passage suggests that Dougherty's main interest lies in the analysis of linguistic argumentation in a neutral metascientific sort of manner. In fact, however, Dougherty's paper presents an attack on generative semantics. The following quote from Dougherty's chapter gives a more accurate indication than the one above of what the "main questions" are for Dougherty:[15]

> It is an empirical question as to whether generative semantics is an incoherent mixture of unit ideas which yields instruments of research like theory exposition or whether it is a new theory of grammar uniting syntax and semantics. All the data of which I am aware supports the former, see Dougherty (1973, 1974). (Dougherty, 1976, p. 136)

Whether a given analysis pursuing the ultimate aim of (22) will or will not reveal anything about the nature of linguistic argumentation depends on, among other things, the analyst's ability to overcome his substantive bias.[16]

8. EVALUATING THE CASE FOR LINGUISTIC HYPOTHESES

In the preceding paragraphs we have looked at six of the aims that linguists have set for their analyses of linguistic arguments. The analyses performed in the pursuit of these six aims are all of them of a deliberate, philosophical, sort. Moreover, all of these analyses are potentially capable of shedding some light on the nature of linguistic argumentation. The nature of the above-mentioned six aims pursued by deliberate analyses of linguistic arguments may be further clarified by contrasting these six aims with a seventh aim set by "ordinary, working" linguists for their analyses of linguistic arguments.

Let us approach this, seventh, aim by considering the assertions below by Chomsky (1972b) and McCawley (1973).

The analysis of the head noun as a nominalized verb requires that we establish abstract verbs that are automatically subject to nominalization. This requires devices of great descriptive power which should, correspondingly, be very "costly" in terms of a reasonable evaluation measure. Nevertheless, it is an interesting possibility. Perhaps the strongest case for such an approach is the class of examples of which (22i) [i.e., "the *author* of the book"—R. P. B.] is an instance. It has been argued, quite plausibly, that such phrases as *the owner of the house* derive from underlying structures such as *the one who owns the house*; correspondingly (22i) might be derived from the structure *the one who *auths the book*, **auth* being postulated as a verb that is lexically marked as obligatorily subject to nominalization. However, the plausibility of this approach diminishes when one recognizes that there is no more reason to give this analysis for (22i) than there is for *the general secretary of the party, the assistant vice-chancellor of the university*, and similarly for every function that can be characterized by a nominal phrase. Another fact sometimes put forth in support of the analysis of these phrases as nominalizations is the ambiguity of such expressions as *good dentist* (*dentist who is a good man, man who is good as a dentist*). But this argument is also quite weak. The ambiguity, being characteristic of all expressions that refer to humans by virtue of some function that they fulfill, can be handled by a general principle of semantic interpretation; further-more, it is hardly plausible that the ambiguity of *good assistant vice-chancelor* should be explained in this way. (Chomsky, 1972b, pp. 31–32)

Chomsky's discussion of his second major argument for a lexicalist treatment of nominalizations and against a transformationalist treat-ment is of necessity somewhat vague, since it deals with details of the relationship between nominalizations and their meanings and none of the existing transformationalist treatments had had much to say on that topic. He gives a list of 14 verb-related nouns and simply says that they have "their individual ranges of meaning and varied semantic relations to the base forms" and concludes that "To accommodate these facts within the transformational approach (as-suming, as above that it is the grammatical relations in the deep structure that determine meaning) it is necessary to resort to the artifice of assigning a range of meanings to the base form, stipulating that with certain semantic features the form must nominalize and with others it cannot" (p. 19). The kind of treatment that Chomsky objects to here is objectionable for precisely the same reason that his own treatment is: each contributes nothing towards an understanding of the question of what nominalizations are possible (though perhaps accidentally non-occurring) and what relationships between a nomi-nalization and its meaning are possible. Either treatment says that the relationship between nominalizations and their meanings are pure chaos. Perhaps nothing is really systematic, as Chomsky seems to suggest; however, it takes more to establish that than a list of 14 words and a comment that their meanings are wildly diverse. (McCawley, 1973, p. 9)

In these two excerpts, Chomsky and McCawley present their appraisal of certain linguistic arguments. They do this in the capacity of "ordinary, working" linguists. That is, they have analyzed the arguments in question not with one or another philosophical aim in mind, but with the following substantively oriented aim:

(23)   *the aim of assessing the strength of the case for or against linguistic hypotheses.*

This constitutes a seventh aim that may be pursued in the analysis of linguistic arguments.

The pursuit of the aim of (23) by "ordinary, working"

linguists does not contribute in any direct manner to our understanding of the nature of linguistic argumentation. For, to analyze linguistic arguments in order to appraise the case for or against linguistic hypotheses is not to be engaged in the study of the nature of linguistic argumentation. To perform analyses of linguistic arguments with the aim of (23) is to be engaged in the study of the nature of human language. Clearly, the analyses carried out in pursuit of this aim are not of the same, deliberate, philosophical, sort as those considered in Sections 2-7. Obviously, a great deal of the intellectual activity of the "ordinary, working" linguist goes into the pursuit of the substantively oriented aim of (23). To study the nature of linguistic argumentation, consequently, is to attempt to gain insight into, among other things, the manner in which the "ordinary, working" linguist pursues the aim of (23).

9. CONCLUSION

We have considered seven of the aims that linguists may pursue when undertaking analyses of linguistic arguments:

(24) a. the aim of identifying and evaluating "substantive" argument forms used in linguistic theory;
   b. the aim of identifying and evaluating "philosophical" argument forms used in linguistic inquiry;
   c. the aim of reconstructing the logic of justification of linguistic inquiry;
   d. the aim of clarifying the reasons why linguists use the argument forms which in fact they use;
   e. the aim of clarifying the epistemological status and methodological roles of theoretical linguistic principles;
   f. the aim of, ultimately, bringing into discredit an entire approach to linguistic inquiry;
   g. the aim of assessing the strength of the case for or against linguistic hypotheses.

The discussion of these seven aims of analyses of linguistic arguments, hopefully, provides a perspective from which the chapters in the present volume may be studied.[17] This perspective, however, is not complete. In order to give it greater substance, the questions of (4b–e) would have to be discussed in some detail as well. For, in order to assess the merit of each of these chapters on the nature of linguistic argumentation, the reader would have to do more than identify the aims set for the analyses of the chapter. Specifically, the reader would have to determine as well whether these analyses do or do not have the properties typical of genuine analyses of scientific arguments, whether these analyses have or have not been carried out by means of appropriate and adequate conceptual tools, and whether these analyses do or do not satisfy the (other) standards of adequacy for analyses of scientific arguments.

APPENDIX

Conventionally, an *argument* is regarded as an ordered set of statements or propositions which belong to one or the other of two categories: conclusions and premisses.[18] *Conclusions* represent propositions which are based on, or affirmed on the strength of, other propositions. These other propositions constitute the *premisses* and, as such, have the function of presenting the evidence for the conclusion. The *evidence* for a conclusion consists of those considerations which are put forward as reasons for accepting the conclusion as true or probably true. Traditionally, a distinction has been drawn between the minor premiss and the major premiss of an argument. The *minor premiss* presents one or more individual data from which the conclusion is drawn. The *major premiss* contains a "guarantee," "warrant," or "inference-licence" in accordance with which the inferential step from the minor premiss to the conclusion may legitimately be taken. The conclusion of an argument and its premisses are related in terms of one or another *logical relation*. The logical relation incorporated in arguments is conventionally designated by expressions such as "is indicated by," "supports," "entails," "follows from," "can be reduced to," and so on.

A fundamental logical distinction drawn in respect to the conventional concept "argument" is the distinction between an argument form and a specific (substitution) instance of some argument form. Copi (1965, p. 18) explicates the basis for this distinction by pointing out that argument forms are conveniently discussed by using small letters from the middle of the alphabet,—"p," "q," "r," "s," and so on—as *statement variables.* Such statement variables are taken to be letters for which, or in the place of which, statements may be substituted. An *argument form,* then, is for Copi (1965, p. 18) "any array of symbols which contains statement variables, such that when statements are substituted for the statement variables—the same statement replacing the same statement variable throughout—the result is an argument." A *(substitution) instance* of an argument form is, for Copi (1965, p. 19), any argument "which results from the substitution of statements for the statement variables of an argument form. . . ."[19]

The explication given above of the content of the concepts "argument" and "argument form" may be made more concrete by applying these concepts to a few real linguistic arguments. Consider the following arguments by McCawley (1968) in support of his thesis that selectional restrictions are definable solely in terms of properties of semantic representations.[20] McCawley argues

that the various nonsemantic features attached to nouns, for example, proper versus common, grammatical gender, grammatical number, and so on play no role in their selection. All the verbs which have suggested themselves to me as possible counter-examples to this assertion turn out in fact to display selection based on some semantic properties. For example, the verb *name* might at first glance seem to have a selectional restriction involving the feature [proper] :

28. They named their son John.

29. *They named their son that boy.

However, there are in fact perfectly good sentences with something other than a proper noun in the place in question:

30. They named their son something outlandish.

The selectional restriction is thus that the second object denote a name rather than it have a proper noun as its head. Regarding grammatical number, verbs as *count* might seem to demand a plural object:

31. I counted the boys.

32. *I counted the boy.

However, there are also sentences with grammatically singular objects:

33. I counted the crowd.

> The selectional restriction on *count* is not that the object be plural but that it denote a set of things rather than an individual. Similarly, there is no verb in English which allows for its subject just those noun phrases which may pronominalize to *she*, namely noun phrases denoting women, ships, and countries. I accordingly conclude that selectional restrictions are definable solely in terms of properties of semantic representations and that to determine whether a constituent meets or violates a selectional restriction it is necessary to examine its semantic representation and nothing else. (McCawley, 1968, pp. 134–135)

The arguments advanced by McCawley in the above excerpt may be explicitly reconstructed as the argument (25) to which is linked the argument (26).

(25) If selectional restrictions are based solely on semantic properties, then the selectional restrictions of all apparent counterexamples should also turn out to display selection based on semantic properties.

The selectional restrictions of all apparent counterexamples turn out to be based on semantic properties.

∴ Selectional restrictions are based solely on semantic properties

(26) If the selection of all apparent counterexamples is in fact based on semantic properties, then the selection of the apparent counterexamples *name* and *count* should be based on semantic properties.

The selection of the apparent counterexamples *name* and *count* is based on semantic properties.

∴ The selection of all apparent counterexamples is in fact based on semantic properties.[21]

In terms of the notions "major premiss," "minor premiss," and "conclusion," (25) and (26) above provide an illustration of the application of the basic logical concept "argument."

Consider now the second basic logical concept: "argument form." First, both the argument (25) and the argument (26) are nondemonstrative arguments. That is, both these arguments are substitution instances of a nondemonstrative argument form. Nondemonstrative arguments have the logical property of not being necessarily truth-preserving: even if the premisses of nondemonstrative arguments are true, their conclusions may still be false.

Second, both the arguments (25) and (26) are substitution instances of a reductive argument form. Reductive arguments, that is, arguments which are substitution instances of the reductive argument form, incorporate a rule of reductive inference. This rule of reductive inference authorizes a scholar, in regard to a conditional statement, to infer the antecedent from a conjunction of the conditional statement with its consequent.[22] The logical "skeleton" of reductive arguments may be presented as follows:

(27) $p \supset q$
$$\frac{q}{\therefore p}$$

Third, two reductive forms of argument may be distinguished: progressively reductive arguments or confirmatory arguments, and regressively reductive arguments or explanatory arguments. This distinction is based on the distinction which Bocheński (1965) draws between "progressive reduction" and "regressive reduction":

> if the reduction is to be done progressively, . . . , the antecedent—whose truth-value is still unknown—is taken as the starting-point, from which the argument proceeds to the known or ascertainable consequent. This progressive reduction is called "verification." Regressive reduction, on the other hand, begins with the known consequent and proceeds to the unknown antecedent. Regressive reduction is called "explanation." (Bocheński, 1965, p. 92)

The two arguments (25) and (26) are instances of the progressive subtype of the reductive argument form. That is, these

two arguments are progressively reductive arguments or confirmatory arguments.[23] In sum, as regards the form of argument
of which they are substitution instances, the arguments (25) and
(26) are nondemonstrative arguments, reductive arguments, and
confirmatory arguments.

NOTES

1. See the chapters in the present volume as well as Botha (1971a, b, 1973,
   and to appear) and Dougherty (1973, and to appear).
2. For a discussion of the nature of scientific crises, see Kuhn (1970,
   chaps. 7 and 8).
3. See Chomsky (1974), G. Lakoff (1974a, b), R. Lakoff (1974), and
   McCawley (1974).
4. "Paradigm" here denotes Kuhn's (1970, pp. 182ff.; 1974, pp. 462-
   463) *disciplinary matrix*. A disciplinary matrix "contains all those
   shared elements which make for relative fullness of professional
   communication and unanimity of professional judgment. These include
   values for judging the adequacy of scientific work, models, ontological
   commitments, symbolic generalizations, a language, with meanings
   specific to that community, for interpreting symbolic generalizations,
   and so on." (Suppe, 1974b, p. 497).
5. The ensuing discussion requires a clear understanding of the content of
   such logical concepts as "arguments," "major premiss," "minor
   premiss," "conclusion," "evidence," "logical relation," "argument
   form," and so on. To make the present chapter more readable I have
   informally outlined the content of these concepts in the Appendix (pp.
   26–30). This outline account of the content of these concepts is
   identical, in the essential respects, to the exposition presented in
   Botha, 1973, pp. 25–27.
6. A third one is mentioned in Section 3 below.
7. In chap. 7 of his *Syntactic Theory*, Bach (1974) discusses arguments of
   this "substantive" form.
8. Postal's arguments in support of the claims (6c–e) incorporate this
   major premiss as well.
9. See also Botha (1973, secs. 5.7, 6.2.4) for an analysis of linguistic
   arguments appealing to a notion of "independent motivation."
10. See also Botha (1971a, sec. 3.2, 1973, sec. 6.2.4.3) for an analysis of
    linguistic arguments appealing to a notion of "linguistically significant
    generalization."
11. For a discussion of various problematic aspects of Dougherty's notions
    "the *theory comparison* argument form" and "the *theory exposition*
    argument form," see Botha (to appear), Sec. 6.8.

12. The numbers in this quote have the following values:

    (6) a. John is easy (difficult) to please.
         b. John is certain (likely) to win the prize.
         c. John amused (interested) the children with his stories.

    (7) a. John's being easy (difficult) to please
         b. John's being certain (likely) to win the prize
         c. John's amusing (interesting) the children with his stories

    (8) a. *John's easiness (difficulty) to please
         b. *John's certainty (likelihood) to win the prize
         c. *John's amusement (interest) of the children with his stories

    (9) a. John's eagerness to please ((21), (4a))
         b. John's certainty that Bill will win the prize
         c. John's amusement at (interest in) the children's antics

    (10) a. John's being eager to please ((2a), (3a))
          b. John's being certain that Bill will win the prize
          c. John's being amused at (interested in) the children's antics

    (12) The stories [+ cause] [$_S$he was amused at the stories]$_S$

13. Thus, McCawley (1973, p. 5) asserts that "the facts ... appear to conflict with both hypotheses: the lexicalist hypothesis implies that all nominalizations of structures derived by cyclic rules are ungrammatical; the transformationalist hypothesis implies that they are all grammatical; but in reality some of them are grammatical and some ungrammatical."

14. Dougherty (to appear) has made an attempt to discredit this study as being a study that deals, not with the logic of justification of transformational grammar, but with the rhetoric of linguistic argumentation. For a rebuttal of Dougherty's criticisms of this study, see Botha (to appear).

15. Insofar as this paper of Dougherty's presents analyses of actual linguistic arguments motivating claims about natural language, it repeats earlier criticisms by Dougherty on a number of arguments to be found in a squib jointly authored by Lakoff and Ross. These criticisms are to be found in Dougherty (to appear). The squib in question is Lakoff and Ross's "Two kinds of *and*" (*Linguistic Inquiry* 1 (1970), pp. 71–72).

16. For a critical analysis of Dougherty's manner of performing methodological analysis, see Botha (to appear).

17. Gopnik's contribution to the present volume has not been considered above in relation to the aims of analyses of linguistic arguments. The

reason for this is that Gopnik's chapter is not *in a direct manner* concerned with the analysis of linguistic arguments. In this chapter Gopnik (1976, p. 217) sets out to analyze "some different ways in which empirical research about language is carried out and to suggest a way in which these different approaches may be related." In particular, she focuses on "the way empirical evidence from fields allied to linguistics, for example sociolinguistics, psycholinguistics, and computational linguistics, interacts with the work in what we may call 'pure' linguistics." Two other contributions to the present volume which have not been considered above are the chapters by Hastings and Koutsoudas, and by Loflin. I did not have the opportunity to examine copies of these chapters.

18. Every assertion made in this Appendix about the content of the logical concepts to be considered is fully documented in Botha (1973). See especially pp. 25–27 of that book.
19. See Copi (1965, p. 19).
20. For a more detailed treatment of these arguments by McCawley see Botha (1973, pp. 124–126).
21. For an alternative reconstruction of this argument see Botha (1973, pp. 126–128).
22. See Botha (1973, p. 36).
23. For a discussion of the role of explanatory and confirmatory arguments in linguistic inquiry see Botha (1973, chap. 3).

REFERENCES

Anderson, S. R., and P. Kiparsky (eds.) (1973) *A Festschrift for Morris Halle.* New York: Holt, Rinehart and Winston.

Bach, E. (1974) *Syntactic Theory.* New York: Holt, Rinehart and Winston.

_____ and R. T. Harms (eds.) (1968) *Universals in Linguistic Theory.* New York: Holt, Rinehart and Winston.

Bocheński, J. M. (1965) *The Methods of Contemporary Thought,* Peter Caws (trans.). Dordrecht, The Netherlands: D. Reidel Publishing Co.

Botha, R. P. (1968) *The Function of the Lexicon in Transformational Generative Grammar.* Janua Linguarum, Series Maior, No. 38. The Hague: Mouton.

_____ (1971a) *Methodological Aspects of Transformational Generative Phonology.* Janua Linguarum, Series Minor, No. 112. The Hague: Mouton.

_____ (1971b) "Le statut méthodologique de la preuve linguistique externe en grammaire générative." *Langages* 6:67–92.

_____ (1973) *The Justification of Linguistic Hypotheses: A Study of Nondemonstrative Inference in Transformational Grammar.* Janua Linguarum, Series Maior, No. 84. The Hague: Mouton.

_____ (to appear) "On the logic of linguistic research." *Working Papers in Linguistic Methodology,* No. 1. Lisse: The Peter de Ridder Press.

Campbell, M. A., (eds.) (1970) *Papers from the Sixth Regional Meeting, Chicago Linguistic Society*. Chicago: Chicago Linguistic Society.

Chomsky, N. (1964) *Current Issues in Linguistic Theory*. Janua Linguarum, Series Minor, No. 38. The Hague: Mouton.

_____ (1972a) *Studies on Semantics in Generative Grammar*. Janua Linguarum, Series Minor, No. 107. The Hague: Mouton.

_____ (1972b) "Remarks on nominalization," in Chomsky (1972a):11–61.

_____ (1974) "Discussing language," in Parret (ed.) (1974):27–54.

Copi, I. M. (1965) *Symbolic Logic*. 2nd ed. New York: Macmillan.

Dinneen, F. P. (ed.) (1974) *Georgetown University Round Table on Languages and Linguistics 1974. Linguistics: Teaching and Interdisciplinary Relations*. Washington, D.C.: Georgetown University Press.

Derwing, B. L. (1973) *Transformational Grammar as a Theory of Language Acquisition. A Study in the Empirical, Conceptual and Methodological Foundations of Contemporary Linguistic Theory*. Cambridge: At the University Press.

Dougherty, R. C. (1973) "A survey of linguistic methods and arguments," *Foundations of Language* 10:423–490.

_____ (1976) "Argument invention: The linguist's *feel* for science," in this volume: 111–165.

_____ (to appear) "The logic of linguistic research," *Foundations of Language*.

Eckman, F. R. (1976) "Empirical and nonempirical generalizations in linguistics," in this volume: 35–48.

Fillmore, C. J., and D. T. Langendoen (eds.) (1971) *Studies in Linguistic Semantics*. New York: Holt, Rinehart and Winston.

Gopnik, M. (1976) "What the theorist saw," in this volume: 217–248.

Kac, Michael B. (1976) "Hypothetical constructs in syntax," in this volume: 49–83.

Kiparsky, P. (1968) "Linguistic universals and linguistic change," in Bach and Harms (eds.) (1968):171–202.

Kuhn, T. S. (1970) *The Structure of Scientific Revolutions*. 2nd ed., enlarged. Chicago: University of Chicago Press.

_____ (1974) "Second thoughts on paradigms," in Suppe (ed.) (1974a): 459–482.

Labov, W. (1972) "Some principles in linguistic methodology," *Language in Society* 1:97–120.

Lakoff, G. (1974a) "Discussing language," in Parret (ed.) (1974):151–178.

_____ (1974b) "Humanistic linguistics," in Dinneen (ed.) (1974):103–117.

_____ and John Robert Ross (1970) "Two kinds of *and*," *Linguistic Inquiry* 1:71–72.

Lakoff, R. T. (1974) "Pluralism in linguistics," in Dinneen (ed.) (1974): 59–82.

Leech, G. N. (1968) "Some assumptions in the metatheory of linguistics," *Linguistics* 39:85–102.

McCawley, J. D. (1968) "The role of semantics in a grammar," in Bach and Harms (eds.) (1968):125–169.

_____ (1973) Review of Chomsky's *Studies on Semantics in Generative*

Grammar. Mimeographed. Indiana University Linguistics Club, Bloomington.

_____ (1974) "Discussing language," in Parret (ed.) (1974):249-277.

Parret, H. (ed.) (1974) *Discussing Language.* The Hague: Mouton.

Partee, B. H. (1971) "On the requirement that transformations preserve meaning," in Fillmore and Langendoen (eds.) (1971):1-21.

Perloff, M. N., and J. R. Wirth (1976) "On independent motivation," in this volume: 95-110.

Postal, P. M. (1968) *Aspects of Phonological Theory.* New York: Harper and Row.

Sadock, J. M. (1976) "On significant generalizations: Notes on the Hallean syllogism," in this volume: 85-94.

Schane, S. A. (1976) "The best argument is in the mind of the beholder," in this volume: 167-185.

Suppe, F. (ed.) (1974a) *The Structure of Scientific Theories.* Urbana: University of Illinois Press.

_____ (1974b) "Exemplars, theories and disciplinary matrixes," in Suppe (ed.) (1974a):483-499.

Zwicky, A. M. (1970) "The Free-Ride Principle and two rules of complete assimilation in English," in Campbell et al. (eds.) (1970):579-588.

_____ (1973) "Linguistics as chemistry: The substance theory of semantic primes," in Anderson and Kiparsky (eds.) (1973):467-485.

2
Empirical and nonempirical generalizations in linguistics

Fred R. Eckman
University of Wisconsin–Milwaukee

SECTION 1. INTRODUCTION

In this chapter, we shall be concerned with the status of a number of nondefinitional statements in linguistics, which, for our purposes, include the assumptions and laws made within the context of a linguistic metatheory or language-specific grammar. Since linguistics is an empirical science, the laws and explanatory principles which linguists formulate about language must have empirical content. Consequently, linguists must seek and provide empirical evidence in support or dissupport of all linguistic hypotheses. In what follows, we shall attempt to show that, in a number of cases, the laws and principles which linguists have stated, and the supporting evidence which has been provided, are devoid of empirical content in that they are not subject to

I would like to express my gratitude to Gerald Sanders for his extensive comments and suggestions on earlier drafts of this paper. I have also benefited from discussions on the topic with Daniel Dinnsen, Andreas Koutsoudas, and Iris Winogrond.

35

falsification by observation of any things or events in the real world.

Before proceeding to concrete examples, we should give a brief characterization of what we have termed nondefinitional statements. It is generally assumed that, at one of the earlier stages of investigation, a scientist gathers a certain amount of data relevant to a given problem and defines a number of pretheoretical notions. These notions are what Northrop (1949) calls "concepts by intuition," which are concepts whose meaning is given by something which is immediately apprehended. Thus, *intuition* means not a speculative hunch but the immediate apprehension of pure empiricism which occurs in direct inspection or pure observation. In linguistics, such pretheoretical notions include concepts like "sentence," "nonsentence," "phonetic segment," "consonant," "noun," etc. The scientist then introduces a number of hypothetical constructs whose meaning is determined by the theory in which they are postulated. Logic is then applied to the system of postulates to deduce a number of theorems or consequences which are checked against the real world. The laws or empirical generalizations are formulated in terms of the constructs of a theory and have the general characteristic that they are statements of universal form which assert a connection between empirical phenomena or between aspects of an empirical phenomenon. Thus, all nondefinitional statements must have empirical consequences which make them subject to falsification. We should point out that the requirement that such statements be empirical is not a requirement that all theoretical constructs postulated in a theory be observable. Rather, following Northrop (1949) we are requiring only that such concepts have empirical implications:

> The only prescription is that these meanings [i.e., the meanings of the postulated constructs, FRE] must be rigorously and precisely designated by being unambiguously prescribed in the postulates of the deductive theory, and that the theory must be verified by way of epistemic correlates with directly inspectable data before what its postulates designate may be said to exist. (p. 123)

SECTION 2

The first example that we shall take up is Ross's (1970) article, "Gapping and the Order of Constituents." In this chapter, Ross is attempting to account for certain language-distribution facts concerning verbal reductions in conjoined sentences. To this end, Ross postulates a rule called Gapping, which deletes an identical verb in conjoined sentences according to the following Directionality Principle:

(1) Directionality Principle: If the identical verbs are left-branching, the rule of Gapping applies forward; if the verbs are right-branching, Gapping applies backward.

For example, since verbs in English branch to the left from the VP node, Gapping applies forward to the structure underlying (2a) to derive (2b):

(2) a. I ate fish and Bill ate rice.
    b. I ate fish and Bill rice.

In languages which have a constituent order different from that of English, there should be a concomitant difference in the application of Gapping. Thus, since Japanese has the surface constituent order SOV (where S, O, and V are convenient mnemonics for *subject, object,* and *main verb,* respectively), it is the case that Gapping in Japanese applies to the structure underlying sentences like (3a) to derive sentences like (3b):

(3) a. SOV & SOV
    b. SO & SOV

Moreover, there are languages like Russian which exhibit surface word orders like both English and Japanese. It should therefore be the case that Russian contains sentences resulting from Gapping which are like both English and Japanese, namely, those in (4a) and (4b):

(4) a. SVO & SO
    b. SO & SOV
    c. SOV & SO

However, in addition to these sentence types, Russian also contains sentences like (4c) above. Thus, the sentence types exhibited in (4) are the sentence types resulting from Gapping which are realized in natural language. Sentence types like (5), however, never occur:

(5) *SO & SVO

Consequently, the theory which Ross is proposing is an attempt to explain the possible range of sentence types which can occur in natural language as the result of Gapping.

To account for the above facts, Ross assumes that, in addition to the rule of Gapping, languages which exhibit both SVO and SOV surface constituent orders contain the rule of Scrambling. This rule converts structures underlying SVO sentence types to SOV sentence types. Furthermore, Ross assumes that Gapping can apply both before and after the rule of Scrambling. The facts concerning Russian can be summarized by the derivations in (6):

(6)   i. Underlying structure
     ii. SVO & SVO— Scramble—SOV & SOV
    iii.   Gap   Gap
     iv. SVO & SO   SO & SOV
      v. Scramble
     vi. SOV & SO

Thus, given these assumptions, Ross can account for the facts of Gapping in English-, Japanese-, and Russian-type languages. What remains to be explained is the nonoccurrence of sentences like (5) in any natural language.

To account for this fact, Ross proposes the following principle:

(7) If a language has SOV order in deep structure, it is a *verb-final language*: its grammar can contain no rule which moves verbs to the left, nor any rule of the form of (23) [i.e., ...A...X ⟶ ...X...A, FRE]. (1970, p. 258)

This principle excludes the occurrence of sentences like (5) by preventing derivations like (8), where Scrambling applies to the output of Gapping in all languages which have SOV underlying order:

(8)   i. Underlying structure
      ii. SOV & SOV
     iii.   Gap
      iv. SO & SOV
       v. Scramble
      vi. *SO & SVO

Given this brief characterization of Ross's theory of Gapping, let us focus on the principle in (7). Superficially, this principle has the appearance of a law in that it is in the form of an unrestricted universal statement which asserts a relation between objects or properties of objects, namely, deep structure constituent order and transformational rules. In the case of (7), however, the properties of the objects involved are not empirical.

What Ross has apparently overlooked in the formulation of (7) is that the order of elements in deep structures is not a fact, rather it is something which is postulated as part of a theory of grammar. Therefore, a principle formulated in terms of deep structure has no empirical consequence because nothing would follow from such a principle. This is true because there is no necessary connection between surface structure constituent order and deep structure order, since transformations have the power to derivationally reorder constituents. Furthermore, there are no initial constraints or pretheoretical notions about deep structures to which the deep structure objects which are postulated must conform. Thus, not only is it possible to posit verb-initial deep structures for languages like English which never exhibit such surface orders in declarative sentences, as was done by Mc-Cawley (1970), but it is possible to postulate deep structures containing complex sentences as underlying representations for simple sentences. This proposal was made by Ross (1972) when he argued that all simple sentences containing verbs of action must be derived from underlying complex structures in which the superficial simple sentence is embedded as a complement clause of a superordinate predicate containing the verb *do*. This being the case, statements about deep structure order are not falsifiable on the basis of any observations about surface structure.

Finally, one might argue that principles formulated in terms of deep structures are empirical because deep structures receive a semantic interpretation. Therefore, properties of deep structures should have consequences in terms of the meaning of a sentence. While this may be true for those properties of deep structure which are relevant to semantic interpretation, this is not true of principles like (7) which make reference to the order of constituents. The rules of semantic interpretation which have been proposed so far make no reference to the order of elements in the underlying representation. Our conclusion is, then, that a principle like (7) is not an empirical statement.

Another example which is closely related to this one involves Bresnan's 1970 article entitled "On Complementizers: Toward a Theory of Complement Types." In this article, Bresnan proposes that complementizers—particles like *that, for–to,* and *'s–ing* in English—be represented in a grammar as elements of the underlying representation rather than being introduced transformationally. Thus, Bresnan is proposing that the grammar of English contain a phrase structure rule like (9):

(9) S $\longrightarrow$ COMP^S

where the node COMP is realized as one of the complementizer particles whenever the clause dominated by S is a subordinate sentence. In addition, Bresnan argues that the so-called Wh-words in English, that is, forms like *who, what, how,* etc., are also complementizers in that they are dominated by the node COMP in the underlying representation.

As justification for this particular assumption, Bresnan argues that, if Wh-words are considered to be complementizers, then an unsolved problem first raised by Baker (1970) can be solved. Thus, Bresnan states:

(10) I will show that if WH is recognized as a complementizer, Baker's Q-universal (Baker, 1970) can be strengthened in a way which immediately explains an unsolved problem noted by Baker—that of relating the universal behavior of relative clauses to that of questions. This result in turn leads to another possible universal and a means of relating underlying word order to the class of transformations possible in a language. (p. 317)

Baker's Q-universal is stated as follows:

(11) Baker's Q-Universal: The first part of the hypothesis is that morphemes such as *if* and *whether*, and other words and particles in other languages in which such elements occur, are introduced into trees as lexical realizations of the Q-morpheme. . . . The second part of the hypothesis is that there is only one possible movement rule for questions, which differs in different languages only in the particular formatives mentioned in place of English *wh* [footnote 12 omitted]:

$$Q \ X \ NP \ Y$$
$$1 \ 2 \ 3 \ \ 4 \longrightarrow 1 \ 3+2 \ \emptyset \ 4$$

Bresnan argues that if her hypothesis that Wh-words are complementizers is correct, then there is no need for the special Q-morpheme posited by Baker, and his universal can be restated as (12):

(12) The Complementizer Substitution Universal: Only languages with clause-initial COMP permit a COMP-substitution transformation.

A COMP-substitution transformation is any rule which moves a constituent over an essential variable into the position of the COMP node (for example, Relative Clause Formation and Question Formation). Bresnan notes, however, that if relative clauses are assumed to be derived from complement clauses, then the Complementizer Substitution Universal can be restated as the Expansion Universal:

(13) Expansion Universal: If R_1 belongs to the PS [phrase structure component] of the grammar of a language, then so does R_2.

For the purposes of this universal, R_1 and R_2 are formulated as in (14):

(14) a. R_1 $NP \longrightarrow N\char`^S$
      b. R_2 $S \longrightarrow COMP\char`^S$

From the quote in (10), we see that the purpose of the Expansion Universal is to explain the universal behavior of relative clauses and questions. This behavior is the fact that languages which have relative clauses following the head noun have clause-initial question words. Putting aside the matter of whether a statement of co-occurrence with respect to rules is an explanation of these facts, it seems clear that the law stated by Expansion Universal is not empirical. This is true because the Expansion Universal is a statement about phrase structure rules which specify the deep structures of sentences, and not their surface structures. The former are hypothetical constructs and therefore are not constrained by any observations about surface structures. Since transformations have the power to reorder constituents, there is no necessary connection between the order of elements specified by R_1 and R_2 and any facts about the order of relative clauses respective to their heads, or about question words in surface structure. Moreover, as was the case in the Gapping example, it is not possible to appeal to semantics, since the meaning of a sentence is independent of the order of constituents in deep structure. Therefore, there are no semantic facts which are deducible from the constituent order defined by R_1 and R_2.

We have discussed two examples from syntax where laws or generalizations are devoid of empirical content because they were stated about theoretical assumptions rather than empirical phenomena. We shall now discuss some similar examples from phonology.

SECTION 3

The first example we shall consider is Hyman's 1970 paper entitled "How Concrete Is Phonology?" In this article, Hyman is concerned with the issue of abstractness of underlying representations. That is, he is facing the question of the extent to which a linguist is justified in postulating underlying segments as part of a phonological description, where these segments are not phonetically realized. Toward this end, Hyman proposes a partial description of Nupe phonology in which he argues that it is necessary to postulate underlying low back and low front vowels

which are not realized on the surface—this nonrealization being
due to a rule of absolute neutralization which collapses these
vowels with the segment [a].

As part of Hyman's description of Nupe phonology, he
proposes a rule which labializes consonants before back vowels
and another rule which palatalizes consonants before front
vowels. In view of these labialized and palatalized consonants
before back and front vowels respectively, Hyman considers
certain problematical forms, namely, those in (15):

(15) a. eg^{w}a 'hand'
      b. eg^{y}a 'blood'
      c. egal 'stranger'

These forms are problematical, on the one hand, since Hyman
would like to account for the occurrence of the labialized and
palatalized consonants before [a], and, on the other hand,
because it does not appear to be entirely clear that in the forms
for 'hand' and 'blood the consonants are labialized or palatalized. Thus, Hyman cites an earlier account of Nupe phonology—Smith (1967)—in which these words are represented as in
(16):

(16) a. egwa 'hand'
      b. egya 'blood'

Consequently, Hyman is faced with the problem of deciding
whether the consonantal segments in these Nupe words represent
instances of a labialized and palatalized consonant, or whether
they represent a sequence of a consonant followed by a glide.

In deciding the question, Hyman argues that, in the underlying representation, the consonantal segments in the forms for
'hand' and 'blood' should not be considered as clusters of a
consonant followed by a glide, since this would violate an
underlying pattern:

> Thus /Cw/ and /Cy/ clusters are exceptional in that . . . they alone
> violate the underlying regularity of (V)CVCV. . . . (p. 60)

In short, Hyman is assuming that the underlying forms for

'hand' and 'blood' in Nupe contain no consonant clusters because this assumption enables him to state a generalization with respect to the underlying representation.

As was the case in the syntactic examples we discussed, the generalization which Hyman is able to make is about hypothetical rather than empirical objects. Since underlying forms can be altered by phonological rules which have the power to delete, insert, and reorder segments, nothing follows from generalizations which are stated about underlying representations. Therefore, any such generalization is without empirical content.

Another closely related example comes from Chomsky and Halle's 1968 discussion of the diphthong [ɔy] in English. Since the description of English phonology which Chomsky and Halle are proposing contains no underlying diphthongs, they would like to derive the sequence [ɔy] from an underlying vowel, V*:

> The optimal solution would be to take V* as some vowel which fills a gap in the phonological system and which is converted to phonetic [ɔy] by independently motivated rules. (pp. 191–192)

The independently motivated rules to which they refer are a rule which inserts a glide after a tense vowel and a rule which makes a [−back] vowel become [+back] when it precedes a [−back] glide. Given these rules, Chomsky and Halle postulate the vowel in (17) as the underlying representation of the diphthong [ɔy].

(17) /ǣ/

In support of this analysis, they offer the following statement:

> In further support of this conclusion is the observation that [ǣ] in fact constitutes an otherwise unexplained gap in the phonological pattern, since the other three tense low vowels (namely, [ǣ], [ā], [ɔ̄]) do appear in lexical matrices. (p. 192)

Thus, the supporting evidence for the postulation of the underlying vowel in (17) in English, even though this vowel is never realized phonetically, is the fact that it regularizes the underlying phonological pattern. However, as in the previous example, this argument must be rejected since the generalization (or regularity) which is statable is about an underlying hypothetical object rather than about an empirical object. Moreover, it is not the case that the assumption that [ɔ̃y] is derived from the vowel in (17) makes it possible to state a generalization about phonetic representations which is otherwise unstatable. The independently motivated rules to which Chomsky and Halle refer state generalizations which are statable independently of whether [ɔ̃y] is derived from the vowel in (17).

SECTION 4

In the preceding paragraphs, we have discussed a number of examples where linguists have formulated certain principles or generalizations which are nonempirical in that these generalizations were made about underlying representations rather than surface representations. We are not claiming, however, that assumptions about underlying structures cannot be justified. Rather, we are claiming that such justification must come from generalizations which are statable about surface structures, and not generalizations statable about hypothetical constructs. Along these lines, we shall consider two examples of assumptions about underlying representations which are empirical.

In his book *Deep and Surface Structure Constraints in Syntax*, Perlmutter (1971) imposes a constraint on the deep structures into which certain lexical items may be inserted. This constraint, termed the Unlike-Subject Constraint, restricts a class of verbs in English from being inserted into a deep structure phrase marker if the subject of that verb is identical to the subject of the object complement sentence. Thus, the Unlike-Subject Constraint allows for sentences like (18a) while blocking those like (18b and c):

(18) a. I screamed for Clyde to commit himself.
      b. *I screamed for me to commit myself.
      c. *I screamed to commit myself.

Perlmutter argues that the Unlike-Subject Constraint must be stated with respect to deep structures instead of surface or intermediate structures. Given this, the question arises as to how this constraint is different from Ross's principle in (7).

The Unlike-Subject Constraint, though formulated on deep structures, is empirical because it is formulated in terms of the notion of identity of constituents. In the theory of grammar which Perlmutter is assuming, transformations may delete constitutents if they belong to the class of indefinites or if they are identical to another constituent in the same phrase marker. Consequently, it is possible to determine whether or not the Unlike-Subject Constraint has been violated with respect to a given sentence on the basis of surface structures. The difference between Ross's principle in (7) and the Unlike-Subject Constraint lies in the fact that the former is stated in terms of underlying order, which is not determinable from surface structures, whereas the latter is formulated in terms of identity, which is determinable upon inspection of surface structures.

An example of assumptions about the underlying representations in phonology being justified on the basis of generalizations about phonetic representations comes from Foley's 1967 paper entitled "Spanish Plural Formation." In this paper, Foley is attempting to give a unified account of the various phonetic manifestations of the plural morpheme in Spanish words like those in (19):[1]

(19)
	Singular	Plural	Gloss
a.	cárta	cártas	letter
b.	bajá	bajáes	pasha
c.	razón	razónes	reason
d.	més	méses	month
e.	lúnes	lúnes	Monday

The problem that Foley is faced with is that of explaining why in the Spanish word for 'letter' the plural is simply [s], whereas in 'pasha', 'reason', and 'month' the plural is [es] and in the word for 'Monday' the singular and plural are homophonous.

Another anomaly about the nouns in (19) is that the placement of stress seems unpredictable, sometimes falling on the last syllable and other times falling on the penultimate syllable.

To account for these facts, Foley assumes that the underlying plural morpheme is /s/ and that the underlying representation of the words in (19) are as in (20):

(20) a. *carta   d. *mese
      b. *bajae   e. *lunes
      c. *razone

Given these underlying representations, Foley can account for the forms in (19) by means of independently motivated rules. Specifically, the correct form for the plural of 'Monday' is derived by a rule of Degemination which deletes one of the two /s/'s formed by adding the plural morpheme to (19e). The other independently needed rule is Apocope, which deletes a word-final, unstressed /e/ in forms like (20b, c, and d).

The justification for assuming underlying representations like those in (20) is that not only are the various realizations of the plural morpheme accounted for by independently motivated rules, but in addition, it is now possible for Foley to formulate a general rule of stress placement for nouns, which stresses the penultimate vowel. Thus, the underlying forms in (21) are supported by the ability to state a generalization about stress, not with respect to underlying representations, but with respect to phonetic representations.

SECTION 5

The conclusion we draw is that, insofar as linguistics is an empirical science, the only viable linguistic arguments are those in which the assumptions and explanatory principles are justified on the basis of generalizations statable about empirical phenomena. The requirement that linguistic hypotheses must have empirical support is not derived from any arbitrary or aesthetic considerations. Rather, this requirement is grounded in the widely accepted goals of linguistic theory, namely, the characterization of the linguistic competence of the native speaker. The nature of these goals requires that any prediction made by a linguistic theory be testable against native-speaker intuitions.

NOTES

1. These forms are represented orthographically, as they appear in Foley's article.

REFERENCES

Baker, C. L. (1970) "Notes on the description of English questions: The role of an abstract question morpheme." *Foundations of Language* 6:197-219.

Bresnan, J. (1970) "On complementizers: Toward a theory of complement types." *Foundations of Language* 6:297-321.

Chomsky, N. (1965) *Aspects of the Theory of Syntax*. Cambridge, Mass.: M.I.T. Press.

_____ and M. Halle (1968) *The Sound Pattern of English*. New York: Harper and Row.

Foley, J. (1967) "Spanish plural formation." *Language* 43:486-493.

Hyman, L. (1970) "How concrete is phonology?" *Language* 46:58-76.

McCawley, J. (1970) "English as a VSO language." *Language* 46:286-299.

Northrop, F. (1949) *The Logic of the Sciences and the Humanities*. New York: Macmillan.

Perlmutter, D. M. (1971) *Deep and Surface Structure Constraints in Syntax*. New York: Holt, Rinehart and Winston.

Ross, J. R. (1970) "Gapping and the order of constituents," in M. Bierwisch and K. E. Heidolph (eds.), *Progress in Linguistics*. The Hague: Mouton.

_____ (1972) "Act," in D. Davidson and G. Harman (eds.), *Semantics of Natural Language*. Dordrecht, The Netherlands, D. Reidel Publishing Co.

Smith, N. V. (1967) "The phonology of Nupe." *Journal of African Languages* 6:153-169.

3

Hypothetical constructs in syntax

Michael B. Kac
University of Minnesota

It is a commonplace of the philosophy of science, constantly reiterated in the recent history of linguistics, that the constructs required in theory formation are necessarily "abstract" and that it is impossible to require of any science that it couch its theories entirely in terms of observables. This claim is valid, and I have no wish to dispute it here. I intend to argue nonetheless that the doctrine of the abstractness of hypothetical constructs has been abused in some of the most influential linguistic work of recent years and that its significance must, as a consequence, be rather drastically reassessed. The central problem currently confronting the generatively oriented study of language, in my view, is not that we have too many alternative theories and too much equivocal data; we have no theory at all, and hence nothing for linguistic data to be relevant to.

Comments and criticisms by Larry Hutchinson on an earlier draft of this chapter are gratefully acknowledged. Portions of the research reported here were carried out during the summer of 1974 under a stipend from the National Endowment for the Humanities.

In making a case for this admittedly pessimistic position, I will proceed as follows:

1. I will first draw, and justify, a distinction between what I will call *valid abstractions* as opposed to *fictions,* and will define certain criteria that must be satisfied in order for an abstract construct to be considered an instance of the former. I will also draw a second distinction, between hypothetical constructs in general (whether valid or fictitious) and *observational representations*—that is, expressions of observation statements in some metalanguage; I will maintain that hypothetical constructs and observational representations have sometimes been confused.

2. Having drawn and justified these distinctions, I will examine some paradigmatic syntactic arguments which will be seen to be invalid either because they fail to satisfy the criteria for argumentation in support of valid abstractions, or because they confuse hypothetical constructs with observational representations.

3. Finally, I will argue that certain claims about abstractness in syntax are erroneous because of a persistent confusion between theories (i.e., collections of hypotheses) and the metalanguages within which these theories are couched. Transformational generative grammarians have opted for a metalanguage of a certain type, within which recourse to certain kinds of representations is considered necessary if the simplest and most perspicuous statements of significant generalizations are to be made; but metalanguages exist in which exactly the same results can be achieved without recourse to such representations, from which it follows that the claim that these representations are required by an adequate syntactic theory is false.

SECTION 1

We must begin by considering what is meant by the terms "abstract" and "abstraction" as they are currently employed in linguistics. This turns out to be rather difficult to do since little has been done by way of careful definition of these terms, and examination of the literature shows them to be used in a variety of senses. The most etymologically strict interpretation identifies "abstract" with "incomplete." To abstract x from y is to remove x from y, the resulting object then being "abstract" in that it is missing some attribute or property. An "abstract general concept," for example, is one specifying only certain properties of the members of a class of objects and not others. For example, the concept of triangularity pertains to a certain kind of geometrical configuration associated with certain objects, but not to their size, ratios of sides or angles, etc.; such properties of individual triangles have been abstracted away in the formation of the general concept. One important difference between empiricist and rationalist philosophy concerns the epistemological validity of such concepts, empiricists holding that if all knowledge is based on experience, then there can be no abstract general concepts since one can never have experience of attributes such as triangularity alone. Abstractness in this sense is also what is involved in the relationship of the classical phoneme to its phonetic counterparts: In specifying a phoneme, and in distinguishing it from others, we deliberately exclude certain phonetic information from the specification.

In a second, but related sense, "abstract" means something like "ideal" or, even better, "idealized." Scientific laws may be formulated with reference to ideal systems, in which certain variables are deliberately ignored. The linguist's notion of the ideal speaker-hearer is also a case in point, the variables being ignored having to do with social pressures, effects of intoxication, limitations of short-term memory, and so on.

The third and loosest sense identifies "abstract" with "unobservable", "known by inference rather than observation." I do not know whether this usage is common in other sciences (e.g., whether a physicist would feel comfortable with the statement "Atoms are abstract entities"), but I think that it is fair to say that this usage is widespread in present-day linguistics. The term "abstract analysis" commonly calls to mind analyses in which structures or segments are posited at some level for which there is no direct observational evidence: If, for example, some language is analyzed as having segments of type s at the underlying level but does not have such segments in its phonetic inventory, then the underlying segments are commonly referred to as "abstract." By contrast, a phonological description of a language which permits only the kinds of abstractions inherent in classical phonemics would typically be called "concrete." It must be emphasized, however, that abstractions of the kind now under discussion need not be confined to underlying levels of analysis: A surface syntactic structure is similarly abstract in that its analysis into constituents is also determined by inference rather than by direct observation. That is, one does not observe the tree or bracketing directly but assigns it hypothetically via a particular chain of inferential reasoning.

Recourse to abstractions of this third type poses significant problems for theories with regard to accountability. Clearly this recourse cannot be unconstrained since if it were there would be no way to distinguish scientific theories from fanciful or mythic accounts of the world. For an abstract hypothetical construct to be valid rather than fictitious, it must satisfy certain specific criteria. Among these, the following two are of special significance:

A. The construct must be shown to be "essential," that is, it must be shown that an adequate account of the facts is possible only if recourse to this construct is permitted.[1]
B. Maintenance of the construct must not come at the cost of the introduction of ad hoc auxiliary hypotheses.

It is important to point out that these criteria were not simply invented so as to provide a foundation for a particular type of argument; they would be accepted as among the necessary conditions on valid theory formation in any established science. Criterion B is critically related to the requirement of falsifiability: If one has unlimited recourse to ad hoc auxiliary assumptions, then one can always insulate an hypothesis from disconfirmation by adding whatever additional assumptions are necessary to protect it; hence, no such additional assumptions are admissible without independent support. We shall see presently that some widely accepted syntactic arguments are in clear violation of this criterion.[2]

An abstraction which fails to satisfy criteria A or B is a fictitious abstraction, or, more simply, a fiction. An abstraction which satisfies A and B meets at least the necessary conditions

for validity; that A and B may not constitute sufficient conditions is due to the fact that they make no reference to the
explanatory or predictive power of hypotheses, normally taken
into account in defining the conditions for validity.

A second distinction must be drawn between hypothetical
constructs (of whatever type) and observational representations.
As noted above, an observational representation is simply an
expression, in some metalanguage, of an observation statement.
Semantic representations, for example, are observational representations; this is so because (a) meanings are observationally
accessible—that is, are part of the data domain of linguistics, and
(b) to assert that sentence S has semantic representation R is
merely to say that S has the meaning of which R is the
expression in the metalanguage chosen for the description of
meanings.[3]

Let us now examine what I would take to be a paradigm case
of a valid argument for an abstract hypothetical construct in
linguistics. In accounting for the ambiguity of the constructional
hononym *old men and women* and parallel examples, the
assumption is generally made that the ambiguity is due to the
fact that alternate constitutent structures may be assigned to
such constructions. The structures may be given as follows:

(1) a.

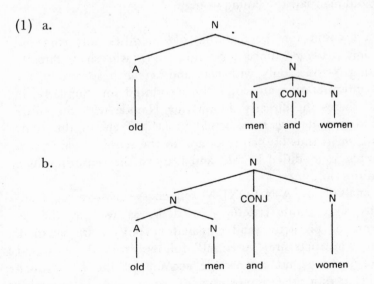

b.

This analysis presupposes the equivalences A-N = N and

N-CONJ-N = N (alternately expressible as phrase structure rules N → A-N and N → N-CONJ-N), which are themselves justified by the significant similarities in behavior observable between A-N and N-CONJ-N sequences and simplex N's.[4] The point is that if one accepts these equivalences, then there is an indeterminacy as to how they are to applied in building up the trees for A-N-CONJ-N sequences; both (1a, b) satisfy the formulae in different ways. In either case, an abstract level of organization is imposed on a linearly arranged sequence of morphemes—the structures imposed being no less abstract for the fact that they are applied to the surface level.

There is one further step, however, which is commonly ignored but which is absolutely crucial. An auxiliary assumption *is* required here, namely that an attributive adjective modifies only the N with which it shares a directly dominating N-node. Notice that unless this assumption is made, there is no way to interpret the two groupings shown in (1); more significantly, it must be shown that the connection between the alternate groupings (1a, b) and the ambiguity of the expression *old men and women* is not a fortuitous one. But the auxiliary assumption must be made in any case since, given a sentence like

(2) The old man saw the young woman.

we must account for the fact that *old* modifies only *man* and *young* only *woman*. Since *old* and *young* will share directly dominating N-nodes only with *man* and *woman* respectively, the facts of interpretation are correctly accounted for. Similarly, in (1a), *old* shares the directly dominating N-node with the entire expression *men and women,* while in (1b) it shares this node only with *men*; thus (1a) corresponds to the sense in which *men and women* is modified by *old* and (1b) to the sense in which *old* modifies only *men*.

This analysis of A-N-CONJ-N sequences involves valid abstractions since both criteria A and B, as well as the requirements of predictive and explanatory power, are satisfied. That the constructs are "essential" follows from the fact that there seems to be no comparable account of the facts which does not permit the imposition of some sort of grouping structure on sequences of morphemes; moreover, though an auxiliary assumption is required, this assumption is non–ad hoc, having independent motivation provided by cases like (2). The predictive and explanatory power of the analysis can be seen from its primary motivation, which is to account for the similarities in behavior between simplex N's and A-N and N–CONJ–N sequences. The relevant rules, which assign the structures $[_N A-N]$ and $[_N N\text{-CONJ-}N]$, jointly predict alternative bracketings for A–N–CONJ–N sequences. This prediction, accompanied by the auxiliary principle of semantic interpretation, explains why such sequences are ambiguous: Depending on which bracketing is assigned, A shares a directly dominating N-node with a different expression, and its scope of modification is accordingly affected.[5]

SECTION 2

I turn now to consideration of two representative analyses from the recent history of the development of generative grammatical theory, both of which involve "abstract" elements and have been widely accepted, but which fail to satisfy criteria A and B, cited in the previous section. Both analyses involve the postulation of underlying structures which do not occur as surface structures, that is, in which elements occur in configurations in which they would not be able to occur in actual sentences of the languages under analysis. These underlying structures are "abstract" since direct inspection of actual sentences of the languages in question will never encounter such configurations.

2.1 Underlying SVO Order in Hindi[6]

Ross (1971) proposes the following constraint governing the directionality of gapping:

(3) The order in which gapping operates depends on the order of elements at the time the rule applies; if the identical elements are on left branches, gapping operates forward; if they are on right branches, it operates backward.

This principle is intended as a general hypothesis by means of which to account for such differences as that between English and Japanese with respect to the nature of gapped coordinations. Specifically, English (which is presumed to have underlying SVO order) can gap only in second conjuncts, while Japanese (whose underlying order is presumed to be SOV) can gap only in first conjuncts. Hindi, however, presents a problem for this hypothesis: Like Japanese, it is verb-final in surface structure, but unlike Japanese (or English) it can gap bi-directionally. That is, either SO–SOV or SOV–SO coordinations may be found in the language, according to Ross, who seeks to reconcile these facts with the principle given in (3) by assuming (a) that Hindi has SVO order in underlying structure, and (b) that there is an inversion transformation which obligatorily derives verb-final surface order. (In point of fact, (b) breaks down into two separate assumptions, both ad hoc: that Hindi has the transformation in question, and that the transformation is obligatory. That these assumptions are logically independent of each other can be seen if we consider a language like Russian, which has both SVO and SOV surface orders; if this is accounted for by a similar inversion transformation, the rule in question is optional.)

The inference from the facts pertaining to gapping in Hindi to the hypothesis that, at a more abstract level, the language has SVO order (even though sentences with this order are not accessible to direct observation through inspection of the language) can easily be shown to be invalid since the overall hypothesis fails to fulfill criterion B. The maintenance of the hypothesis requires two ad hoc auxiliary assumptions: that Hindi has an inversion rule for deriving verb-final order, and that this rule is obligatory. (Notice also that the hypothesis has no predictive power; it serves merely to insulate (3) from possible disconfirmation.)

The problem here is that the facts have been misread, the misreading resulting from a confusion as to what can be taken as fact and what is to be taken as hypothetical. Notice that (3) contains the qualification "at the time the rule applies"; thus, the correlation postulated between constituent order and gapping is not based on the empirically observable surface orders of languages. Since there are no principled limitations (at least in the theory assumed by Ross) on what can be a possible nonsurface order of constituents (whether or not it is the order at the most deeply underlying level), one is free, given the statement of (3), to set up whatever apparatus is necessary to guarantee the correct results. But then (3) could itself never be falsified; since all that is required is that the correlation between constituent order and directionality of gapping be maintained with regard to structures at arbitrarily selected points in derivations, and since there are no constraints on possible orders of constituents at any of these points, the entire analysis is vacuous.

If we confine ourselves solely to facts (at least insofar as they pertain to Ross's sample of languages), we discern a different picture. The real generalization is as follows,

(4) a. Full SVO–SVO coordinations may not have corresponding SO–SVO gapped coordinations.
     b. Full SOV–SOV coordinations may have corresponding SO–SOV gapped coordinations.

where SOV and SVO designate surface constituent order exclusively. What is of cardinal importance here is that (4) does not claim that SOV structures should admit either bidirectional gapping or backward gapping exclusively; it states only that full conjunctions in the form SOV–SOV are a necessary condition for the possibility of backward gapping. This statement is thus consistent with both the Hindi and Japanese facts, these languages being alike just insofar as they both have backward gapping and surface verb-final order. It is also worth pointing out that it is not clear why Ross chose Japanese to serve as the paradigm case of a verb-final language with regard to gapping since the majority of such languages in his sample behave like Hindi (Turkish, German, Russian, Latin) and only one other language (Siouan) shows the same pattern as Japanese. In other words, bidirectional gapping is the expected case for verb-final languages, with the unidirectional situation in Japanese and Siouan being exceptional.

The overall mode of argumentation used by Ross is more than slightly reminiscent of that employed by proponents of the phlogiston theory in seeking to falsify the hypothesis that combustion is due to combination with oxygen. To explain the weight gain observed after oxidation, they suggested that if phlogiston were assumed to have negative weight, its release by the substance in combustion would naturally cause an increase in its weight. The attribution of negative weight to phlogiston is a textbook example (see for example, Hempel, 1964) of recourse to an ad hoc auxiliary assumption to protect an hypothesis from disconfirmation.[7]

2.2. Equi-NP Deletion and Associated Structures

It is commonly (though not universally) claimed by transformational generative grammarians that sentences like (5a) derive from underlying structures like (5b):

(5) a. Harry wants to go.
     b. [$_S$ Harry wants [$_S$ Harry go]]

Structures like (5b) are "abstract" since they do not conform to well-formed sentences of English; for such a structure to be rendered grammatical as a surface structure, the embedded clause Subject must be either deleted or reflexivized and the complementizer *to* must be inserted ahead of the verb. (The matter of complementizer insertion will not concern us here.) In keeping with current terminological practice, I will call (5b) an "Equi-structure" and the transformation deriving (5a) from (5b) "Equi-NP Deletion"; (5a) itself will be called a "truncated complement structure" or "TC-structure."

Arguments of several different kinds have been given for the analysis of TC-structures whose outlines have just been sketched. I would like to consider one such argument in the form which it takes in a recent textbook.[8] First, the following paradigm is presented:

(6) I want Bill to go.
(7) Bill wants me to go.
(8) You want me to go.
(9) I want you to go.
(10) You want Bill to go.
(11) Bill wants you to go.

(12) a. *You want you to go.
      b. You want to go.
(13) a. *I want me to go.
      b. I want to go.
(14) a. *Bill wants Bill to go.
      b. Bill wants to go.

concerning which the author says the following:

> On the basis of sentences [(6–11)] it is apparent that *I*, *you*, and *Bill* (like an indefinite number of other noun phrases) can occur as either the subject of the main clause or as the subject of the subordinate clause. However, the (a)-expressions in [(12–14)] seem to vitiate this otherwise valid generalization. Although [(12a–14a)] contain no main or subordinate clause subject that does not appear in the same role in [(6–11)], these sentences are ungrammatical.

> Closer examination reveals this irregularity to be only apparent. The ungrammatical sentences are not randomly distributed . . .; they are exactly those in which the main and subordinate clause subjects are identical. Moreover, each of the ungrammatical (a)-sentences is paralleled by a grammatical sentence—namely the corresponding (b)-sentence—that is identical to it except for the lack of a subordinate clause subject. The (b)-sentences fill the gap in an otherwise regular pattern that is created by the ungrammaticality of the (a)-sentences.

> These facts suggest that a syntactic rule of English requires the deletion of the subject in subordinate clauses . . . when the subject happens to be identical to a noun phrase in the main clause. Thus [(12a–14a)] can be posited as underlying representations; at the level of underlying representations, the generalization is maintained that *I*, *you*, *Bill*, and so on, can function either as main or subordinate clause subjects. This regularity is obscured somewhat in surface structure by the operation of the subject deletion rule which derives the (b)-sentence from the underlying (a)-structures. . . . We see consequently, that underlying structures such as *I want I/me to go* have a certain amount of syntactic motivation. By positing them as underlying structures, we avoid having to mar an otherwise regular pattern by excluding structures in which the two subjects happen to be identical. (p. 106)

This explanation is an example of what is sometimes called the "hole-in-the-paradigm" argument form: The underlying representations called for are presumed to be motivated on the grounds that they fill the holes, thus providing, at some level of representation, a fully regular set of structures despite the "irregularity" of the surface paradigm. It is commonly asserted that analyses which do not permit such abstract structures as Equi-structures "miss a generalization" in that they must provide ad hoc devices for assigning certain properties to the irregular structures (TC-structures in this instance). On the other hand, if the irregular cases are derived from abstract regular ones, then the devices motivated for the regular cases will handle the irregular ones as well. In this sense, an "apparent" irregularity can be eliminated and certain "deeper" analogies shown between superficially distinct kinds of structures.

This particular type of argument can, however, be shown to be empty. The reason is that the analyses it leads to are no more general (or less ad hoc) than more concrete alternatives. Let us develop this claim further, since it contains the key to the demonstration that Equi-structures are fictions if taken as hypothetical constructs.

We first of all consider how the paradigm would be treated if Equi-structures were not posited as underlying the particular class of constructions that we are calling TC-structures, and the TC-structures were themselves regarded as underived. We would thus need the following phrase structure rules:

$$(15) \quad VP \rightarrow \begin{Bmatrix} V–S \\ V–VP \end{Bmatrix} \quad \begin{matrix} a. \\ b. \end{matrix}$$

Rules (15, a, b) are involved in the generation of sentences like (16a) and (16b) respectively:

(16) a. [$_S$Harry knows [$_S$Bill is smart]]
     b. [$_S$Harry wants [$_{VP}$to kiss Maxine]]

To block sentences like

(17) *Harry wants Harry to kiss Maxine.

that is, to prevent the generation of Equi-structures, we adduce the following output constraint:

(18) Mark as ill-formed any sentence in which two identical

nonpronominal NP's occur in a configuration such that either commands the other.[9]

(Given the rules (15a, b), sentences like (17) actually are generated but only as garbage to be filtered out by (18). This is in contrast to the situation in the abstract analysis, where a structure like (17) would be considered well-formed at some level.) The constraint (18) will block (17) since the first occurrence of *Harry* commands the second.

It might appear that this analysis is ad hoc in two respects: First, it requires the phrase structure rule (15b), ostensibly not required under the abstract analysis, and second, it requires the output constraint (18). But the abstract analysis turns out to be no less ad hoc since it requires (a) a phrase structure rule corresponding to (15a), (b) a transformation of Equi-NP Deletion, and (c) a statement to the effect that this transformation is obligatory. That the obligatoriness of the rule must be dealt with by some such independent statement follows from the fact that there is no way to know a priori whether a given transformation will be obligatory or optional. The number of distinct devices required by the abstract Equi analysis (three) is thus exactly the same as that required by the concrete analysis. But further investigation reveals that, in fact, the concrete analysis is *less* ad hoc than the Equi analysis for the simple reason that the constraint (18) has broad applicability. Consider the following paradigm:

(19) a. *Harry likes Harry.
      b. *Harry kissed the girl that liked Harry.
      c. *Harry is happy because the girl kissed Harry.
      d. Harry likes Maxine and Maxine likes Harry.
      e. Harry came and Harry left.
      f. Harry likes Fred and Maxine likes Fred.

In (19a–c), one of two occurrences of *Harry* commands the other and thus (18) predicts, correctly, that all should be ill-formed. Significantly, however, the sentences in question are not Equi-structures; in other words, (18) would be required in any case in a concrete syntactic theory and is not adduced ad hoc for the case of Equi-structures. In the coordinate sentences

(19d–f), no command relation obtains in either direction between identical occurrences of *Harry,* and thus, the sentences are well formed.

The difference between the two analyses, in short, is that under the concrete analysis, the nonoccurrence of Equistructures is accounted for by a general, independently motivated constraint on output, whereas under the abstract analysis in its usual form, such structures are blocked by an ad hoc obligatoriness specification attached to a particular rule. It is, of course, possible to modify the Equi analysis in such a way as to retain the abstract underlying structures while accounting for the surface facts via constraint (18) rather than via extrinsic rule application constraints; but since exactly the same syntactic facts can be accounted for without assuming such structures, insofar as the "hole-in-the-paradigm" considerations presented above are at issue, there is no evidence in favor of the abstract analysis over the concrete one.

Let us now return to the textbook argument cited above. What was centrally at issue there was an apparent "irregularity" which was claimed to be able to be eliminated if the Equi analysis is adopted; or, as the author puts it, assuming that there is an abstract underlying level at which Equi-structures occur as well-formed objects, it is possible to "avoid having to mar an otherwise regular pattern." The invalidity of this rationale as support for the Equi analysis can be clearly seen against the backdrop of the foregoing discussion. Observe first of all that the author has confused the idea of *capturing* or *expressing* a generalization with *inventing* or *creating* one. By positing Equistructures to "fill the holes," we merely conjure up an artificial world, so to speak, in which the facts are as we would like them to be rather than as they are. That we gain nothing in terms of true generality by this approach becomes immediately evident when we see what must be done to make up for the discrepancy between our idealized hypothetical state of affairs (in which all structures are "regular") and the actual state of the language: We must adduce ad hoc rules to indicate just what modifications must be made in the ideal structures before they can be read out as sentences. It is thus not true that the need to "mar the pattern" can be avoided—since the pattern will, even given access to abstract Equi-structures, be marred by the fact that just these structures have to undergo some sort of transformation before they can be accepted as well-formed sentences. There is, in other words, no way to really fill the holes; regardless of the analysis adopted, abstract or concrete, TC-structures have to be viewed as having certain special properties. We can, however, attempt to establish some sort of link between the gap in the paradigm (6–14) and between similar gaps in other paradigms—which is precisely what the output constraint (18) permits us to accomplish. The ultimate result is that the entire argument is turned on its head, since not only does the Equi analysis not capture the generalization to which it lays claim (there being no such generalization to be captured), it misses a valid and significant generalization at least insofar as it depends on the use of ad hoc extrinsic rule application constraints. If such constraints are employed, then Equi-structures are fictions since criterion B for valid abstractions is violated; but if they are supplanted by an output constraint such as (18), Equi-structures are still fictitious since (18) is consistent with a concrete analysis and thus essentiality for Equi-structures cannot be shown, in violation of criterion A.

Let us now consider a different type of argument, which runs in two parts as follows:[10]

(i) If we compare TC-structures with sentences like

(20) Harry wants Bill to go.

we perceive an analogy. Comparing (20) to

(21) Harry wants to go.

we note that *Harry* plays the roles of *Harry* and *Bill* in (20). In other words, even though the relevant semantic information is not encoded in a structure like

(22) *Harry wants Harry to go.

the interpretation of (21) corresponds to what would be the interpretation of (22) if the latter were actually a sentence of English. It thus seems plausible to suppose that speakers of English have some sort of psychological access to Equi-structures even if they do not normally employ them, and regard them as deviant when encountered.

(ii) But further, if we accept the foregoing, then we can account simultaneously for the semantic facts and the syntax: While the concrete analysis can handle the former only at the expense of an ad hoc rule of semantic interpretation just for TC-structures, the abstract Equi analysis requires no such special extra device since, by virtue of deriving TC-sentences from Equi-structures, it predicts that truncated sentences should have exactly the semantic properties that they actually do have; but the required transformation, Equi-NP Deletion, has independent motivation since it accounts for the syntax, that is, for the fact that Equi-structures are inadmissible on the surface, by obligatorily converting them into TC-structures.[11]

The problem with this argument is that the (ii)-section is false—or at least misleading—since it ignores a crucial difference between the abstract and concrete accounts of the facts. I have myself ignored this difference up to this point because nothing hinged on it; but it becomes crucial now, and must be discussed. As a beginning, let us again compare the two analyses as to the devices imputed to them so far:

Equi Analysis	Concrete Analysis
1. Phrase structure rule (15a)	1. Ditto
2. Equi-NP Deletion	2. Phrase structure rule (15b)
3. Application constraint on Equi-NP Deletion	3. Constraint (18)

On this comparison, the two are equivalent in terms of number of devices needed—three for each. Let us consider now a phenomenon not yet discussed, namely the fact that the application of Equi-NP Deletion (or, in theoretically more neutral terms, the capacity of a verb to enter into TC-structures) is governed. To illustrate, we examine the four verbs *believe*, *expect*, *want*, and *condescend*, which exhibit these various possibilities:

(23) a. Harry believes (that) he will win.
       b. *Harry believes to win.

   c. Harry expects that he will win.
   d. Harry expects to win.
   e. *Harry wants (that) he will win.
   f. Harry wants to win.
   g. *Harry condescended (that) he would go.
   h. *Harry condescended (for) himself to go.
   i. Harry condescended to go.

Confining ourselves for the moment just to *believe, expect,* and *want,* we must, regardless of approach, indicate the following in the lexicon by some appropriate means: (a) that all three verbs may take complements in the Object relation (that is, that the Object of all three may be a predication), and (b) that the three differ with regard to the types of surface configurations into which they may enter. Thus, under any analysis, two kinds of statements are needed, one to specify a certain semantic property of the verbs in question, and another to control surface contexts of such verbs. Now consider *condescend*: This is a paradigmatic like-Subject verb, that is, one which requires that its Subject and that of its complement be identical. In an abstract treatment, there are several alternative ways of accounting for the properties of such verbs:

(i) One possibility is to make use of strict subcategorization and rule features, marking all like-Subject verbs as [+__ S, +EQUI]; if, for any reason, Equi-NP Deletion should be inapplicable at any point in a derivation of a sentence containing a verb so marked, then all sentences derivable from the underlying structure in which the verb is inserted will be ill-formed.

(ii) A second possible device would be that of a positive absolute exception. To make use of such a device would be to make two statements relative to *condescend*: first, that it must enter into a structure which satisfies the SD of Equi-NP Deletion, and second, that this structure actually undergo the transformation involved. If either condition is failed, then the structure into which *condescend* or any similar verb is inserted is ill-formed.

(iii) Finally, we could make use of a device like Perlmutter's deep structure constraints[12] according to which verbs like *condescend* are marked as obeying the restriction that identity must obtain between their own Subject and the complement Subject.

In addition, all such predicates must be marked [+EQUI-NP DELETION], as in the first account. (This could be accomplished via a redundancy rule [+LIKE-SUBJECT] → [+EQUI-NP DELETION].)

All three treatments have a crucial property in common: They all require that *two* statements be made about like-Subject verbs—one to control the underlying structures into which such verbs are inserted, and one to guarantee that these structures surface only as TC-structures. Now consider what will happen under a concrete analysis: All that will be required is that like-Subject verbs be marked as entering only into TC-structures. One statement to this effect will account completely for the surface facts; it will, of course, also be necessary to account for the semantic facts, and hence some sort of rule will be needed to specify that in a sentence like (23i), *condescend* and *go* are understood to have the same Subject.[13] But this rule, however formulated, will apply to all TC-structures, not just to those containing like-Subject verbs. Now let us compare the Equi analysis and the concrete analysis: Under both, it is necessary to make distinct statements about non-like-Subject verbs marking predicates such as *believe, expect,* and *want* as taking Object complements and as entering into certain types of surface configurations but not others. Under the former, it is also necessary to make two kinds of statements about like-Subject verbs; but under the latter, it is necessary to make only one kind of statement (confining such verbs to occurrence in TC-structures), though it may be necessary to have a principle of semantic interpretation in the latter not required in the former (see fn. 13). There is, in other words, an exact tradeoff, summarized as follows:

Equi Analysis	Concrete Analysis
1. Phrase structure rule (15a)	1. Ditto
2. Equi-NP Deletion	2. Phrase structure rule (15b)
3. Application constraint on Equi-NP Deletion	3. Constraint (18)
4. Remote structure restriction on non–like-Subject verbs taking complements	4. Ditto
5. Surface structure restrictions on non–like-Subject verbs taking complements	5. Ditto

6. Remote structure restriction on like-Subject verbs	6. Rule of semantic interpretation (subject to qualification in fn. 13)
7. Surface structure restriction on like-Subject verbs	7. Ditto

In short, the abstract analysis is able to account for the syntax and semantics of TC-constructions via a single device (i.e., an obligatory Equi-NP Deletion rule applied to Equi-structures); it does so at the cost of requiring a more complex treatment of like-Subject verbs than would be required in the concrete analysis—even though the latter does not give a "uniform" account of the syntactic and semantic facts. The criteria for choice between the two thus cannot be based on considerations of generality or lack of ad hocity since they correspond point-by-point in number of distinct devices required.

Yet a third defense of the Equi analysis might be mounted as follows: Suppose the requirement of syntactic motivation for underlying representations is dispensed with entirely, underlying structures being presumed valid if they exhibit semantic properties of the sentences to which they correspond with a certain degree of transparency. For example: A TC-structure such as

(24) Harry wants to go.

consists of a single clause, but expresses two distinct prepositions or predications. In order to exhibit its semantic organization more transparently, therefore, it is regarded as being derived from the Equi-structure

(25) [$_S$ Harry wants [$_S$ Harry go]]

in which, among other things, there is an S corresponding to each predication in the meaning of the sentence. Given that one adheres to certain principles for the interpretation of underlying P-markers, (25) may also be taken as indicating that *Harry* is the Subject of both verbs, that the embedded predication is the Object of *want*, and so on. These principles, or reading conventions, are what permit particular underlying configurations to be associated with particular semantic interpretations.[14] (That (25) cannot itself *be* a semantic representation follows from the

fact that it is subject to further interpretation by these conventions.) The argument continues: Since underlying structures
need be motivated only by semantic considerations (this motivation consisting in showing that some specified structure is the
most transparent one given the meaning of the sentences with
which it is associated, and that the correct interpretation follows
when the appropriate reading conventions are applied to this
structure) and since (25) and similar structures may be presumed
adequate on these grounds, therefore a theory with recourse to
such structures is justified.

   In responding to this hypothetical argument, I will not
attempt to deal with matters of validity or invalidity, confining
myself to the following claim: If it is granted that the argument
is valid, it nonetheless fails to support the claim that abstract
underlying structures are valid hypothetical constructs in syntactic theory since, so motivated, they fail to be hypothetical
constructs at all. They are, rather, observational representations—that is, translations of observation statements into a
particular metalanguage. This is so because (a) statements about
meanings of sentences, or, more accurately, statements of associations of meanings with sentences, are observation statements; and (b) structures like (25) are, on the view currently
under discussion, intended solely as translations into a syntactic
metalanguage of a series of semantic statements about sentences
like (24). For example, the semantic statement '(24) expresses
two propositions' is translated into the syntactic statement '(24)
is derived from a structure containing two S's'; similarly, 'Harry
is the subject of *want* and *go* in (24)' translates into '(24)
derives from an underlying structure in which *Harry* has two
occurrences, once as the NP directly dominated by the S most
directly dominating *want*, and once as the NP directly dominated by the S most directly dominating *go*'. In order to motivate
a particular underlying representation for a sentence S, one need
know only (a) the meaning of S, and (b) the translation rules
(equivalent to the reading conventions alluded to above) by
which a full description of the meaning of S is converted into a
P-marker. The key point here is that hypothetical constructs are,
by definition, posited via a chain of inference; but a structure
like (25), if presumed to be motivated solely by semantic
considerations, is based not on inferential reasoning from facts

but on translation via a conventional procedure of observation statements form one expressive medium to another.

The third type of motivation for Equi-structures (and abstract underlying structures in general) seems to me to be both the most sound and the one most true to the actual working practices of transformational grammarians regardless of orientation—even though it fails to provide a basis for the claim that certain kinds of hypothetical constructs are required in syntactic theory. On this view, a transformational generative grammar may be reasonably viewed as a perspicuous algebraicization of the discrepancies between surface syntactic organization and an ideal type of organization dictated by certain semantic considerations. Since one central goal of syntactic theory is to explain why particular types of semantic information get encoded in certain ways and not others, it should be clear that there is much to be gained from careful descriptions of this sort.

Before concluding this portion of the paper, I would like to comment briefly on an analysis of English reflexive constructions of much the same kind as the Equi-analysis, and for which argumentation has been given which parallels that in the second argument considered above. As paradigm sentences, take

(26) a. Harry loves himself.
      b. *Harry loves Harry.

Concerning such sentence pairs, Postal (1969) says the following:

> to prevent the derivation of structures like [(26b)] and their analogues would require *adding* [original emphasis] special restrictions to the grammar prohibiting identical 'subjects' and 'objects' with a single verb. . . . . But now if structures like [(26b)] are enumerated they provide a simple means for describing correctly reflexive sentences if one simply adds the rule that the second noun phrase in a structure NP_1 + Verb + NP_2 + X is replaced by the appropriate reflexive pronoun when NP_1 = NP_2. This correctly derives just those reflexive strings which meet the equivalence condition stated before and permits retention of the noncomplicated verb–'object' and 'subject'–verb selection rules by eliminating the need for special restrictions to prevent the enumeration of the analogues of [(26b)]. *This follows because this new reflexive rule converts* [(26b)] *and all similar phrase markers into the superficial*

phrase markers which must represent the occurring sentences like [(26a)] *and these must be described anyway* [emphasis added, MBK]. But this analysis of reflexives provides an explanation [*sic*] of why an English speaker *understands* [original emphasis] reflexive sentences to refer [*sic*] to 'objects' identical to their 'subjects'. (p. 25)

Postal is arguing that the analysis he advocates is desirable because it employs a single device (i.e., the Reflexive transformation) to (a) circumvent an ad hoc restriction on identity of Subject and Object NP's in simple S's, and (b) account for the semantic interpretation of sentences like (25a). But the argument is fallacious because the emphasized statement to the effect that the reflexive rule converts all structures like (26b) into sentences like (26a) does not follow from the premises. Merely stating a rule to convert full NP's under requisite conditions of identity does not of itself guarantee that *all* structures meeting the SD for the rule will actually undergo the pertinent structural change. This is so because the rule could in principle be optional; the only way to guarantee that it applies to all structures meeting its SD is to add some further device to the grammar which guarantees that the rule will be obligatory. Hence it is not the case that the proposed Reflexive transformation accounts simultaneously for the surface restriction on identical Subjects and Objects and for the facts of interpretation; the rule itself accounts only for the latter, while the ad hoc obligatoriness specification is what accounts for the former. In a concrete analysis, the surface facts would be accounted for via the independently motivated constraint (18), while the semantics would be handled via an appropriately formulated rule of interpretation, the result being a treatment no more complex or ad hoc (and perhaps less so) than the one Postal advocates.

SECTION 3

I have tried to show in the foregoing section that certain typical arguments in favor of abstract analyses either fail to fulfill criteria A and B set down in Section 1, or turn out to be irrelevant to the question of validity of abstractions. Although I have discussed only a few such arguments, I believe they can be

taken as genuinely representative and that their form is repli-
cated again and again in the literature on transformational
generative grammar. In this final section, I would like to make
some general observations about the current state of syntactic
theory, particularly with a view toward clearing up some con-
fusions that currently impede its progress.

In the preceding section, I suggested that the most reasonable
view of transformational generative grammar (and the one truest
to the practices of its proponents) was such that a transformational description of a language is essentially an algebraicization of the relationship between surface syntax and semantically ideal syntactic organization. Transformational grammar in general may be viewed as providing a specific metalanguage within which to make statements about this relationship—statements whose utility and interest I do not question. It is important to stress, however, that there is a crucial
difference between a metalanguage and a theory. A theory is a
set of hypotheses for the explanation of facts concerning the
behavior of some system (whether it be 'natural' or 'formal', or,
in the case of human language, a mix of both), whereas a
metalanguage is merely a medium via which to express statements about the system (of both a hypothetical and an observational nature). It is thus mistaken to say that transformational generative grammar provides a theory of syntax; it
merely provides a metalanguage within which to couch such a
theory. It is, for certain purposes at least, a reasonable metalanguage, though it is neither the only one that could be
conceived for the purposes to which it is put nor the best for all
purposes for which a theory of the nature of language would be
desirable. I would like to suggest moreover that the best we can
hope to do with transformational generative grammars is to give
precise representations of facts; we cannot thereby explain the
facts. Furthermore, just as a metalanguage cannot be identified
with a theory, neither can a particular algebra or calculus
couched within a given metalanguage. A transformational grammar, viewed as an algebra of correlations between surface
syntactic structures and underlying, semantically based structures, is no more a theory of these correlations than propositional calculus is a theory of propositional logic or a set of
algorithms for ordinary arithmetic a theory of arithmetic. A

calculus for the manipulation of a system cannot be identified with a statement of the underlying principles of a system (i.e., a theory), though the discovery of such a calculus may assist in the discovery of those principles. We can construct underlying representations and posit transformations as components of an algorithm for mapping between these representations and surface structures, but we cannot thereby explain why the set of possible mappings turns out to have the properties it may then be observed to have. This does not mean that we do not sometimes have explanations at hand; but in such cases, it is the explanation which determines the form of the algebra, not the other way around. Let us illustrate this point with a standard example, namely the ambiguity of sentences like

(27) The chicken is ready to eat.

Such sentences are commonly cited as providing evidence that sentences must be described transformationally—that is, that they must be assigned structural descriptions at two distinct levels, thus necessitating transformational rules to map between the two. The essential rationale is that since only one surface structure is assignable to such a sentence, in this case

(28)

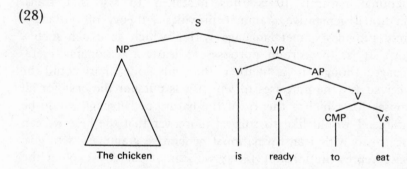

the ambiguity in question cannot be accounted for unless a second, abstract, level of analysis is introduced at which two distinct structures may be assigned. This argument is fallacious, in its usual form, since it erroneously assumes that the only way to represent the ambiguity of a grammatically (as opposed to lexically) ambiguous sentence is to assign it alternate P-markers at some level of representation. While this may be true in some cases, it is not true in all; all that is crucially necessary is that for an n-ways ambiguous sentence, there be a principled means of assigning n semantic representations to the sentence (in whatever formal medium has been selected for semantic representation—there being many possibilities) such that each representation correspond to one of the actual meanings of the sentence. It could be the case that a given ambiguous sentence has only one P-marker but, because of its particular properties, is such that certain principles of interpretation apply to it in such a way as to yield more than one result. We could indeed view (27) as just such a case; the facts, described as neutrally as possible, are the following:

F1. The verb *eat* can occur on the surface without an overt Object, in which case its Object is semantically unspecified.

F2. Any predicate can occur without an overt Subject, also construed as semantically unspecified, when embedded under an adjective like *ready*. The subordinate nonovert Subject, moreover, *must* be so construed if the Subject of the adjective is taken as the Object of the subordinate predicate. Thus, in the sentence

(29) The meat is ready to eat.

the meat must be taken as Object of *eat*, and the Subject of *eat* as unspecified.

F3. If a verb embedded under *ready* (or another adjective of the same class) has an unspecified Subject, then the Subject of *ready* must be the Object of this verb; thus *the meat* in (29) must be understood as the Object of *eat* in (29).

F4. Where selectional restrictions permit, however, the Subject of *ready* can also be the Subject of the embedded predicate, as in

(30) Harry is ready to go.

The facts F1–4 are stated with sufficient explicitness so as to be taken as actual grammatical rules. Returning to (27) we see that, in the light of these four statements, there is more than one conclusion that could be drawn about this particular structure. On the one hand, it could be assumed that *eat* occurs in this sentence with an unspecified Object; this means that *the chicken* could not be the object of *eat*; but *eat* requires a Subject, which, according to F4, may be the Subject of *ready*. We thus obtain the following characterization of the interpretation of (27) in crucial respects:

(31) a. Object of *eat*: unspecified (by F1)
      b. Subject of *eat*: *the chicken* (by F4)

On the other hand suppose we assume, following F3, that *the chicken* is the Object of *eat* by virtue of this verb being presumed to have an unspecified Subject (following F2); we thus assign the other possible interpretation such that

(32) a. Object of *eat*: *the chicken* (by F3, F2)
      b. Subject of *eat*: unspecified (by F2)

What is central to the explanation is the interaction of several properties of particular predicates and a specific type of syntactic construction; the properties, and their interaction, can be described, as they were above, entirely with reference to pretheoretical notions such as "Subject," "Object," "selectional restriction," and so on. At no point is it necessary to mention "underlying structures" or "transformations." In other words, we can state our explanation in a metalanguage which is completely neutral as to how the explanation might be translated into a particular type of algebraicization. One type of translation might involve assignment of alternate P-markers to (27) at a "deeper" level and the postulation of rules such that the structure in (28) is derivable from either; a different one might involve specification of procedures for inspecting surface P-markers and determining the various construals in terms of grammatical relations that could be assigned to it given particular properties of the specific construction and the lexical items it contains. The claim that the ambiguity of (27) can only be accounted for transformationally is false since (a) there is more than one algebraic translation of the explanation, and (b) the explanation itself can be stated independently of any such translation. Note that this is not to say that the standard transformational account of the facts is erroneous; all that is being claimed is that such notions as "transformation" and "underlying structure" play no essential role in the discovery or the articulation of the explanation, being merely terms of the metalanguage via which the explanation is expressed.

Consider now another case in point, namely the well-known analysis of English auxiliaries given in Chomsky (1957). This example deserves attention since it is one in which purely syntactic considerations motivate the underlying structures and transformations posited. What is at issue is the formation of English compound tenses as in

(33) a. Harry is kissing Maxine.
      b. Harry has kissed Maxine.
      c. *Harry is kissed Maxine.
      d. *Harry has kissing Maxine.
      e. *Harry is/has kiss Maxine.
      f. *Harry kissing Maxine.

There is, in other words, an auxiliary-affix dependence which holds across an intervening verb, or across an intervening auxiliary as in

(34) Harry has been kissing Maxine.

Such a situation, Chomsky argues, calls for an 'abstract' analysis since phrase structure rules in and of themselves cannot adequately handle discontinuous dependencies. His proposed solution (ignoring modals) is to expand the VP thus:

(35) VP → Aux-V-...

and Aux as follows:

(36) Aux → C-(have-en)-(be-ing)

where C is the agreement marker ultimately realized as s, $\emptyset$, or Past (as in *kisses, kiss, kissed*). A transformation of Affix Hopping is posited, which interchanges the position of a given affix (C, *en*, or *ing*) with the element to its immediate right:

(37) en-kiss ⇒ kiss-en (⇒ kissed)
      ing-kiss ⇒ kiss-ing
      C-kiss ⇒ kiss-C (⇒ *kisses, kiss, kissed*)[15]

The transformation may be stated thus:

(38) X-AF-*v*-Y ⇒ 1-3-2-4
      1 2 3 4
           where v = V, *have*, or *be*, and AF is a realization of C, or
           en or *ing*

Let us now consider precisely what factual claim this analysis makes. It may be viewed as specifying a mechanical procedure (algorithm) by which to generate VP's such that the following condition is always met by the structure generated:

(39) a. C is always attached to the end of the first v;
      b. *en* and *ing* attach to the end of the v to the immediate right of *have* and *be* respectively.

There are several points to raise in this regard:

(i) As long as C and v are adequately defined, the facts can be accounted for without any reference whatsoever to phrase structure rules, transformations, or underlying structures; Chomsky's rules are merely a translation of (39), which is given in what we might call a "descriptive" metalanguage, into a particular type of "procedural" metalanguage, that is, one associated with an algorithm for mechanically "cranking out" all and only these VP's with the requisite structural properties. The procedural expression of the facts happens to require certain kinds of statements; but insofar as truth claims about the structure of English are concerned, it makes no difference whether or not such a translation is made. The statement (39)—given a sufficiently rigorous definition of C and v—is every bit as precise as Chomsky's rules even though it is entirely neutral as to how one might formulate an algorithmic procedure for generating English VP's such that the relevant restriction is always satisfied. To say that (39) is formulated in a descriptive metalanguage is to say that the statement gives an explicit specification of what conditions must be satisfied by an English

VP in order to be well-formed as regards the placement of affixes and the relationship between affixes and auxiliaries; to say that (35), (36), and (38) are in a procedural metalanguage is to say that, without being as explicit as (39) as to the conditions to be satisfied, they specify how one might mechanically construct all and only those VP's meeting the aforesaid conditions. The central point is that there is no reason to suppose that this specific procedural metalanguage—or *any* such metalanguage, for that matter—must be adopted in order for the facts to be expressed in an explicit way. Indeed, the procedural statement is *less* explicit than the descriptive one in that for a direct statement of the restriction in question, it substitutes a procedure which states the restriction implicitly in specifying how it is to be satisfied in the mechanical construction of VP's by a certain type of algorithm. But then it follows that the claim that such structures as

(40) Harry–C–have–en–be–ing–kiss–Maxine

underlie sentences like

(41) Harry has been kissing Maxine

is merely an artifact of the adoption of a specific procedural metalanguage; the "abstract" structures and associated rules are merely elements of a complex representational device which is empirically exactly equivalent to (39). Since Chomsky's rules and (39) are thus notational (i.e., metalinguistic) variants of each other, structures like (40) have no critical theoretical role—since an account of the facts in a descriptive metalanguage, empirically equivalent to the procedural one, does not require mention of such structures.

(ii) The foregoing indicates that there are really two separate problems to be faced in accounting for the paradigm in (33): First, one must discover the relevant constraint on positioning of affixes and dependency between affixes and auxiliaries; second, one must—if one desires—find the appropriate expression of the constraint in procedural terms. Whether such an expression is presumed necessary, however, depends on what one is trying to accomplish. For many descriptive purposes, no such translation is necessary; if, on the other hand, one's selected problem is precisely that of discovering what procedural metalanguages are sufficient to express the relevant generalizations (and this is a legitimate question), then the matter of translation becomes significant. But to say that a language is a formal system of a particular type (i.e., that it is describable by a particular type of metalanguage) is not to explain its formal properties; it is merely to represent them. It is also important to bear in mind that there are many substantive questions in linguistics which need not presuppose any procedurally oriented analysis; it is widely recognized that there is a difference between discovering "what's going on" in a body of data and translating one's discovery into some particular expressive medium—whether it be that of transformational grammar, tagmemics, stratificational grammar, or whatever. Moreover, we have all been frustrated at one time or another, I suspect, by an excessive preoccupation in some segments of the literature with mechanical details at the expense of substantive insight. I do not mean to belittle concern with formalization by this remark; my point is that there are many ways to achieve formalization, and that they are a means to an end, not an end in themselves.

In the first paragraph of this paper, I made the remark "We have no theory at all, and hence nothing for linguistic data to be relevant to." I wish to conclude by briefly outlining the basis for this claim, in the light of the preceding discussion. First of all, for a theory to be worthy of the name, the argumentation by which its claims are supported must have a certain degree of rigor and sophistication; I am at present unconvinced that the most common types of syntactic argumentation employed by generative grammarians have attained a sufficiently high level. There appears to be widespread confusion as to the nature of necessary conditions to be met by valid arguments in favor of abstract constructs, and as to what is and is not a hypothetical construct in the first place. In addition, there is a pervasive tendency to confuse theory with metalanguage; much of the concern of recent work in syntax from a generatively oriented point of view has been with the capabilities of particular metalanguages to express particular kinds of generalizations (as illustrated by the preoccupation with "limiting the power of grammars" and with debate on the necessity of specific types of expressive devices such as global rules, arbitrary syntactic features, extrinsic ordering constraints, the transformational cycle, and so on), and hence with questions involving representation rather than explanation. Such questions are valid, but they hardly exhaust the concerns of a genuinely theoretical enterprise, which must be as concerned with explanation as with representation. Only when convincing and solidly supported explanations appear will we have what we presently lack and so urgently need: a theory of syntax.

NOTES

1. As stated, this criterion is perhaps overly strong since it may be read as implying that one can demonstrate necessity for empirical hypotheses; we must therefore qualify the criterion so as to identify 'essentiality' of a construct with the *preferability* of an account containing this construct to whatever alternate accounts are available at the time.
2. Note that it is not auxiliary assumptions themselves which are being disallowed; any auxiliary assumption that can be given independent motivation may then take its rightful place in a valid theory. The oxygen theory of combustion, for example, depends on the assumption of the law of conservation of mass; but this law appears valid for all chemical reactions and hence is an auxiliary hypothesis of a non-ad hoc character.
3. This does not mean that it is always immediately obvious what the meaning of a given sentence is—as any philosopher of language will be quick to point out. But the task of finding out, in an obscure case, what the meaning of an expression is is not one of theory construction; it is analogous, rather, to that in the natural sciences of obtaining accurate measurements. The claim that the meanings of expressions are accessible to observation does not imply that they are accessible to casual observation.
4. Among these similarities are distributional ones—for example, that N, N-CONJ-N, and A-N can all occur in the environment DET-___. But there are others as well. For example: Simple N's may undergo *one*-pronominalization, as in

   (i) Harry kissed the girl from Minneapolis and Fred kissed the one from Duluth.
   (ii) Harry kissed the girls from Minneapolis and Fred kissed the ones from Duluth.

   Now compare:

(iii) a. Harry kissed the pretty girl from Minneapolis and Fred kissed the one from Duluth.

   b. Harry kissed the women and girls from Minneapolis and Fred kissed the ones from Duluth.

The antecedents of *one* and *ones* in these cases are A–N and N–CONJ–N sequences respectively. I make an issue of this matter only because of the arguments in Postal (1964) against assuming the equivalences in question. Significantly, Postal presents no evidence against the equivalences and merely makes the *ex cathedra* pronouncement that they are "counterintuitive." He also attempts to argue that the required rules for generating such structures violate certain restrictions on phrase structure rules; but this is true only for phrase structure rules interpreted as rewriting rules—his conclusion does not apply to interpretations which omit derivations and define trees directly (cf. McCawley, 1968). Perhaps the most peculiar facet of the entire argument (which is directed principally against Harris's model of string analysis) is that it attempts to translate the rules in question into a metalanguage unsuited to them and then seeks to fault the rules because of this failure of translation.

5. Once the role of auxiliary assumptions is recognized, an apparent paradox of constituent structure analysis disappears. The equivalence N = N–CONJ–N can lead to alternative bracketings in cases of multiple conjunction; for example:

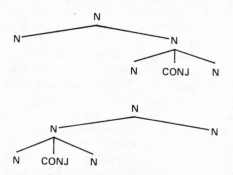

And yet there are unambiguous instances of such multiple coordinations. This is a paradox only if the assumption is made that a string with two constituent structures is necessarily ambiguous, an assumption which is false. A string with two constituent structures is ambiguous only if the alternate groupings affect the outcome of the application of principles of semantic interpretation. In the A–N–CONJ–N case, this is clearly so; but multiple coordinations with *and* may, if the *and* is construed as having the same meaning as the logical connective "&", have alternate groupings without ambiguity since this particular connective is associative. (That is, any expression of the form $(\alpha$ & $\beta)$ & γ is logically equivalent to α & $(\beta$ & $\gamma).$) Thus, given a sentence like

(iii) Harry and George and Max held up the First National Bank.

on its normal interpretation, there would be no ambiguity even though the coordinate N could be bracketed either as in (i) or as in (ii). By contrast, since $(\alpha$ & $\beta)$ v γ is not logically equivalent to α & $(\beta$ v $\gamma)$, (iv) will be ambiguous:

(iv) Harry and George or Max held up the First National Bank.

On the other hand, there are other senses of *and* than the "logical" one: For example, there is an "aggregating *and*," which serves the additional function of indicating that conjuncts refer to individuals or entities which are either naturally or conventionally associated as members of a group. In such cases, ambiguities can arise, as in the following situation: Max is married to Martha, but is having an affair with Laverne; Martha, in turn, is having an affair with Sidney. A party takes place at which all four are present, grouped as couples. Suppose this situation is described thus:

(v) Laverne and Max and Martha and Sidney were all at the party.

It is not possible to determine (unless intonation cues of some sort are provided) whether Max and Martha came as a couple or whether the couples present were Laverne and Max, and Martha and Sidney. Thus, with aggregating *and* there must be an interpretive principle which defines "scope of aggregation"; such a principle is naturally formulable in terms of constituent structure and would assign different readings to an expression assigned either the structure (i) or (ii).

6. For additional commentary on Ross's claims concerning the correlation of constituent order and directionality of gapping, see Eckman (this volume).

7. The problem is not that negative weight is an absurd notion, but that the claim that phlogiston has negative weight was never given independent support. Jon Ringen has pointed out to me that the phlogiston theory could have regained some credibility at the time it was first challenged if it could have been shown that attribution of negative weight to phlogiston could account for such additional phenomena as buoyancy. Suppose, for example, it could have been demonstrated that the buoyancy of a substance varied directly with the amount of phlogiston it was presumed to contain, all else held constant; such a demonstration would have had considerable force, but no such defense of the negative-weight hypothesis was ever successfully undertaken.

8. Langacker (1972): My reason for choosing a textbook as my source is

to emphasize the extent to which the argument in question is accepted as a standard one.

9. The qualification that the identical NP's must be nonpronominal is required because of well-formed sentences such as *You think you're smart.*

10. I know of no place in the literature where this precise argument is advanced; nonetheless, it closely parallels a well-known argument (Postal, 1969) for an abstract source for English reflexive constructions. This latter argument will be discussed at the end of Section 2.

11. This is presuming, of course, that transformations are meaning-preserving.

12. Though we would have to come to grips with the fact that the identity conditions affecting like-Subject verbs involve the *derived* Subject of the complement, not the deep structure Subject.

13. Actually, the necessity for such a rule is not clearly established. If it is assumed that every predicate in a sentence must have a Subject, and that a given NP in the sentence must play this role if its identification as Subject violates no other principles, then special Subject-identification rules are not needed for the TC-structures. For further discussion, see Kac (in manuscript and 1974).

14. The use of the term "convention" is important here. Any rules connecting such structures as (25) to semantic representations have to be viewed as nonempirical since without independent access to such hypothetical structures, we cannot make factual claims about their meanings.

15. Actually, in Chomsky's analysis, the morphological realization of C is effected before this affix is moved into its surface position—a point which leaves this discussion unaffected.

REFERENCES

Chomsky, N. (1957) *Syntactic Structures.* The Hague: Mouton.

Hempel, C. G. (1964) *Philosophy of Natural Science.* Englewood Cliffs, N.J.: Prentice-Hall.

Kac, M. B. (1974) Explanatory adequacy and the Complex NP constraint. Mimeographed. Indiana University Linguistics Club, Bloomington.

—— (in manuscript) Corepresentation of Grammatical Structure.

Langacker, R. W. (1972) *Fundamentals of Linguistic Analysis.* New York: Harcourt Brace Jovanovich.

McCawley, J. D. (1968) "Concerning the base component of a transformational grammar." *Foundations of Language* 4:243–269.

Postal, P. M. (1964) *Constituent Structure: A Study of Contemporary Models of Syntactic Description.* The Hague: Mouton.

_____ (1969) "Underlying and superficial grammatical structure," in D. Reibel and S. A. Schane (eds.), *Modern Studies in English*, pp. 19-37. Englewood Cliffs, N.J.: Prentice-Hall.

Ross, J. R. (1971) "Gapping and the order of constituents," in M. Bierwisch and K. E. Heidolph (eds.), *Progress in Linguistics*, pp. 249-259. The Hague: Mouton.

4

On significant generalizations: Notes on the Hallean syllogism

Jerrold M. Sadock
University of Chicago

The famous argument against autonomous phonemics given by Halle (1959) has become a model for generative grammatical methodology. Several attempts to copy it (including one by the present author) have been made, usually with the same intent: to demonstrate one linguistic model to be superior to another. Here I wish to examine that argument form on its philosophical merits. I will attempt to demonstrate that the conclusion that Halle came to was much too strong, and that, in general, the conclusions which generative grammarians reach on the basis of arguing from the loss or capture of generalizations are too strong. I am not arguing that generative phonology is wrong nor am I trying to resurrect phonemic theory, but I do wish to establish that arguments of the form of Halle's should not be used in the way they have been.

In outline, Halle showed that autonomous phonemics imposed upon the grammarian a treatment of Russian in which two separate, but complementary, voicing assimilation rules were required. In a grammar without an autonomous phonemic level, however, he showed that it was possible to describe the voicing alternations in Russian in terms of one general, and hence simple, voicing assimilation rule. From these facts Halle concluded that there is no level of autonomous phonemics. As the argument stands, this conclusion is clearly a non sequitur. Why should the mere fact that an intuitively appealing generalization is available spell doom for a supposedly empirical theory which forces on the grammarian a nongeneral account of selected data? I can think of two sorts of background assumptions which would make Halle's conclusion follow from his demonstration: (a) that we have a priori knowledge that the general solution is correct in Russian, or (b) that general descriptions are *always* the correct descriptions of selected data in natural language. Either additional premise would allow us to conclude that the correct description of Russian cannot be given within phonemic theory while it can within the theory of generative phonology. Thus the superiority of the generative grammar model over the phonemic model would follow.

But I am quite sure that neither of these additional assumptions is tenable. The first assumption would reduce linguistic analysis to vacuity since, if we had a priori knowledge of the correct description of natural language facts, all we would need to do in describing a language would be to examine our intuitions as to the correct description. The very fact that there are controversies over linguistic descriptions indicates that we have no such a priori knowledge. (I need hardly mention that I reject the assumption that Professor Halle, or any other individual, has a priori knowledge denied to the rest of us.) It might be the case, of course, that we have *independent* knowledge that the general solution is correct in this case, but this is quite a different matter. Adding to Halle's argument a demonstration of the independent preferability of the general solution changes the argument form radically. We would end up with a much more familiar argument form, one which argues for one theory over another on the basis of empirical superiority. The two theories would make equivalent predictions with regard to the phenomenon of voicing assimilation but would make different predictions with regard to other data, and if it turned out that Halle's theory was the one which jibed with these additional data, we would have a clear empirical reason for rejecting the phonemic theory. Some additional data which distinguish the competing theories would have to lurk behind any "independent knowledge" we could have of the correctness of the more general description. Empirical arguments such as this are not, I presume, to be questioned. But here I am interested in arguments based solely upon the greater generality (or, equivalently, simplicity) of one description over another and not on solid empirical differences between two theories.

The second assumption—that general solutions are always correct—is patently false. The reason is that spurious generalizations can easily be found among real-world data (including, and perhaps especially, natural-language data). The phlogistonists, for example, wished to capture the "generalization" that combustion involved emanations of heat and light and was accompanied by a loss in weight of the burned matter. This they did by supposing there to exist a substance which all combustible materials gave off when they burned. This one assumption therefore accommodated both facts. In the modern theory of combustion, the loss in weight that often accompanies burning is seen as essentially unrelated to the emanation of heat and light. Today's chemistry claims (on the basis, of course, of the *empirical* superiority of the theory) that the attractive generalization which inspired the phlogistonists is entirely spurious and that a more adequate theory *must* not recognize it as a general fact.

Spurious generalizations are easy enough to come by in linguistics as well. The complementary distribution of [h] and [ŋ] in English is a well-known case in point. It is possible to choose one of these segments arbitrarily, say [h], and claim that an abstract version underlies both [h] and [ŋ]. Then a rule could be supplied to obligatorily change the segment to [ŋ] when it doesn't precede a stressed vowel. Thus the "generalization" that these two segments are in complementary distribution would be captured. Since the competing analysis says that there are two unrelated segments which just happen to be distributed in a nonoverlapping way in morphemes, a Hallean argument in favor of the former analysis could be given. But we feel (on independent grounds?) that the complementary distribution of [h] and [ŋ] is an essentially accidental fact, and that the argument on the basis of the loss of a generalization would lead to a false conclusion in this case. Thus the hypothesis that all intuitively available generalizations amount to true descriptions must be rejected and, with it, the strong conclusion with which Halle's argument ends.

As far as I can see, the most that can be made to follow from Halle's argument is the very much weaker conclusion that (all other things being equal) the theory in which the general solution is possible is to be *preferred*. For even this to hold, a few tacit assumptions must be made explicit. One way for this weak conclusion to follow would be to assume something like Popper's (1965) idea of degree of falsifiability as a measure of relative goodness of theories. Popper showed that the intuitive simplicity of a theory correlated inversely with the number of freely adjustable parameters and hence directly with the ease with which the theory could, in principle, be falsified.

Consider, by way of illustration, a hypothetical case in which only two data points involving the simultaneous measurement of some property P and some property Q are known. Let us say that the values are $(P = 1, Q = 2)$ and $(P = 2, Q = 4)$. Now let us consider three theories of the relation between P and Q:

Theory 1. P and Q lie along a straight line, i.e., $P = aQ + b$ where a and b are constants.

Theory 2. P and Q lie along a circle, i.e., $aP^2 + bQ^2 = c^2$ where a, b, and c are constants.

Theory 3. P and Q lie along a figure that can be described in terms of integral powers of P and Q, i.e., $aP^n + bQ^n + cP^{n-1} + dQ^{n-1} + \ldots xP + yQ = z$.

Now it is clear that the first theory is intuitively simpler than the second and the second simpler than the third. Moreover, given two data points, the line is completely determined, and there are no freely adjustable parameters. In the present case, then, the equation determined by the two data points is $P = \frac{1}{2}Q + 0$. Two points do not fully determine a circle, however, and any one of the three constants in the equation can be freely adjusted and still produce a circle which passes through the two data points. Theory 3, the most complicated theory both mathematically and intuitively, allows one to choose freely the value of arbitrarily many constants in the equation and still accommodate the data.

Exactly because there are no adjustments that can be made in the first theory, it is the easiest to falsify. It is possible, indeed, for a single additional datum to falsify the straight-line theory. The circle theory, on the other hand, allows for some adjustment if only two data points are known; because of this, no single additional datum could show the theory to be wrong. Through any three points a circle can be drawn. The minimum number of additional data points that need to be found to falsify the claim that the circle theory makes is two. The last of our three theories cannot be falsified at all since there is always room for adjustment. In fact, because it cannot be proved wrong, even in principle, Popper would not dignify it with the name "theory."

In some cases the notion of a generalization in linguistics corresponds to this kind of simplicity since the theory that captures the generalization leaves little room for after-the-fact adjustment and hence is easier to disprove in principle. As far as the day-to-day business of empirical science is concerned, more general, more easily falsifiable theories are superior in that they serve as better guides for research. They point out exactly where critical experiments ought to be performed. whereas, at the other extreme, nontheoretical (metaphysical) statements make no suggestions whatever about what data to gather. Thus, if it could be shown that the difference between Halle's analysis and the phonemic analysis amounted to a difference in ease of falsifiability—with Halle's being the more easily falsifiable theory—then the weak conclusion that Halle's theory should be examined first (rather than the strong conclusion that phonemic theory should be rejected out of hand) could at least be drawn.

It is easy to see that Halle's analysis is indeed easier in principle to prove wrong. There is a class of possible facts which would disprove Halle's thesis (in the sense that additional hypotheses would have to be added to bring the theory in line with the data) but would not disprove the phonemic theory. The bare bones of the two theories are:

(1) Halle's theory: All obstruents assimilate in voicing to following obstruents.[1]
(2) The phonemic theory:
    a. Some obstruent morphophonemes assimilate in voicing to following obstruents.

b. Some obstruent phonemes occur as the voiced allophones before voiced obstruents.[2]

Now if Russian were characterized by the same alternations that we find, with the exception that [c], say, failed to alternate, Halle's theory would be disconfirmed: An additional clause (e.g., "except for [c]") would have to be added to the theory to make it compatible with the facts. It is, of course, never possible to falsify an empirical theory so completely that it cannot be made to accommodate new data by the addition of assumptions. If a proponent of the straight-line theory (mentioned above) came across a bad third datum, he could always say, "I'm sorry, it's a straight line and a point not on the line." When a number of different facts of this kind come to light, the theory ceases to be attractive and tends to look like a mere bundle of unrelated, ad hoc observations; a "crisis state" (to use Kuhn's (1970) term) is reached. In this sense, then, the hypothetical failure of [c] to alternate with a voiced segment in appropriate contexts would disconfirm the Hallean theory since the theory would have to be patched up by the addition of a statement to accommodate the new datum.

The phonemic theory of such an unusual set of alternations, on the other hand, would not be falsified. For the phonemic theory to be shown wrong would require a circumstance under which *all* morphophonemes or *all* phonemes failed to alternate. The possible states of affairs that could disprove the phonemic theory are a proper subset of the possible states of affairs that could disprove Halle's theory. Therefore the latter is seen to be considerably more constraining and more easily disprovable in principle. It goes much farther out on an empirical limb, and since it would serve as a better guide for research, it should, ceteris paribus, be the first theory we try to disprove.

This result is a far cry, however, from the conclusion that phonemic theory is flat-out wrong. The power of Halle's argument, it seems to me, lies partly in the gross difference in testability between his treatment and the phonemic treatment. While Halle's theory is incompatible with what we feel to be highly improbable linguistic states of affairs, such as the one described above, phonemic theory says nothing at all about them. A second factor which undoubtedly contributed to the enormous success of Halle's argument against phonemic theory is that his analysis is probably correct and could, I suspect, be argued for on entirely empirical grounds. But my point is that the correctness of the analysis was not demonstrated by his argument.

I have argued thus far that no argument based solely on the capturing or missing of intuitively valid generalizations can be construed as an argument that the less general treatment is false, but, at most, as an argument that the more general treatment should be examined as a working hypothesis before the less general treatment is. In the recent history of American linguistics, however, the Hallean syllogism has become an archetype of argumentation. This has resulted in an overweening fondness for intuitively reasonable generalizations, which has, I feel, engendered many essentially empty controversies that have occupied far too much of our time.

Several rancorous debates of the last half-dozen years turn out, if scrutinized closely, to be essentially arguments over whether certain facts do indeed amount to significant generalizations in synchronic descriptions. The lexicalist–generativist debate, the argument over the need for global rules in syntax, and the one concerning the proper treatment of indirect speech acts are of this kind.

In the battle between lexicalists and generativists, Hallean arguments are to be found in the arsenals of both camps. McCawley (1968, 1973) aimed one celebrated Hallean blast at the theory of syntax with an autonomous level of deep structure; Chomsky (1972) fired back at generative semantics. I think it bears out my contention about the lack of force of the Hallean syllogism that neither side admitted to having suffered a scratch.

Chomsky's argument is especially interesting since it illustrates so clearly the dangers of infatuation with unexamined generalizations. He attributes to Jackendoff the observation that if generic-ness and specific-ness are interpreted from surface structure, the following can be stated: "At the level of deep structures, there is a very simple generalization governing such sentences . . .: any noun phrase can be followed by any verb phrase" (Chomsky, 1972, p. 89). Of course if generic-ness and specific-ness were represented in underlying structure, this "simple regularity" would be missed. Chomsky exhorts the reader to compare his argument with Halle's.

All right, let's. Halle's argument, we saw, was easily falsifiable. What sorts of facts could disprove, even in principle, the contention that in deep structure any noun phrase goes with any verb phrase? Perhaps the failure to find certain combinations in surface structure? No, for Chomsky points out in a footnote that not all combinations are grammatical in surface structure and insists that their sources are nevertheless generated by the base component. Apparently, then, it is not possible to disprove this claim by adducing empirical evidence. Thus Chomsky's putative generalization is not even a theory in Popper's sense. It resembles in all essentials the untestable Theory 3 discussed above, or the statment that languages can vary in infinite and unpredictable ways. The fact that we know of no language in which, say, all prime-numbered segments starting from the beginning of a word are devoiced doesn't falsify this infinite-variability hypothesis but only casts doubt on it. All predictive statements with empirical content must entail not only that "P" will be true but also that "not P" will not.

In this instance I think there is a principled reason for rejecting a putative generalization, but often there is none. In such cases theoretical splits are based on mere differences of opinion over what is or is not a significant generalization. For example, the disagreement between the advocates of very abstract underlying phonological representations and those who argue for a more superficial level is clearly a disagreement as to what is and what is not a synchronic generalization. The fact that nonalternating nasal vowels in French occur only before consonants, as in the word *Inde* [æ̃d], could be handled as a general fact by providing such words with underlying oral vowel–nasal consonant sequences and giving them a free ride, in Zwicky's (1970) terms, on the independently needed nasalization and deletion rules which account for alternations such as *fin* [fæ̃], *final* [finál]. But it is also possible to argue that the fact that nonalternating nasal vowels occur only before consonants is a mere historical artifact, that is, to deny that there is any synchronic generalization at all.

What is needed to settle this case and all similar ones is independent motivation for one or the other view in the form of additional data. If, as often seems to be the case, there are no data of the traditional sort which could decide the issue, then the data base of linguists should be widened to include kinds of evidence that have not been considered before. Unfortunately, the tendency has been just the opposite. Proponents of opposing views have in some cases attempted to narrow the range of data which they are willing to consider, for instance, by excluding certain data as performance, semantics, or pragmatics. Empirical science does not work that way.

Even if arguments based on the capture of significant generalizations cannot be construed as arguments for the correctness or falseness of competing theories, it is still possible that the search for distributional generalizations is a useful heuristic. That is, it might turn out more times than not that intuitively satisfying generalizations reflect what is really going on in language. There is, I am sure, a demonstrable tendency for purely formal generalizations governing the distribution of linguistic items to arise and spread. On the other hand, there are powerful forces at work that serve to break up formal generalizations. This has been amply demonstrated for phonology by Kiparsky (1972).

NOTES

1. It should be mentioned at this point that this version of Halle's theory is in fact wrong. The voiced obstruent [v] fails to produce voicing in a preceding voiceless obstruent. This fact was handled by analyzing [v] as a glide at the point of application of the voicing assimilation rule.
2. It is quite possible that this formulation of the phonemic theory is unfair to the spirit of the phonemic theory. But fair or not, it is the windmill that Halle tilted at.

REFERENCES

Chomsky, N. (1972) "Some empirical issues in the theory of transformational grammar," in S. Peters (ed.) *Goals of Linguistic Theory.* Englewood Cliffs, N.J.: Prentice-Hall.

Halle, M. (1959) *The Sound Pattern of Russian.* The Hague: Mouton.

Kiparsky, P. (1972) "Explanation in phonology," in S. Peters (ed.), *Goals of Linguistic Theory.* Englewood Cliffs, N.J.: Prentice-Hall.

Kuhn, T. (1970) *The Structure of Scientific Revolutions*. Chicago: University of Chicago Press.

McCawley, J. (1968) "The role of semantics in a grammar," in E. Bach and R. T. Harms (eds.), *Universals in Linguistic Theory*. New York: Holt, Rinehart and Winston.

——— (1973) "The annotated respective," in J. McCawley, *Grammar and Meaning*. Tokyo: Taishukan.

Popper, K. (1965) *The Logic of Scientific Discovery*. New York: Harper and Row.

Zwicky, A. (1970) "The free-ride principle and two rules of complete assimilation in English," in *Papers from the Sixth Regional Meeting of the Chicago Lingusitic Society*. Chicago: Chicago Linguistic Society.

5

On independent motivation

Michael N. Perloff
Jessica R. Wirth
University of Wisconsin-Milwaukee

In contemporary linguistics a style of argument has begun to play an increasingly important role. That style of argument claims that a proposal or hypothesis is independently motivated. Since different linguists use arguments from independent motivation in different ways, it seems to us to be of some importance to undertake an analysis of independent motivation, and to see how that style of argument is to be assessed. In the course of this analysis we shall offer some ideas about the nature of evidence in linguistics.

Upon setting out to produce a discussion of independent motivation in contemporary linguistics our initial step was to do some empirical research among contemporary linguists. One of the authors sought out various linguists and asked each of them to characterize "independent motivation." All of the responses to this request described independent motivation as evidence for a hypothesis when the hypothesis accounts for some set of facts and additionally accounts for another set of facts different from, or independent of, the first set. In this informal poll some respondents noted spontaneously that it would be difficult to provide a precise account of "independent." And though no one was willing to try a precise account of "independent," some respondents claimed that there were arguments utilizing independent motivation which did not appeal to facts which were really independent.

We then speculated that while to our knowledge no one had ever proposed a criterion of independence, some criterion might be found to underlie all, or most, of the arguments concerning independent motivation. We first noted that there is general agreement that "independent motivation" is an evidential relation, in that if some fact is independent motivation for a particular proposal, the fact is evidence for that proposal. Since claims that one thing is evidence for another may be right or wrong, we decided that the criterion we were looking for should be both used by linguists and defensible as an evidentiary relation.

But this proved to be a real problem, for on those accounts which were plausible and for which the evidentiary relation held, the account of "independence" was unsatisfactory. Consider the suggestion that a hypothesis H which accounts for some set of facts F_1 is independently motivated just in case H *unexpectedly* accounts for a distinct set of facts F_2. The failure of this suggestion is its reliance on expectations. Are we to judge the expectations of the proponent of the hypothesis, or an opponent of the hypothesis? Neither of these two alternatives seems satisfactory. Listen to Botha's sardonic commentary on how to argue manipulating expectations.

> Divide the data which you know beforehand can be reduced to your hypothesis/theory into those which are "explained" by the hypothesis/theory and those which are unexpectedly (!) "predicted" by the hypothesis/theory, and then commend this hypothesis/theory for its unexpected "predictive success." (1973, p. 332)

Perhaps this suggestion would be acceptable if "expectation" were understood as a generalized expectation of experts in the field. But in such a case the facts in question are independent only until the hypothesis which accounts for them both is accepted. Suppose one expert has an insight in which it is seen that two facts not so far demonstrably related can be accounted for by a new hypothesis. A breakthrough in the theory comes when the expert produces a hypothesis which relates in sufficient detail the facts. The generalized expectation of the experts was that the facts were independent, but as these experts accept the hypothesis they must give up their expectation that the facts are unrelated. Notice that it would be unreasonable for anyone to claim that the evidence for the new hypothesis was less strong after the generalized expectations of experts in the field had changed, since there was no longer independent motivation for the hypothesis.

The moral of this story is not merely that an account of independence in terms of expectations fails, but that any similar account is bound to fail. For two facts, or two sets of facts, *cannot* be independent if they are accounted for by the same hypothesis. An example from another field may help to reinforce this idea. Consider a cat which is a male cat, which is white, which is blue-eyed, and which is sterile. To a nonbiologist these properties seem quite independent. But to a biologist whiteness, blue-eyedness, and sterility are not at all independent in male cats, for they are related in the same chromosome. The properties may have seemed independent, but it is an important discovery that they are not.

On the basis of the foregoing considerations it seemed that we might not be able to find a satisfactory account of the notion of independence where "independence" was understood to describe distinct sets of facts accounted for by the same hypothesis. But this momentary despair freed us from our preconceptions, and upon another review of the literature we found that arguments appealing to independent motivation were quite different in their structure than the structure we had been looking for.

We shall contend that given a rather rigid, though accurate, characterization of "linguistic hypothesis," independent motivation provides ancillary evidence for a hypothesis by providing evidence for one part of that hypothesis. Before going on to explain and argue the truth of this claim, we shall look at an example from contemporary linguistics which utilizes arguments from independent motivation, and show in further detail why we reject the characterization we first considered.

The example we shall be concerned with is taken from an

article by Perlmutter and Orešnik (1973), "Language-Particular Rules and Explanation in Syntax." Their discussion of the Orphan Accusative, and their claim of independent motivation for their account, is an interesting and illuminating representative of the sort of argument with which we are concerned. In the Slovenian language the Orphan Accusative is a particular accusative form of an adjective which appears in the absence of a head noun. The Orphan Accusative shows up most often in question–answer discourse, where the answer is a reduced form of sentence, and in a partially reduced coordinate construction. The most interesting feature of the Orphan Accusative is that it does not have the phonological shape which it would have if the noun were present. Perlmutter and Orešnik set out to explain the occurrence in Slovenian of the Orphan Accusative. In essence their proposal is that the nonoccurrence of the head noun is due to a deletion process which takes place in two steps. The first step is a pronominalization yielding a pronoun in place of the full head noun. The pronoun has constant gender and number, not varying with the gender and number of the noun it replaces. The second step is deletion of the pronoun. They contend that after step one, Pronominalization, but before step two, Deletion, a rule of Concord applies, whereby the adjective is made to agree in gender, number, and case with the head of the construction. After the deletion the result is the Orphan Accusative. An example of the facts to be accounted for appears in (1).

(1) črn površnik   'black overcoat'
    *črn ∅
    črnega ∅   'black one'—Orphan Accusative

A sample of the derivation is given in (2).

(2) D.S.

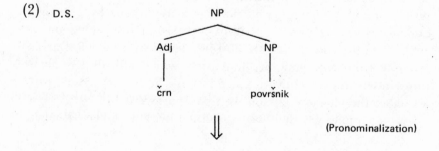

(Pronominalization)

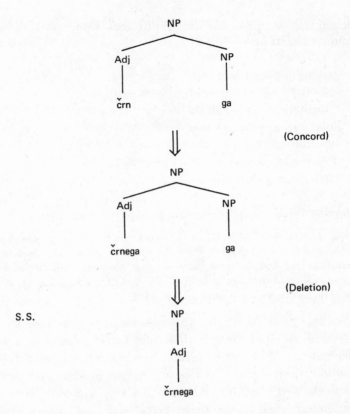

Perlmutter and Orešnik make two claims that there is independent motivation for their proposal. First they assert that
the rule of Concord "is needed in the grammar anyway,
completely independently of the cases at issue here" (p. 427).
They provide as evidence for this assertion the facts listed in (3).

(3) a. Stane ima star<u>o</u> rjav<u>o</u> hiš<u>o</u>
         'Stane has an old brown house'.
     b. Stane ima star rjav površnik
         'Stane has an old brown overcoat'.

In sentences of the type illustrated in (3), the Orphan Accusative does not appear, and in sentences of this type the
adjective agrees with a noun that is present in the surface
structure.

They also assert that the effects of the rule of Concord
appear when the pronoun form is present, and that this is

independent support for the claim that Concord applies after Pronominalization.

(4) Želel sem pojesti ves riž
    wanted eat up all rice
    'I wanted to eat up all the rice'.
(5) Želel sem ga pojesti vsega
    wanted it eat up all
    'I wanted to eat up all of it'. (it = rice)
(6) *Želel sem ga pojesti ves

Referring to the facts presented in (4)-(6), they note:

> This [referring to (4)-(6)] is a remarkable fact. And it shows that, completely independently of the Orphan Accusative, the pronoun *ga* must be marked in some way so that Concord will produce the genitive-like form *vsega* instead of the ordinary accusative *ves* if [(4) and (5)]are to be accounted for. (p. 440)

Assume now that for this proposal to be independently motivated, it had to be that the facts accounted for were independent. Under this assumption, which we would like to show to be misguided, someone might produce an argument which claimed that the facts in (1), (3), and (4)-(6) were not independent, and since these facts were not independent the Perlmutter-Orešnik proposal had no independent motivation.

One such argument might go as follows. In their introduction of the term "Orphan Accusative," Perlmutter and Orešnik characterize as members of the class of Orphan Accusatives adjectives which have a genitive-like accusative and appear in the absence of a head noun. They say, "because the genitive-like accusative *navadnega* [rather than *navaden*] appears in the absence of a head noun, we will refer to it as the "Orphan Accusative" (p. 421). One might, the argument continues, interpret the phrase "in the absence of a head noun" either as "a head noun appears nowhere in the sentence," or as "a head noun does not appear adjacent to the adjective with the genitive-like accusative form." Given the second interpretation of the phrase the facts in (4)-(6), especially (5), are simply further instances of the Orphan Accusative. Therefore the facts cited in (4)-(6) are not independent and so cannot be independent motivation for the proposal. Additionally, it might be argued, since the facts cited in (1), (3), and (4)-(6) are related in their connection with the rule of Concord, they are on that basis alone not independent. Thus, on the assumption that the facts must be independent for there to be independent motivation, the Perlmutter-Orešnik claim of independent motivation is at least shown to be doubtful.

If the two arguments presented above seem a bit strained, that is no accident. For however one understands the phrase "in the absence of a head noun" and whether or not the facts of (1), (3), and (4)-(6) are independent, the Perlmutter-Orešnik hypothesis has the *same* evidential support. That is, their hypothesis does account for the data of (1) and (4)-(6), and their arguments concerning the scope of the rule of Concord provide further evidence for their hypothesis. Is it of any consequence, then, whether or not the facts in question are independent? We submit that it is of no consequence at all. Since independent motivation is an evidentiary connection, and the weight of evidence is not altered by the independence or nonindependence of the facts, the independence of those facts is irrelevant.

But there remains the additional, or independent, evidence for the Perlmutter-Orešnik hypothesis. If the independence of the facts is not crucial, how are such arguments understood? We stated above our contention that independent motivation is a way of providing ancillary evidence for a hypothesis by providing additional support for one part of the hypothesis. Having, we think, dealt with the most likely alternative, we turn to the explanation and justification of our own contention. To make our case we shall characterize what we take to be essential in a hypothesis and show how the notion of "hypothesis part" is to be understood. We then go on to discuss some feature of evidence for a hypothesis, evidence for a hypothesis part, and how this last is independent motivation for a hypothesis.

Although the word *hypothesis* is used in linguistics to describe almost any proposal anyone puts forth, there seems to us to be one class of proposals which might be called *standard hypotheses*. A standard hypothesis consists of three items: (a) an underlying structure, (b) a set of rules, and (c) an ordering of the rules. A standard hypothesis accounts for, explains, or predicts a linguistic fact or set of linguistic facts just in case the rules in the hypothesis when applied to the underlying structure in the order specified produce the surface structure.

In the sample derivation of the Perlmutter-Orešnik discussion (see (2) above), the three parts of a standard linguistic hypothesis can be seen clearly. The underlying structure is revealed in the top tree diagram. The rules are named in parentheses, and the order of those rules is obvious from their serial arrangement. The three items taken together yield the surface structure, and in so doing explain, account for—predict—the surface structure, and thereby also explain some linguistic fact or facts. A consistent set of standard hypotheses which together generate all and only the surface structures of a language is a grammar of that language.

We are now in a position to understand why arguments from independent motivation, of the sort typified by the Perlmutter-Orešnik case, play an important part in contemporary linguistics. Any standard hypothesis which generates a surface structure has some evidence in its favor, simply in virtue of the fact that it does generate that surface structure. That is, when a standard hypothesis which does not violate some theoretical constraints *does* account for some linguistic facts, it has some confirmatory evidence.

But if every standard hypothesis which generates a surface structure has some evidence in its favor, this kind of evidence alone will not suffice to establish the superiority of one hypothesis over another. Since there is *no* reason to believe that a hypothesis which accounts for one sort of sentence has more evidence than a hypothesis which accounts for another sort of sentence, the weight of evidence must be the same in all such cases. Similarly if two distinct hypotheses both account for the same facts, their equal ability to account for the facts yields equal evidence in their favor.

Therefore, if one is to establish the superiority of one among competing hypotheses, ancillary evidence must be produced. And it is just this ancillary evidence which arguments from independent motivation claim to produce. In its ideal form the argument from independent motivation produces additional evidence for one hypothesis by showing that one part of the hypothesis has additional evidence for it, because that hypothesis part has a place within an already established hypothesis. Presumably, the hypothesis part carries its share of the evidential weight from the already established hypothesis to the newly proposed hypothesis.

Notice that this sort of argument is intragrammatical, where a grammar is understood to be a complete, consistent set of standard hypotheses. That is, if an argument from independent motivation is to be successful, the different hypotheses, and so the hypothesis parts, must be from the *same* projected grammar. If there were a proposed grammar of Slovenian which did not contain the rule of Concord, within that proposed grammar there would be no independent motivation for the Perlmutter-Orešnik proposal. But we are now left with a problem. Since intragrammatical evidence is not also evidence for one grammar rather than another, must we choose among proposed grammars simply on the bases of simplicity and personal preference?

Some writers think that this is precisely the situation. In a recent article called "Methodological Reflections on Current Linguistic Theory," W. V. Quine asks us to

[i]magine two systems of English grammar: one an old-fashioned system that draws heavily on the Latin grammarians, and the other a streamlined formulation due to Jespersen. Imagine that the two systems are *extensionally equivalent*, in this sense: they determine, recursively, the same infinite set of well-formed English sentences. In Denmark the boys in one school learn English by the other system, and those in another school learn it by the other. In the end the boys all sound alike. Both systems of rules *fit* the behavior of all the boys, but each system *guides* the behavior of only half the boys. Both systems *fit* the behavior also of all us native speakers of English; this is what makes both systems correct. But neither system guides us native speakers of English; no rules do, except for some intrusions of inessential schoolwork. (p. 442)

The conclusion Quine draws from a discussion of this thought experiment is that contemporary linguistic theoreticians can justifiedly settle for any grammar which provides a complete, consistent account of a language (see pp. 443 ff.). He subjects this decision only to considerations of simplicity. While Quine does not deny the possibility of there being nontrivial criteria for deciding among rival grammars, he is not sanguine about their likelihood. This, because it seems to Quine that if there are to be criteria for deciding among hypotheses, and if these criteria are to be nontrivial, they must arise from the connections between linguistics and some form of behavioristic psychology.

Insofar as Quine is claiming that as linguistics stands now there are no natural and nontrivial criteria for deciding among rival grammars, we agree. But insofar as he is claiming that there are not liable to be such criteria, we disagree. For though he is surely right in expecting these criteria to be specified in the connections of linguistic theory to other empirical theories, some form of behavioristic psychology is not the only alternative. It seems to us that as linguists begin to produce clear and detailed theories of language production, language comprehension, and language acquisition, there will also be produced theories relating these fields to grammatical and phonological theories. It seems to us that as there are further theoretical developments not only in behavioristic psychology, but in neural psychology, social psychology and anthropology, linguists will begin to produce theories of the interconnections between linguistics and these other disciplines. Once these theories are produced, and the relationships begin to become clear, criteria for deciding among rival grammars will appear which will be neither trivial nor nonempirical.

However, we must note that if linguists do not take Quine's argument seriously, and do not set about to produce the sorts of theories we have just talked about, Quine will turn out to have been correct. For the forms of argument used in linguistics will merely be ways of demonstrating consistency, completeness, or aesthetic preferability.

Before concluding our discussion of arguments from independent motivation, we should like to discuss two arguments which rely heavily on claims of independent motivation, but which are not of the form displayed above. We shall consider the Partee–Lakoff debate about whether there is independent motivation for the IMP node, and the Lakoff–Partee debate about whether there is independent motivation for the causative analysis. Partee (1971) argues for the IMP node claiming that there is independent motivation, and against the causative analysis claiming there is no independent motivation. Lakoff argues against the IMP node (1971) claiming there is no independent motivation, and for the causative analysis (1970) claiming that there is independent motivation.

Careful examination of these kinds of debates had led one thoughtful commentator to observe that

[a]t the basis of these noncongruous judgements of independent motivation lies the fact that there are crucial respects in which the transformationalist notion or principle of independent motivation is unclear. (Botha, 1973, p. 249)

This unclarity is not an accident, for first, the notion of independent motivation is stretched and altered so that it is only vaguely related to other arguments using the notion, and second, these arguments propose not simply different hypotheses for the same grammar, but different grammars. Thus the argument is not about independent motivation but is at its deepest level concerned with the value of evidence from within linguistic theory, and how such evidence is to be used in determining the acceptability or nonacceptability of competing sets of hypotheses and competing grammars.

Although the proposals in the debates we shall look at are usually called hypotheses, we shall want to distinguish them from the standard hypotheses characterized above. Since what is at issue is the shape and nature of whole sets of standard hypotheses, that is, a generalized account of standard hypotheses, we shall call these proposals *generalized hypotheses.*

The generalized hypothesis of the IMP node as presented by Katz and Postal and defended by Partee is that every standard hypothesis which generates an imperative sentence contains an abstract marker IMP, which does not appear in the surface structure; and that in every standard hypothesis which generates an imperative sentence there is an obligatory *you* deletion rule, which, among other things, deletes the IMP node. Support for this hypothesis comes from two sources: first, a class of syntactic facts such as the nonoccurrence of either sentence adverbs or negative preverbs in imperatives, and the non-occurrence of imperatives conjoined with declaratives; second, the claim that "I order you" is part of the meaning of all imperative sentences, and the IMP node is associated with the semantic representation *I order you.*

Lakoff (1971) argues against the generalized IMP node hypothesis:

The meaning of the imperative construction in a sentence like *Come here* must be given in terms of a three-place predicate relating the speaker, the addressee, and a sentence describing the action to be performed, as expressed overtly in the sentence *I order you to come here*.... The arbitrary syntax position would maintain in this case that the 'deep structure' of *Come here* would not contain such a three-place predicate, but would instead contain an arbitrary marker. In recent studies such a marker has been given the mnemonic IMP, which may tend to hide its arbitrariness. (p. 283)

His argument appeals to independent motivation when he goes on to claim that "it requires independent justification to be given for choosing each proposed arbitrary marker over the independently motivated semantic representation" (p. 288). It is obvious that this is not an appeal to independent motivation in the sense discussed above; but it is not obvious that the appeals to independent justification and independent motivation are irrelevant to the argument. What is disguised by raising the issue of independent motivation is that Lakoff is proposing a generalized hypothesis about the shape of the underlying structure of imperative sentences; that is, that there are no IMP nodes in that structure. And he argues for this generalized hypothesis from the following claims:

(i) the meaning of an imperative sentence is given in terms of a three-place predicate;
(ii) the underlying structure of an imperative sentence must display the three-place predicate;
(iii) the semantic representation of an imperative sentence must reflect the three-place predicate.

On the basis of (i), (ii), and (iii), Lakoff's conclusion appears to be that the IMP node hypothesis either does not meet the requirements of his claims, or if it does it does so in an unsatisfactory manner.

There is more to this argument than has been presented here. But we hope that it has begun to be clear that the argument is not about any sort of independent motivation but rather is an argument about the shapes of sets of hypotheses. In such cases the weight of the evidence has nothing to do with independence or nonindependence; rather, it has to do with whether certain claims are true, and whether, if true, such claims actually do provide evidence for the proposed hypothesis.

We find a similar situation in the debate about Lakoff's causative hypothesis. Although Lakoff's proposal (1970) is put forth in the form of a standard hypothesis, its intended scope is that of a generalized hypothesis. Lakoff proposes that sentences like "John killed Bill" are to be explained by hypotheses like that of (7) below. This is a generalized hypothesis because it really involves a much wider range of sentences than those containing the transitive verb *kill*.

(7)

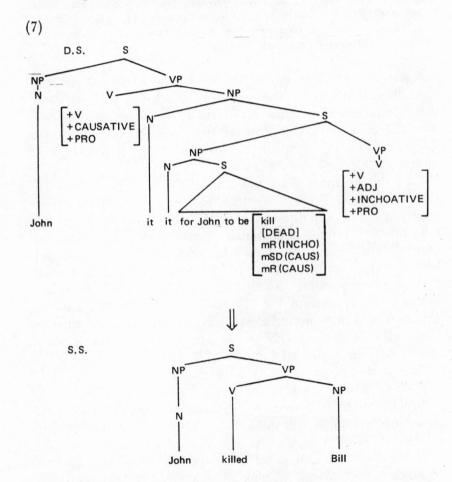

The following features of the hypothesis show up on inspection of the hypothesis: There is an abstract element CAUS in the underlying structure of the sentence; this element CAUS is not the lexical item *cause* (this can be seen in that the abstract element triggers an obligatory rule, the causative transformation, so that the abstract element never appears in the surface structure); and the abstract element CAUS is a verb in the underlying structure.

Partee's objection to the causative hypothesis claims that the independent motivation for the hypothesis is inadequate:

> since no independent reasons are given for this dummy trigger element being analyzed as a verb, let alone for its being related in any principled way to the verb *cause*, the empirical claim that seems to be made by the statement that English has a causative transformation is greatly weakened. (1971, p. 8)

Again, independent motivation or the lack of independent motivation is not really the issue here at all. For it seems to us that the proposed grammar of which the causative analysis is a part differs in important respects from the proposed grammar Partee appeals to when she denies that there is independent motivation for the causative analysis.

And this is the crucial point in the two debates between Partee and Lakoff which we have looked at: The issue is not merely differing hypotheses within the same proposed grammar, but different proposed grammars. Partee and Lakoff seem to have different conceptions of the shapes of the hypotheses which, taken together, will be the grammar of English. But since their arguments claim to rely on there being, or not being, independent motivation for a hypothesis, this broader issue is obscured. But it is nevertheless an important issue, for what is really at stake is the nature and weight of evidence for deciding among different proposed grammars.

And if this is, as we think it is, the heart of the issue, *two* important points need to be made. First, for there to be empirical, nontrivial criteria for deciding among rival grammars, these rival grammars will need to be tested against the relevant results of other theories. As we said above, once there are sufficiently precise and detailed theories in disciplines allied to linguistics, the varying weights of evidence for different proposed grammars will become clearer. That is, the arguments will not depend on purely intratheoretical considerations and spurious claims of independent motivation, as they seem to do in the Lakoff–Partee debates. Rather the arguments will rely on intertheoretical considerations. And in such cases, though linguists may have left the term behind, there will be genuine independent motivation.

The second point is that while proposing complete, consistent grammars is not a trivial undertaking, as all linguists know, intertheoretic considerations will be more easily weighted for and against complete grammars than for and against standard, or even, generalized hypotheses. Therefore, one reasonable methodological stance with respect to the IMP node hypothesis, the causative hypothesis, and other similar disputes is to wait for the complete grammar to be produced before judging the preferability of one proposal to another. Another reasonable methodological stance, and the one more likely to be adopted by linguists with strong feelings on these issues, is to set about producing complete, consistent grammars which integrate those hypotheses believed to be preferable. Incidentally, the task of producing a complete, consistent grammar of a language is even harder than it seems. For while it might be easy to decide whether or not a grammar is consistent, how is one to decide when a grammar is complete? That is, how does one decide that the proposed underlying structures, together with the rules which generate the surface structures, are the totality of underlying structures and rules?

Finally, what we hope to have shown here is that there is a clear and useful sense of "independent motivation" which can be appealed to in providing evidence for linguistic hypotheses. That is the sense in which independent motivation produces ancillary evidence for a hypothesis by showing that one part of the hypothesis has additional evidence for it. But there are also arguments which claim to appeal to independent motivation where what is at issue is the nature and weight of the evidence. In these latter cases one must search beneath the veil of the claim of independent motivation for what are truly the central issues.

REFERENCES

Botha, R. (1973) *The Justification of Linguistic Hypotheses*. The Hague: Mouton.

Lakoff, G. (1970) *Irregularity in Syntax*. New York: Holt, Rinehart and Winston.

———— (1971) "On generative semantics," in D. D. Steinberg and L. A. Jakobovits (eds.), *Semantics: An Interdisciplinary Reader in Philosophy, Linguistics, and Psychology*. Cambridge: At the University Press.

Partee, B. (1971) "On the requirement that transformations preserve meaning," in C. Fillmore and D. Langendoen (eds.), *Studies in Linguistic Semantics*. New York: Holt, Rinehart and Winston.

Perlmutter, D., and J. Orešnik (1973) "Language-particular rules and explanation in syntax," in S. Anderson and P. Kiparsky (eds.), *A Festschrift for Morris Halle*. New York: Holt, Rinehart and Winston.

Quine, W. V. (1972) "Methodological reflections on current linguistic theory," in G. Harman and D. Davidson (eds.), *Semantics of Natural Language*. Dordrecht, The Netherlands: D. Reidel Publishing Co.

6

Argument invention: The linguist's "feel" for science

Ray C. Dougherty
New York University

Every work of science great enough to be remembered for a few generations affords some exemplification of the defective state of the art of reasoning of the time when it was written; and each chief step in science has been a lesson in logic. It was so when Lavoisier and his contemporaries took up the study of Chemistry. The old chemist's maxim had been "Lege, lege, lege, labora, ora, et relege." Lavoisier's method was not to read and pray, but to dream that some long and complicated chemical process would have a certain effect, to put it into practice with dull patience, after its inevitable failure, to dream that with some modification it would have another result, and to end by publishing the last dream as a fact. (Charles Sanders Peirce, 1966, 5.363)

1. THE EMPIRICAL JUSTIFICATION OF ARGUMENT FORMS

Chomsky, Halle, and Ross (1971) contend, quite rightly I believe, that the ability to invent sound arguments of a type

I wish to thank my colleagues for comments on the ideas presented in this paper. I am especially indebted to Stevan Stoddard-Apter, Joan Bachenko, Marilyn Bart, Eileen Fitzpatrick, David Halitsky, Marianne Lonergan, Ruth Palaszewski, Diane Raulerson, and Virginia Sterba.

This work was supported by a grant-in-aid from the American Council of Learned Societies.

previously unknown comprises the main route of advance for any particular science:

> One of the most acute problems that a beginning student in syntax encounters is how to gain some facility in following a syntactic argument. . . .
> Comprehending such arguments is, of course, only a part of the battle. The next task is to gain insight into what makes a good argument in syntax so that one may then construct such arguments himself. . . . If [syntactic arguments] are presented in such a way as to stimulate the students' minds rather than to burden their memory, a great deal can be learned. Needless to say, learning to appreciate and to construct good arguments is a never-ending task, for the invention of good arguments of a type previously unknown is the major step whereby advances in any scientific discipline are achieved. (p. ix)

As Chomsky, Halle, and Ross point out, the forms of arguments used by linguists are not given a priori. They are intellectual tools which are invented and shaped by the linguist, and they are subject to empirical verification and refutation in a way illustrated in this chapter. For ease of reference, a linguist's methods, argument forms, working assumptions, etc., will be called the instruments of research. A linguist cannot escape the implications of having adopted definite instruments of research— be they good or bad. These instruments of research lead him to record particular kinds of facts using specific procedures and to present arguments organized and structured in accordance with certain patterns specified by a particular logic.

At any given time, just as there will be many alternative theoretical mechanisms being proposed, there will be many different methodologies in use and many different methodologies being proposed. Each instrument of research, whether it is in use already or newly proposed, must, through confrontation with empirical facts, be validated or refuted no less than the theoretical proposals which the instruments are used to justify. How these instruments, in particular the argument forms, can be isolated and identified, and further, how they can be evaluated for strength, will be the main questions of this investigation.

The criteria which are relevant in choosing between alternative instruments of research are determined by the goals of research.

Once a person realizes where he wants to go, he can determine the best way to get there. Once a scientist has selected his goals, he can evaluate alternative argument forms, methods, and research strategies to achieve those goals. We can only decide the strength of an argument if we have specific goals, that is, if we know what our arguments must accomplish.

We are seduced when we assume an argument to have a strength which it does not in fact possess. As we shall see, a researcher unclear about his goals may think that his argument justifies a conclusion which it does not. We open ourselves to seduction if we are uncertain of our goals or if in formulating arguments we attribute to other goals which they do not accept and explicitly reject.

My main concern is to evaluate certain forms of argument used by linguists in practice. I am interested in understanding the intellectual frame of a researcher's thoughts (about the status of linguistics as a science, the nature of explanation, the goals of research, etc.) as this frame is reflected in the actual organization and structure of his arguments. The actual frame of a researcher's thoughts determines the questions he asks, the answers he is willing to accept, and the detailed results he will enumerate. This study provides a perspective from which we can analyze the structure of arguments linguists actually use to motivate their proposals over alternative analyses. Precisely what types of evidence does a linguist offer to show that one grammar provides a more insightful explanation of the principles of sentence construction than does another grammar? It is my goal to indicate errors in fact and reasoning, and more fundamentally, to indicate how these errors arise from weakness in method that can only be avoided by serious reflection on the status of linguistics as a science and the interactions of goals and methods.

Within the scope of this paper my goal can best be attained by concentrating on selected topics, and by investigating, in specific cases, the arguments employed by the authors to substantiate their claims. What justifications do they offer for their grammars? For this investigation, it is not crucial if the authors still subscribe to these grammars. Presumably each author feels that his article is or was a serious, well-argued contribution to the field.

Since my objective is to be critical and not encyclopaedic, my data is selective rather than exhaustive. I believe, however, that the examples which I have selected from current literature illustrate typical practices. In particular, I feel that further investigation extending to more articles would not refute, but would further substantiate, my conclusions.

Let us begin by offering some reflections on the status of linguistics as a science, and the relation of linguistics to other sciences. The following sketch is intended to be suggestive rather than assertive: It is intended as a working hypothesis to govern future research into linguistic methodology.

2. MATHEMATICS, NATURE, AND THE SCIENTIST

One might argue with much justification that the rise of science ties in directly with the idea of uniting mathematical analysis with the study of nature. The analysis of natural phenomena in terms of mathematical concepts is basic to our conception of science. Mathematical analyses seem to be "scientific" in that they are exact, explicit, etc.

There are at least two ways of uniting mathematics and the study of natural phenomena. Some mathematical views of nature involve a mechanical conception of its operations, other mathematical views do not. By the *typological view* I shall mean the study of nature whose goal is to find the harmonies (correlations) which exist between the properties of nature and the properties of mathematical concepts (numbers, geometric patterns, etc.). By the *mechanical view* I shall mean the study of nature whose goal is to invent a mathematical (deductive) model from which one can deduce consequences which can be compared with certain observable aspects of nature. These inadequate definitions can best be clarified by example.

A person doing research in the typological view will attempt to express mathematically formalizable relations between natural phenomena. He may, for example, feel that three is an important number owing to the religious significance of the Father, the Son, and the Holy Ghost. Or he may feel that six is important because it is a perfect number: $1 + 2 + 3 = 1 \cdot 2 \cdot 3 = 6$. Research consists of seeing how many things in the world can be analysed into groups of three or six. The mathematical harmonies can be suggested by any number of sources. The usual source is a metaphysical system which the investigator considers important: religion, mysticism, astrology, etc.

Kepler's research was in the typological view. He sought mathematical regularities (both numerical and geometric) in natural phenomena. Kepler sought to empirically motivate Copernicus's theory by showing that it led to many more mathematical harmonies than the Ptolemaic theory. He offered several arguments for the Copernican view, including these two:

Kepler's first argument. A planet is in solar opposition if a line drawn from the planet to the sun would pass through the earth, and the earth is between the planet and the sun; that is, if an observer on earth can face a planet only by turning his back to the sun. It was long known that the planets Mercury and Venus never occur in solar opposition, although the other known planets (Mars, etc.) do. If, according to Ptolemy, the sun and the planets go around the earth, it should be possible that any planet could be in solar opposition: It remains a mystery why some do and some do not. If, according to Copernicus, all planets go around the sun, and if Mercury and Venus are closer to the sun than the earth is, then these assumptions explain why Mercury and Venus never occur in solar opposition: It would be impossible for these two planets to be on one side of the earth while the sun is on the other. Mars, etc., being farther from the sun than the earth is, would occasionally occur in solar opposition.

Kelper's second argument. Kepler felt that he had explained why there were only six planets. He had established a mathematical harmony between the six planets and the five regular Platonic solids. According to Burtt (1924), Kepler regarded the discovery of this geometric harmony as his greatest accomplishment:

> But the discovery which yielded Kepler the most inordinate delight and to which he referred for many years as his most important achievement, was the discovery published in his first work, the *Mysterium Cosmographicum* (1597), that the distances between the orbits of the six planets then known bore a certain rough resemblance to the distances which would be obtained if the hypothetical spheres of the planets were inscribed in and circumscribed

about the five regular solids properly distributed between them. Thus, if a cube be inscribed in the sphere of Saturn, the sphere of Jupiter will approximately fit within it, then between Jupiter and Mars the tetrahedron, between Mars and the earth the dodecahedron, etc. Of course, the performance has remained entirely unfruitful—the correspondence is rough, and the discovery of new planets has quite upset its underlying assumptions—but Kepler never forgot the pristine enthusiasm which this achievement awoke in him. In a letter penned shortly after the discovery he wrote: "The intense pleasure I have received from this discovery can never be told in words. I regretted no more the time wasted; I tired of no labour; I shunned no toil of reckoning, days and nights spent in calculation, until I could see whether my hypothesis would agree with the orbits of Copernicus or whether my joy was to vanish into air." (p. 62)

A person doing research in the mechanical view will attempt to formulate a theory which can be expressed in mathematical terms to comprise a deductive system, which is tentatively advanced as a possible description, or explanation, of the phenomena under investigation. The theory (mechanical model) derives its total empirical motivation from the comparison of the consequences deduced from the theory with observable phenomena. A theory is an invention of the human imagination, a conjecture about the processes underlying the patterns in the data.

Newton's research was in the mechanical view. He developed a mathematical (deductive-mechanical) model of dynamics which led to empirically testable consequences. "Newton's aim," says Einstein (1927, p. 201), "was to find an answer to the question: Does there exist a simple rule by which the motion of the heavenly bodies of our planetary system can be completely calculated, if the state of motions of all these bodies at a single state be known?" Einstein continues: "Newton succeeded in explaining the motions of the planets, moon, comets, down to fine details, as well as the ebb and flow of tides and the precessional movement of the earth—this last a deductive achievement of peculiar brilliance" (p. 203).

Holton (1973) tersely expresses the difference between the mechanical view and the typological view as he discusses the differences between Newton and Kepler:

[The goal of research is to characterize] the *nature* of heavens, the *nature* of bodies. How, then, is one to recognize whether a postulate or conception is in accord with the nature of things?

This is the main question, and to it Kepler has at the same time two very different answers, emerging, as it were, from the two parts of his soul. We may phrase one of the two answers as follows: *the physically real world, which defines the nature of things, is the world of phenomena explainable by mechanical principles.* This can be called Kepler's first criterion of reality, and assumes the possibility of formulating a sweeping and consistent dynamics which Kepler only sensed but which was not to be given until Newton's *Principia.* Kepler's other answer, to which he keeps returning again and again as he finds himself rebuffed by the deficiencies of his dynamics, and which we shall now examine in detail, is this: *the physically real world is the world of mathematically expressed harmonies which man can discover in the chaos of events.* (p. 78)

Both Kepler and Newton looked for universal physical laws based on terrestrial mechanics in order to comprehend the whole universe in its quantitative details. They both attempted to apply mathematics to the study of astronomy. Since Kepler, for various reasons, never developed an adequate theory of mechanics, he frequently had to formulate his problems in the terms of this explanation: *"the physically real world is the world of mathematically expressed harmonies which man can discover in the chaos of events."* This is the *typological view.* This led him to ask questions such as, Why are there exactly six planets? Why are the planets exactly the distances they are from the sun? He answered the first question by pointing out that there were six planets because there were five Platonic solids. The second question he answered by contending that the planets were spaced at harmonic intervals.

Newton's work is, in a sense, based on Kepler's earlier studies, but in another sense, it is quite different. By offering a new concept of explanation, Newton redefined what was to be considered important data. For example, the problems in Kepler's system—Why are there exactly six planets? Why are the planets exactly the distances they are from the sun?—are not answerable in terms of the concepts of Newton's theory. In fact, Newton's system would work equally well for any number of planets spaced at any distances from the sun. Newton, by offering mechanical principles which could explain certain facts in the world of phenomena, redefined the nature of explanation in astronomy and physics. He simultaneously redefined the class of answerable questions and important data.[1]

Newton's goal—to find a mechanical model, differs considerably from Kepler's goal—to find mathematical harmonies. As discussed earlier, the value of an argument is a function of our goals. Since Newton and Kepler had different goals, one might expect they assigned different strengths to arguments.

Consider Kepler's two arguments for Copernicus's system. Suppose that the planets really did fit into the Platonic solids as Kepler postulated. Kepler thought that the second argument, concerning the Platonic solids, was stronger than the first argument, concerning solar oppositions. In Newton's system, the argument on solar oppositions is stronger than the argument on Platonic solids. In fact, the argument on Platonic solids is a particular example of an argument type which is irrelevant to Newton's concept of explanation based on a mechanical model. To Newton, if it were true that the planets fit the Platonic forms, it would be considered a fact which, although not without intrinsic interest, has no bearing on the empirical adequacy of his mathematical-mechanical analysis.

This leads to an important fact:

(1) In the change from the typological view to the mechanical view, certain of the arguments which possessed great force to the researchers in the typological view have no force and are irrelevant to the researchers in the mechanical view.

3. TYPOLOGICAL AND MECHANICAL VIEWS OF LANGUAGE RESEARCH

The typological view of science has in linguistics been dubbed the taxonomic view. Many taxonomists have sought to construct a catalog of the elements that function in language and indicate the restrictions on their distribution. The taxonomic view most in line with the typological search for mathematical harmonies would be something like this:

(2) Typological (Taxonomic) View of Language. The goal of research is to use algebraic tools (slot-filler tests, diagnostic environments, co-occurrence tests, paraphrase tests, trans-

formations, etc.) to express this or that claim about particular grammars or the general theory of grammar.

The mechanical view of language research has been called the generative view. According to the view of *Syntactic Structures* and *Aspects*, the goal of research in linguistics is to offer a principled account, based on the mechanical principles of sentence construction (phrase structure rules, transformations, etc.) of the ability a speaker has to recognize certain sentences as well-formed and others as ungrammatical. The mechanical view might be stated as follows:

(3) Mechanical (Generative) View of Language. The goal of research is to use algebraic tools to formalize the mechanical principles of sentence construction and to construct a theory (a grammar) from which one can deduce consequences (the sentences generated) which can be verified or refuted in comparison with observable data (the primary data of the language studied).

For any given school of linguistic research, one might ask if it is in the typological or the mechanical view. For example, one might ask if generative semantics is in the typological or the mechanical view. Postal in his 1969 paper delivered at the Texas conference, Goals of Linguistic Theory, offered this insightful analysis:

In the early days of transformational study . . . we naively assumed that it was actually possible at the time to construct generative grammars for human languages, and people set about seriously attempting just this. These efforts have unquestionably taught us a great deal. It is a fact, however, that actual grammar construction in the sense of early works like Chomsky's *Syntactic Structures* (1957), Lee's *Grammar of English Nominalizations* (1960), etc., probably stopped at least by the mid-sixties, and, in any event, certainly does not go on at the present [footnote 50, see below]. If the pursuit of generative grammar has not led to the construction of viable generative grammars, it has led to a deepening appreciation of just what a fantastic system each human has articulated within him. The pursuit of a precise formulation of grammar, although it has not brought precise formulations which are valid, has created a correct attitude, an attitude which previous work did not engender. (pp. 160–161)

[Footnote 50]: If generative research does not consist of the construction of generative grammars, it is important to ask what it does consist of. In a no doubt never-to-be-written paper, Lakoff, Postal, and Ross (forthcoming) argue that today such research consists in the construction and validation of arguments supporting this or that claim about particular grammars, or the general theory of grammar. This carries on a strand of activity which dates to the beginning of generative work. For example, Chomsky's demonstration of the inadequacy of finite-state devices was work of just this sort. For a time, this kind of activity was pushed into the background by the goal of pursuing here and now the construction of actual grammars. As the latter goal has come to be seen as more and more unrealistic, the other has naturally expanded to fill the gap. (p. 168)

Consider some of the points made by Postal:

(4) "It is a fact, however, that actual grammar construction in the sense of early works like Chomsky's *Syntactic Structures* . . . probably stopped at least by the mid-sixties, and, in any event, certainly does not go on at the present."

This is simply false. The construction of generative grammars has continued unabated since 1957 (see Chomsky, 1973, and references cited there). Postal would seem to be correct, however, if we consider his own proposals and perhaps those of Lakoff and Ross (as we shall see below).

(5) "If generative research does not consist of the construction of generative grammars, it is important to ask what it does consist of. . . . Lakoff, Postal, and Ross argue that today such research consists in the construction and validation of arguments supporting this or that claim about particular grammars, or the general theory of grammar."

This statement reflects a fundamental confusion about basic issues. Postal feels that generative research is taxonomic research. This is a category mistake. Generative research, being in the mechanical view, differs categorically from taxonomic research, which is in the typological view. Postal formulates his arguments in the taxonomic (typological) view.

Recall that arguments which have strength in the typological view may have no relevance in the mechanical (generative) view (see (1) above).

We can now understand why generative grammarians, like Chomsky, have regarded most, if not all, of Postal's arguments to be not merely incorrect, but rather irrelevant. Chomsky delivered a paper at the same Goals of Linguistic Theory conference at which Postal's paper was presented. Concerning Postal's main argument against Chomsky's lexicalist position, Chomsky states: "Postal's counterargument is based on a misunderstanding. He overlooks the essential claim of the lexicalist hypothesis.... Hence, nothing follows from Postal's observations, so far as the lexicalist hypothesis is concerned" (1969, p. 95).

More recently, Chomsky reflects on Postal's arguments in these terms:

> Much of what I will describe here recapitulates or is an outgrowth of ideas presented in Chomsky (1973). See Postal (1974) for a critique of the latter, and Lightfoot (forthcoming) for an argument, which I think is correct, that the critique is beside the point, quite apart from questions of truth and falsity. The debate, of course, continues, and there is more that I would like to say about it, but this is not the place. (to appear; fn. 2)

The fact that Postal's critiques of generative proposals fail to touch the relevant issues follows in large measure but not entirely, as we shall see below, from the fact that Postal's arguments, while they may be significant in the typological view of language he champions, have little, if any, significance in the mechanistic view in which Chomsky and others offer proposals.[2] I return to discuss particular examples in Section 4. Now consider the rest of the Postal statement quoted in (5):

(6) "the construction... of arguments supporting this or that claim about particular grammars, or the general theory of grammars... carries on a strand of activity which dates back to the beginning of generative work"

This is an understatement. This "strand of activity," being nothing other than taxonomic research as performed by

Bloomfield, Gleason, Lamb, etc., predates the mechanistic view of research introduced by *Syntactic Structures*. Postal's view of the status of linguistics as a science is firmly in the tradition of typological (or taxonomic) research. We are offered old wine in new bottles. Postal's claim that "Chomsky's demonstration of the inadequacy of finite-state devices was work of just this sort" indicates a basic misunderstanding of Chomsky's goals, methods, and arguments. Postal states:

(7) "For a time, this kind of activity [taxonomic studies] was pushed into the background by the goal of pursuing here and now the construction of actual grammars."

This is accurate. The taxonomic strand of activity as developed by Bloomfield and others received a setback with the publication of *Syntactic Structures*. Postal, in attempting to rescue the typological strand of activity, has as his intent the rehabilitation of Bloomfieldian goals and argumentation.

Generative semantics, as discussed by Postal, seems to differ from the *Syntactic Structures–Aspects* view concerning the goals of research. Let us next examine if these two schools differ in argumentation.

4. GOALS AND THE STRENGTH OF ARGUMENT FORMS

The goals of linguistic research in the mechanical view are detailed in *Syntactic Structures–Aspects*. The theory-comparison argument form, discussed in many places—including Dougherty (1974), seems to be the main form of argument to achieve rational progress in research. In brief, the argument form is like this:

(8) The theory-comparison argument form requires a researcher to:
　　a. consider all previously proposed or "natural" alternatives to his proposals;
　　b. formulate the descriptive devices of each theory sufficiently to make clear what each theory claims about the data to be considered;

   c. determine where the alternative grammars differ in empirical consequences;

   d. compare the alternative grammars with the data and with each other;

   e. search for crucial examples and arguments by which to choose one grammar over the others. Crucial examples arise in areas where the competing grammars make different claims about a given range of data. They provide substantive reasons for selecting one grammar over the others.

A proposed grammar is a guess about the principles of sentence construction in a particular language and in language in general. At any point in our research, we want to have the best available model, that is, a model meeting at least these conditions:

(9) A theoretical model is tentatively to be accepted if:

   a. it has interesting formal properties: as a minimum it must be a noncontradictory set of assumptions from which we can deduce unequivocal assertions;[3]

   b. it must be testable: it must make about language innumerable claims capable of experimental verification or refutation—it must be empirical;

   c. it must be refutable:[4] it must offer principled reasons for why the patterns of grammatical and ungrammatical sentences take the form they do—it must be explanatory;

   d. it must make claims which are verified in a number of significant cases;

   e. it must be demonstrably superior to previously proposed or "natural" alternatives.

A grammatical model is demonstrably superior to alternatives if we can cite specific examples (crucial examples) which indicate that the claims of the model are more accurate and, in some sense, more insightful than the claims of the competing models, and if further, we can construct solid arguments indicating precisely *how* and *why* those examples are relevant. Our theory is interesting not because the data *could* be described under its assumptions, but because the data *should* be described under its assumptions and not under other assumptions which might be a priori equally plausible.

Let us now analyze some actual arguments.

Lakoff and Ross (hereafter, L&R) (1970) discuss the relative merits of two grammatical models proposed to describe sentences containing coordinate conjunctions and quantifiers: the conjunction reduction (CR) hypothesis and the phrase structure rule (PSR) hypothesis. The CR hypothesis, advocated by L&R, would transformationally derive the following (b) examples by a conjunction reduction transformation from underlying structures with essentially the order of constituents in the (a) examples. The PSR hypothesis, which L&R disagree with, would not transformationally relate the (a) and (b) examples. Instead, the base generates deep structure phrase makers—or underlying structures—with essentially the order of constituents in (10a, b), (11a), and (12a, b). Sentence (11b) would be transformationally derived from an underlying structure with essentially the order of constituents in *Ann and John each dislike the other*.

(10)   a. Ann is erudite and John is erudite.
       b. Ann and John are erudite.

(11)   a. Ann dislikes John and John dislikes Ann.
       b. Ann and John dislike each other.

(12)   a. Ann laughed and John cried.
       b. Ann and John laughed and cried respectively.

The CR hypothesis and the PSR hypothesis differ considerably in what they claim is an underlying form, which sentences are derived by optional transformations, which sentences are transformationally related, what constructions are grouped into natural classes, etc. The choice between these hypotheses is an empirical question. Let us look at the type of argument and the nature of the evidence that L&R adduce to choose between these alternative grammars. L&R state (pp. 271-272):

It has long been realized that certain sentences, e.g. (1a), containing conjoined constitutents are paraphrasable by conjoined sentences.

but that others, e.g. (1b), are not (cf. (2)).

(1) a. Ann and John are erudite.
  b. Ann and John are similar.

(2) a. Ann is erudite and John is erudite.
  b. *Ann is similar and John is similar.

There are several syntactic facts which correlate with this difference in paraphrasability, and which suggest that (1a) should derive from (2a), while (1b) should be (essentially) basic.

Thus note that (3) is ambiguous (for many speakers): it can derive from (4a) or (4b).

(3) Harry scratched his elbow and I did too.

(4) a. Harry scratched his elbow, and I scratched his elbow too.
  b. Harry scratched his elbow, and I scratched my elbow too.

Note that when (1b) is embedded, it can also have two meanings: (5) can derive from (6a) or from (6b).

(5) John$_i$ said that Ann and he$_i$ were similar, and I did too.

(6) a. John$_i$ said that Ann and he$_i$ were similar, and I said that Ann and he$_i$ were similar too.
  b. John$_i$ said that Ann and he$_i$ were similar, and I said that Ann and I were similar too.

However, when either (1a) or (2a) appears as the object of *said*, as in (7), the resulting sentence is unambiguous: the sentences in (7) can only derive from (8), not from (9).

(7) a. John$_i$ said that Ann and he$_i$ were erudite, and I did too.
  b. John$_i$ said that Ann was erudite and he$_i$ was erudite, and I did too.

(8) a. John$_i$ said that Ann and he$_i$ were erudite, and I said that Ann and he$_i$ were erudite too.
  b. John$_i$ said that Ann was erudite and he$_i$ was erudite, and I said that Ann was erudite and he$_i$ was erudite too.

(9) a. John$_i$ said that Ann and he$_i$ were erudite, and I said that Ann and I were erudite too.
  b. John$_i$ said that Ann was erudite and he$_i$ was erudite, and I said that Ann was erudite and I was erudite too.

Thus if both sentences in (7) have the same source ((8b) would be the least abbreviated form of this source), an analysis which is traditional in transformational grammar, the fact that (7a) is un-ambiguous is reducible to the fact that (7b) is, if some trans-formational rule of *Conjunction Reduction* relates the two. Thus the contrast between (5) and (7a) supports the postulation of such a rule. In addition, the fact that the sentences in (10) are unambiguous, paralleling (7a), and not (5), suggests that the sentences in (10) are also to be derived from conjoined structures by some process of reduction.

(10) a. John$_i$ said that Ann and he$_i$ had laughed and cried, respec-
          tively, and I did too.
      b. John$_i$ said that Ann and he$_i$ disliked each other, and I did
          too.

These facts thus provide evidence for the traditional transformational analysis of *respectively* and *each other* and provide counterevidence to the alternative analysis of these constructions which has recently been proposed by Dougherty (see Ray C. Dougherty, *A Transforma-tional Grammar of Conjoined Coordinate Structures* (1968), un-published doctoral disseration, M.I.T.).

Another interesting set of facts which supports a transformational derivation for certain coordinate phrases, but not for all, is the following. While some speakers accept (11b) (as an approximate paraphrase of (11a)), no one finds (12) grammatical, to the best of our knowledge.

(11) a. Who is similar to whom?
      b. Who and who are similar?

(12)   *Who and who are erudite?

If (2a) is converted to (1a), by some rule of *Conjunction Reduction*, then the ungrammaticality of (12) can be explained on the basis of the fact that (13) is ungrammatical.

(13)   *Who is erudite and who is erudite?

As might be expected, *respectively*-sentences and *each other*-sentences, which the facts of (10) suggested should be derived by some transformational process of reduction, cannot occur with *who and who* coordinate NP's.

(14) a. *Who and who laughed and cried, respectively?
      b. *Who and who dislike each other?

L&R offer two arguments to choose between the CR hypothesis and the PSR hypothesis: the first based on sentences (1-10), the second based on sentences (11-14).

I renumber L&R's data for reference in my text. The derivation of (13b) from (13a) parallels the derivation of (10b) from (10a). Similarly, the derivation of (14b) from (14a) parallels the derivation of (12b) from (12a).

(13)   a. *Who is erudite and who is erudite? (L&R #13)
       b. *Who and who are erudite? (L&R #12)

(14)   a. Who laughed and who cried?
       b. *Who and who laughed and cried respectively? (L&R #14a)

L&R state: "the ungrammaticality of [13b] can be explained on the basis of the fact that [13a] is ungrammatical." But how will the CR hypothesis block (14b)? If, as L&R assume, sentence (14b) is derived by a reduction transformation from (14a)—a sentence conspicuously absent from L&R's discussion— then the logical expectation would be that (14b) should be well formed. I can only wonder why L&R state: "As might be expected, *respectively*-sentences . . . cannot occur with *who and who* coordinate NP's."

Under the assumptions of L&R's grammar, which derives (12b) from (12a), the logical expectation is that (14b) should be well formed since (14a) is well formed. This expectation of the CR hypothesis is at odds with the primary data of English. Consequently, the example cited by L&R as support for their grammar, L&R's example (14a), is actually a counterexample to their grammar.

Let us consider a hypothetical situation: Suppose that L&R's example (14a) were not a counterexample to their own proposals. Then their argument, instead of being invalid, would simply offer weak affirmative support for their grammar. That is, the most L&R's form of argument could assert is that the data *could* be described under the assumptions of their system. Their argument would not show that the data *should* be described under their assumptions.

Which part of L&R's discussion of examples (1–14) shows that these data "provide counterevidence to the alternative analysis [the PSR hypothesis] . . . which has recently been proposed by Dougherty . . . (1968)"? The passages quoted above constitute the entire article penned by L&R. They have omitted a crucial step: L&R do not demonstrate what the PSR hypothesis claims about examples (1–14). L&R barely mention the PSR hypothesis. They invoke a logic which assumes that by claiming their grammar describes the data they "provide counterevidence to the alternative analysis," and therefore, the "alternative analysis" need not be discussed. L&R's strategy is no stranger to the kangaroo court where many a defendant has been sentenced in absentia. L&R have not provided a valid argument since their discussion lacks the obvious necessary step: a demonstration that the PSR hypothesis cannot describe the data in any non-ad hoc way. Lacking this step, L&R's argument is merely rhetorical. They are not justified in concluding anything (positive or negative) about the PSR hypothesis.

L&R's argument form, rather than an example of theory comparison, seems to be an example of theory exposition. At no point does L&R's discussion get above this form of argument:

(15) The theory-exposition argument form requires a researcher to:

    a. consider in depth only the championed analysis, although alternative analyses may be mentioned slightly, perhaps as an aid in clarifying his own analysis;

    b. formulate descriptive devices sufficiently to describe a few illustrative examples;

    c. cite selected examples where the championed analysis works to illustrate his meaning and intentions;

    d. consider counterexamples to the analysis in any of three ways: (i) Counterexamples are to be cataloged by a "theory of exceptions," which may factor whatever inductive generalizations there may be among the exceptions. (ii) Consider, as in L&R (1970), counterexamples to the championed analysis to provide evidence for the championed analysis and against the alternative proposals. (iii) Consider the counterexamples as providing insight into the mysterious nature of language by regarding them as discoveries about how the data should be (see Postal, 1966, and Dougherty, 1974, for discussion of this issue).

If our goal is to achieve an explanatory theory of language structure in the mechanical view, then the theory-comparison (TC) argument form is superior to the theory-exposition (TE) argument because TC will give us a model meeting the conditions in (9), but TE will not.

The TC argument form yields not certainty but probable knowledge. If our arguments are coherent, our model will possess a stability and degree of security proportional to the quality of the data involved in the arguments. The TC argument form, and its reliance on comparing theories with each other and with the data, reflects our idea that what distinguishes the scientist is not *what* he believes but *why* he believes it. Ideas, even if correct, do not amount to a scientific theory unless there exists a specific type of reason for believing them. A scientist, via the TC argument form, knows what justifies his beliefs and just how, why, and to what extent that justification is sufficient.

The TE argument form shows, at most, how data *could* be described, not how data *should* be described. It is ideally suited to factor (or "motivate" the factoring) of algebraically formalizable generalizations from large masses of data. The superficial perspicacity of this type of analysis will appeal to those who think but do not think critically.

The instruments of research are frequently taken for granted and are often assumed to be the same for all linguists who contend they are working in generative studies. (See the articles by Searle, Maclay, McCawley, etc., cited in the References.) Clearly this is not the case. Those researchers working in the *Syntactic Structures-Aspects* perspective use TC and not TE as their research tool for advancing their insight into languages processes. The TC argument form was introduced into linguistics in *Syntactic Structures* as a means for developing transformational generative grammars meeting the conditions in (9). What is the source of the TE argument? Does the TC argument precede *Syntactic Structures*? What is the source of methodology and argumentation? Let us examine briefly a perspective in which the scientific revolution in linguistics caused by *Syntactic Structures* might be analyzed.

LOVEJOY ON THE SOURCES OF
METHODOLOGY AND ARGUMENTATION

Arthur O. Lovejoy, in *The Great Chain of Being*, develops the thesis that the doctrines and tendencies designated by familiar names ending in *-ism, -ity, -ics,* or *-ology,* although they may be, usually are not, organized around a single idea. The total body of doctrine of any philosopher or school is almost always a complex and heterogeneous aggregate—and often in ways which the followers of the doctrine do not suspect. Most doctrines, philosophic systems, etc., can be analyzed into their component parts, which Lovejoy calls *unit ideas.* A unit idea, though it may be decomposable into simpler concepts and subject to analysis, functions as a unity by being a basic building block of the movements ending in *-ism, -ity,* etc. According to Lovejoy, the number of distinctly different unit ideas, the components of which philosophic systems are composed, is decidedly limited. He feels that most philosophic systems are original or distinctive rather in their combinations of unit ideas than in their actual component unit ideas.

Lovejoy presents a reasonable scheme for dissecting a complex system into its unit ideas and shows how one might trace the history of a given unit idea through various philosophic systems. He states:

> By the history of ideas I mean something at once more specific and less restricted than the history of philosophy. It is differentiated primarily by the character of the units with which it concerns itself. Though it deals in great part with the same materials as the other branches of the history of thought and depends greatly on their prior labors, it divides that material in a special way, brings the parts of it into new groupings and relations, views it from the standpoint of a distinctive purpose. Its initial procedure may be said—though the parallel has its danger—to be somewhat analogous to that of analytic chemistry. In dealing with the history of philosophical doctrines, for example, it cuts into the hard-and-fast individual systems and, for its own purposes, breaks them up into their component elements, into what might be called their unit ideas. (p. 3)

Lovejoy warns that it may not be a simple process to isolate the unit ideas:

just as chemical compounds differ in their sensible qualities from the elements comprising them, so the elements of philosophical doctrines, in differing logical combinations, are not always readily recognizable, and, prior to analysis, even the same complex may appear to be not the same in its differing expressions, because of the diversity of the philosopher's temperaments and the consequent inequality in the distribution of emphasis among the several parts, or because of the drawing of dissimilar conclusions from partially identical premises. To the common logical or pseudo-logical or affective ingredients behind the surface-dissimilarities the historian of individual ideas will seek to penetrate (p. 4)

Lovejoy offers some simple examples:

doctrines and tendencies that are designated by familiar names ending in *ism, -ology*, etc. . . . commonly constitute compounds to which [our] method of analysis needs to be applied. *Idealism, romanticism, transcendentalism, pragmatism*—all these trouble-breeding and usually thought-obscuring terms, which one sometimes wishes to see expunged from the vocabulary of the philosopher and the historian altogether, are names of complexes, not of simplexes. . . . They stand, as a rule, not for one doctrine, but for several distinct and often conflicting doctrines held by different individuals or groups to whose way of thinking these appellations have been applied, either by themselves or in the traditional terminology of historians; and each of these doctrines, in turn, is likely to be resolvable into simpler elements, often very strangly combined and derivative from a variety of dissimilar motives and historic influences. (p. 6)

Lovejoy observes:

In [a] whole series of creeds and movements going under [a single] name, and in each of them separately, it is needful to go behind the superficial appearance of singleness and identity, to crack the shell which holds the mass together, if we are to see the real units, the effective working ideas, which, in any given case, are present. (p. 6).

We might utilize Lovejoy's approach in order to isolate and define the unit ideas in linguistics and to trace them through various systems of linguistic analysis.

Some unit ideas in linguistics might be: *constituent structure, pair tests, phonology, syntax, semantics, autonomy, phoneme, distinctive feature, transformation, discovery procedure, theory testing, innate ideas, paraphrase, co-occurrence, sentence, dis-*

course, word, morpheme, level, etc. These are unit ideas because they act as conceptual units—building blocks of systems of linguistic analysis. These unit ideas can be traced historically through various schools of thought. They are to some extent independent and can be combined in various ways. Thus, they summarize the conceptual distinctions requisite to determining the interrelations of the various schools internal to the movement known as linguistics.

Though an interesting project would be to isolate and define the unit ideas in linguistics, a more modest task might be to isolate the unit ideas in a single area of linguistics—transformational generative grammar (TGG). Lovejoy's observation might be restated: In the whole series of movements going under the one name, TGG, and in each of them separately, it is needful to go behind the superficial appearance of singleness and identity, to crack the shell which holds the mass together, if we are to see the real units, the effective working ideas, which, in any given case, are present. How can we factor TGG into its unit ideas?

The name TGG derives from two specific ideas: *transformational grammar* and *generative grammar.* These ideas are independent. There are generative nontransformational grammars and nongenerative transformational grammars. The concept "generative grammar" relates to the goals and methods of research, the concept "transformational grammar" relates to the specific theoretical proposals about the rules which describe the data and the structure to be assigned to each sentence. For example, Chomsky would argue that a generative nontransformational grammar, such as a generative phrase structure grammar or a generative Markov grammar, is theoretically inadequate to describe the principles of sentence construction in human language. On the other hand, he would argue that the construction of a nongenerative transformational grammar is not a reasonable goal of linguistic research. A nongenerative transformational model may give an economical survey of a certain body of data, but it will not enable the linguist to pose interesting questions concerning the principles underlying sentence construction.

Four possibilities can, and in fact do, exist: (a) a nongenerative, nontransformational grammar is the type offered by American structuralists; (b) a transformational generative

grammar is offered by Chomsky (1957); (c) a nontransformational generative grammar is championed by Dik (1968),
who states: "I fully agree with *generative grammar*, but I am
quite critical of many aspects of *transformational grammar*" (p.
4); (d) a nongenerative transformational grammar is presented by
Harris (1957, 1965). Table 1 shows how the two unit ideas
(transformational grammar and generative grammar) can be used
to classify different approaches to linguistic research.

Although it would require long and tedious study to prove, it
seems plausible that the number of basic unit ideas in linguistics
is smaller than the number of different schools, movements, and
systems of linguistic analysis which have been proposed since
antiquity. A good case could be made that various linguistic
schools differ from one another more in the combinations of
unit ideas rather than in any really new unit ideas. A new school
of linguistic thought is really a new compound. To the extent
this is true, the best way to gain an understanding of the many
ongoing research activities, and to gain a perspective on the past
history of research activity, is to gain an understanding of the
basic unit ideas. Our work parallels that of the analytic chemist:
We take apart a compound and only then recognize that it is
composed of old familiar elements, which when in compounds
seem to lose their familiar properties although they do retain
their character.

Unit ideas have several properties: (a) they may or may not
be independent; (b) a unit idea may be complex and analyzable
into simpler ideas; (c) a unit idea may assume a variety of
complexions due to the emphasis of its different aspects in
relation to other unit ideas.

Unit ideas in linguistics may be of different types. Theoretical
unit ideas might be: *phrase structure rule, constituent structure,*

TABLE 1. Two unit ideas define four schools of linguistics

	Transformational grammar	Generative grammar
Chomsky (1957, 1965)	+	+
Harris (1957, 1965)	+	−
Dik (1968)	−	+
American structuralists	−	−

*phrase marker, transformational rule, syntactic structure, ab-
stract structure, distinctive feature,* etc. Methodological unit
ideas might be: *generative grammar, derivation, testability, empirical claim, crucial example, falsifiable claim, evaluation measure, discovery procedure, abduction, induction, explanatory
power,* etc.

These are unit ideas to the extent they act as conceptual units
and function as building blocks of systems of linguistic analysis.
That is, they are unit ideas to the extent they summarize the
conceptual distinctions requisite to understanding systems of
linguistic analysis diachronically, as they have evolved over time,
and synchronically, as they face off against each other at any
point in time. Can the above listed unit ideas be traced through
various movements? Can they be used to determine the interrelations of the various schools of thought internal to the
movement known as linguistics? To what extent are they useful
in understanding the distinctions between the various movements stemming from *Syntactic Structures?*

A strong case could be built that Chomsky's theory of
grammar (TGG) is best regarded as a unique new combination of
old unit ideas, each of which has a history in language studies.
What has been called *taxonomy* is a certain compound of unit
ideas. There are some unit ideas which are shared by TGG and
taxonomy.

A study of scientific revolutions in terms of unit ideas would
enable us to understand many facts about scientific revolutions
in general and linguistics in particular. For example, a unit-ideas
theory predicts that there is no qualitative difference between a
revolution and a lesser change in a science. The change of a few
unit ideas is a small change, a lot of unit ideas is a revolution.
Possibly all unit ideas are not equivalently basic. C. S. Peirce had
the idea that a change in methodology (i.e., a change in
methodological unit ideas) in a science is more revolutionary
than a change in theory (i.e., the adoption or rejection of
certain theoretical unit ideas).

A unit-ideas theory predicts that after a scientific revolution,
three groups will exist. One group accepts the old combination
of unit ideas. Another group accepts the new combination of
unit ideas. A third group accepts a combination of unit ideas
drawn from the new and the old combinations. This latter

group, working in a confused perspective perhaps, may assume arguments to have a strength which they do not in fact possess.

One might well argue that the theory-exposition argument form is an incoherent combination of unit ideas drawn from the generative framework introduced by *Syntactic Structures* and the taxonomic framework of structuralism. Within the taxonomic framework much excellent work has been done, for example, the *Oxford English Dictionary*, the studies of Bloch, Harris, Jespersen, etc. Within the generative framework as defined by *Syntactic Structures-Aspects* much excellent work has also been done (see Chomsky, 1973, and works cited there). Within the incoherent framework formed by taking unit ideas from the taxonomic and generative frameworks to yield such arguments as theory exposition, it is not clear what research has yielded. In the unit-ideas analysis, generative semantics is an incoherent blend of unit ideas from the generative and taxonomic perspective.

Searle, in an interesting survey of the state of linguistics, offers these reflections:

> Much as Chomsky once argued that structuralists could not comfortably accommodate the syntactical facts of language, so the generative semanticists now argue that his [Chomsky's] system cannot comfortably account for the facts of the interpenetration of semantics and syntax. There is no unanimity among Chomsky's critics—Ross, Postal, McCawley, Fillmore (some of these are among his best students). . . . (p. 20)

Searle neglects to mention that the young turks leading the new generative semantics revolution—Ross, Postal, and Lakoff—were also among the best students of the leading structuralists—Harris, Bloch, and Householder.

Some people who studied taxonomic linguistics with leading structuralists moved into Chomsky's camp after the appearance of *Syntactic Structures*. These people who studied taxonomy and then generative grammar would, in a sense, represent the "interface" of the scientific revolution in linguistics, that is, the precise point of meeting of the old and the new. It is not a coincidence that generative semantics is a blend of taxonomic and generative methodology. This simply represents mixing or diffusion at the surface boundary.

It is an empirical question as to whether generative semantics is an incoherent mixture of unit ideas which yields instruments of research like theory exposition or whether it is a new theory of grammar uniting syntax and semantics. All the data of which I am aware supports the former (see Dougherty, 1973, 1974).

6. THE CURRENT STATUS OF LINGUISTIC ARGUMENTATION AND GOALS

My hypothesis can be briefly stated:

(16) Conjecture about the current state of linguistic argumentation:
   a. The strength of an argument form is a function of our goals: In particular, strong arguments in the typological view may be judged weak, or irrelevant, in the mechanical view.
   b. Generative grammar (GG), as defined by *Syntactic Structures–Aspects*, sets the goals of linguistic research internal to the mechanical view.
   c. Generative semantics (GS), as defined by Postal, Lakoff, and Ross, sets the goals of linguistic research internal to the typological view, at best.

From this hypothesis we can deduce these consequences:[5]

(17) Consequences deduced from (16):
   a. GS researchers will use the theory-exposition form of argument and not the theory-comparison form of argument.
   b. It is to be expected that researchers in GG and GS will each contend that the opposing faction's arguments are irrelevant, vacuous, meaningless, etc.

It is certainly true that GS researchers use the theory-exposition form of argument and not the theory-comparison form; (17a) is true. In this article I have examined only one example in detail to show the form of the argument. For many more examples of the GS use of theory exposition, see

Dougherty (1970, 1973, 1974, and forthcoming) for a discussion of Fillmore (1966, 1968, 1969), Postal (1966, 1969), McCawley (1968, to appear), and Lakoff and Peters (1966). See also Botha (1973) for some discussion of GS argumentation.

Consequence (17b) is verified. Passages cited earlier indicate that Chomsky feels that GS arguments all too frequently carry no force and are irrelevant to the main issues. Not to be surpassed in this regard, GS authors make similar claims about Chomsky's arguments. Seuren (1974), in his recent book of GS articles by McCawley, Lakoff, etc., uses the term *semantic syntax* to refer to GS and *autonomous syntax* to refer to work by Chomsky, etc. Seuren begins his introduction:

> The purpose of this collection of papers is to give an idea of the essential issues involved in the development, in the wake of Chomsky's *Aspects of the Theory of Syntax*, of what is widely known as "generative semantics." . . .
>
> This book is partisan in that a favorable view is taken of semantic syntax as against the theory of autonomous syntax defended by Chomsky and others. This is, in a way, a matter of course, since the writers who have expounded the theory of semantic syntax most clearly have also promoted it. Apart from that, however, the partisan attitude is motivated by the feeling that the arguments advanced against semantic syntax do not, on the whole, carry conviction. They are sometimes based on a false conception of the essential issues involved, sometimes also on incorrect reasoning. And where they do cut ice, they reveal problems which are indifferent to the issue at hand because they will have to be faced by anyone who attempts an explanation of the facts of language by providing an adequate description of linguistic competence and the innate capacity for language acquisition. There is, moreover, a conspicuous tendency in autonomous syntax to be casual about the explanation of semantic facts. (pp. 1-2)

Lakoff and Ross (1970) appeared a few short months after the following passage, Lakoff (1970), appeared in the Preface to the published version of Lakoff (1965), *Irregularity in Syntax*. Lakoff reflects upon the low state of argumentation in 1965— recall that *Aspects* appeared in 1965. With the appearance of Lakoff and Ross (1970), however, a new age of linguistic argumentation seems to have dawned. Lakoff (1970) states:

> The discerning reader will observe that the level of argumentation in this work [Lakoff, 1965], though normal for 1965, is appallingly

low by contemporary standards. The reason is simple enough. In 1965, so little work had been done in transformational grammar that analyses were rarely in conflict, and no alternative theories had been seriously proposed. That situation changed radically within a year. (p. x)

Apparently in the new, more sophisticated logic of 1970 Lakoff feels that theory exposition is superior to theory comparison, at least as theory comparison is developed in *Aspects*. It is interesting to reflect on Lakoff's statement, "that situation changed radically within a year." Consider 1966. Lakoff and Peters (1966) wish to motivate their *conjunction reduction-conjunct movement* analysis over the analysis of coordination offered by Gleitman (1965). But each and every distribution of data cited by Lakoff and Peters to choose their proposal over Gleitman's actually would select Gleitman's grammar over their own. The one example they offer as a counterexample to Gleitman's grammar is actually irrelevant, that is, a neutral example (see Dougherty, 1971, 1973). The form of argument in Lakoff and Peters seems to be an example of theory exposition.

Lakoff, along with Seuren, feels that Chomsky's arguments carry little weight. On September 10, 1972, the *New York Times* carried a half-page article surveying the field of linguistics. The reporter had interviewed several linguists. Concerning Chomsky, Lakoff stated:

it's virtually impossible to talk to Chomsky about these things [i.e., various aspects of language which Lakoff considers to be serious problems]. He's a genius, and he fights dirty when he argues. He uses every trick in the book. . . .

The mind at any stage of growth has its own logic. This logic specifies the form and organization of the arguments a researcher will use to advance his proposals. In general, the form and organization of the arguments used by a linguist to advance his proposals directly reflect his attitude about the status of linguistics as a science. A critic of arguments must ask, What are the assumptions defining the perspective in which questions are raised and criticisms are offered? To what extent do these assumptions reflect attitudes about what is "science," "explanation," "theory," etc.?

7. THE STRATEGY OF SCIENCE:
THE STATUS OF LINGUISTICS
AS A SCIENCE

James B. Conant, in his Foreword to the *Harvard Case Studies in Experimental Science*—a collection of essays sketching the invention and early justification of the ideas basic to our present-day scientific understanding—states:

> Experience shows that a man who has been a successful investigator in any field of experimental science approaches a problem in pure or applied science, even in an area in which he is quite ignorant, with a special point of view. One may designate this point of view "understanding science"; it is independent of a knowledge of the scientific facts or techniques in the new area. Even a highly educated and intelligent citizen without research experience will almost always fail to grasp the essentials in a discussion that takes place among scientists concerned with a projected inquiry. This will be so not because of the layman's lack of scientific knowledge or his failure to comprehend the technical jargon of the scientist; it will be to a large degree because of his fundamental ignorance of what science can or cannot accomplish, and his subsequent bewilderment in the course of a discussion outlining a plan for a future investigation. He has no "feel" for what we may call "the tactics and strategy of science." (p. vii)

Let us reflect upon Conant's scientist, focusing attention on his "feel" for "the tactics and strategy of science." Following Conant, this "feel" has at least two aspects:

(18) Goals. A scientist has a "feel" for what science can or cannot accomplish.

(19) Methods. A scientist pursues a rational strategy in the course of discussion outlining a plan for future investigation.

In setting his goals, Conant's scientist will realize that science is an invention of the human mind, a specific way of thinking. The form of scientific thinking with which we are most familiar was invented by Galileo, Descartes, Kepler, Newton, and others.

These men, in particular Newton, indicated by word and deed what science, or scientific thought, can and cannot be expected to accomplish.

Science, being an invention of the human mind, continues to develop. There may or may not be anything absolute in our present-day scientist's concept of what science can and cannot accomplish. Conant's scientist, however, will realize that, given the development of scientific thought as it is today (including methodology, argumentation, metaphysics, etc.), there are limits to what science can and cannot do, or at least to what a present-day scientist can and cannot do.

Conant's scientist will set his goals as high as possible consistent with what he believes science can accomplish. That about which he feels science can say little he may consign to his metaphysics, or (essentially) equivalently, may factor from his analysis by methodological assumptions.[6] For his goals, he will have a minimum requirement and an upper limit:

(20) Minimum requirement for goals. A scientist should strive to develop a formal, deductive (mechanical) model and not content himself merely by offering a collection of "mathematical harmonies," that is, formalizable generalizations which are true of the data.

(21) Upper limit on goals. A scientist should seek to formalize the mechanical (deductive-mathematical) principles characterizing *how* nature operates and not be discouraged if he cannot formalize the principles characterizing *why* nature operates as it does.

Sciences like physics, chemistry, and astronomy have developed in the mechanical view. The proposals of *Syntactic Structures–Aspects* develop the science of linguistics in the mechanical view. Accepting the mechanical view, the minimum requirements for the goals of linguistics might be summarized thusly:

(22) Minimum goals for linguistics. Our research is aimed toward the development of an explanatory model (a TGG) which generates all and only the grammatical sentences of

a particular language L by appealing to strong assumptions which narrowly constrain the notions "language" in general and "L" in particular. In a TGG, algebraic tools (phrase structure rules, transformations, lexical devices, etc.) are used to formalize the mechanical principles of sentence construction into a theory (a grammar) from which one can deduce consequences (the sentences generated) which can be verified or refuted in comparison with the observable data (the primary data of the language studied).

If these comprise our minimum goals, then linguistics as a science is methodologically equivalent to the more developed sciences of physics, chemistry, etc. Conant's scientist would sense that his "feel" for the tactics and strategy of science was satisfied by linguistic argumentation.

What does Conant mean by the phrase "what science can or cannot accomplish"? In particular, what is it that science *cannot* accomplish? What is the upper limit on the goals of scientific research? Let us examine what Chomsky (1968) calls "methodological parallels" in this passage:

It seems to me quite possible that at that particular moment in the development of Western thought [i.e., right after Descartes, RCD] there was the possibility for the birth of a science of psychology of a sort that still does not exist, a psychology that begins with the problem of characterizing various systems of human knowledge and belief, the concepts in terms of which they are organized and the principles that underlie them, and that only then turns to the study of how these systems might have developed through some combination of innate structure and organism–environment interaction. Such a psychology would contrast rather sharply with the approach to human intelligence that begins by postulating, on a priori grounds, certain specific mechanisms that, it is claimed, *must* be those underlying the acquisition of all knowledge and belief. The distinction is one to which I will return in a subsequent lecture. For the moment, I want merely to stress the reasonableness of the rejected alternative, and what is more, its consistency with the approach that proved so successful in the seventeenth-century revolution in physics.

There are methodological parallels that have perhaps been inadequately appreciated between the Cartesian postulation of a substance whose essence was thought and the post-Newtonian acceptance of a principle of attraction as an innate property of the ultimate corpuscles of matter, an active principle that governs the motions of bodies. (p. 6)

What are the "methodological parallels" of which Chomsky speaks in discussing *mind*, that is, a substance whose essence is thought, and *gravity*, that is, a principle of attraction which is an innate property of the ultimate corpusculum of matter?

Essentially, if we develop a psychology "that begins with the problem of characterizing various systems of human knowledge and belief, the concepts in terms of which they are organized and the principles that underlie them, and that only then turns to the study of how these systems might have developed through some combination of innate structure and organism-environment interaction," then we are developing our science precisely as physics was developed in the seventeenth century, that is, in accord with the upper limit on goals (21) and the minimum requirement for goals (20).

Consider these passages from Koyré (1957):

It is—or should be—a well-known fact that Newton did not believe in attraction as a real, physical force. No more than Descartes, Huygens, or Henry More could he admit that matter is able to act at a distance, or be animated by a spontaneous tendency. The empirical corroboration of the fact could not prevail against the rational impossibility of the process. Thus, just like Descartes or Huygens, he tried at first to explain attraction—or to explain it away—by reducing it to some kind of effect of purely mechanical occurrences and forces. But in contradistinction to the former, who believed that they were able to devise a mechanical theory of gravity, Newton seems to have become convinced of the utter futility of such an attempt. He discovered, for example, that he could indeed explain attraction, but that in order to do so he had to postulate repulsion, which, perhaps, was somewhat better, but not very much so.

Fortunately, as Newton knew full well, we need not have a clear conception of the way in which certain effects are produced in order to be able to study the phenomena and to treat them mathematically [my emphasis, RCD]. Galileo was not obliged to develop a theory of gravity—he even claimed his right to ignore completely its nature—in order to establish a mathematical dynamics and to determine the laws of fall. Thus nothing prevented Newton from studying the *laws* of "attraction" or "gravitation" without being obliged to give an account of the real forces that produced the centripetal motion of the bodies. It was perfectly sufficient to assume only that these forces—whether physical or metaphysical—were acting according to strict mathematical laws (an assumption fully confirmed by the observation of astronomical phenomena and also by well-interpreted experiments) and to treat these "forces" as *mathematical* forces, and not as real ones. Although only a part of the task, it is a very necessary part; only when this preliminary stage is accomplished can we proceed to the investigation of the real causes of the phenomena.

This is precisely what Newton does in the book so significantly called not *Principia Philosophiae*, that is, *Principles of Philosophy* (like Descartes'), but *Philosophiae naturalis principia mathematica*, that is, *Mathematical Principles of Natural Philosophy*. He warns us that: "I here use the word 'attraction' in general for any endeavor whatever made by bodies to approach each other, whether that endeavor arise from the action of the bodies themselves, as tending to each other or agitating each other by spirits emitted; or whether it arises from the action of the ether or of the air, or of any medium whatever, whether corporeal or incorporeal, in any manner impelling bodies placed therein toward each other. In the same general sense I use the word *impulse, not defining in this treatise the species of physical qualities of forces, but investigating the quantities and mathematical proportions of them, as I observed before in the definitions* [my emphasis, RCD]. In mathematics we are to investigate the quantities of forces with their proportions consequent upon any conditions supposed; then, when we enter upon physics, we compare these proportions with the phenomena of Nature, that we may know what conditions of these forces answer to the several kinds of attractive bodies. And this preparation being made, we argue more safely concerning the physical species, causes, and proportion of the forces" (Newton: book I, section XI, prop. LXIX). (pp. 176–178)

According to Koyré, therefore, in the *Principia* Newton made no effort to explain what gravity was and instead offered an account of its mathematical properties. Koyré indicates that many people misunderstood Newton's statements about gravity:

In his *Letters* (written five years after the publication of the *Principia*) to Richard Bentley who, like nearly everybody else, missed the warning just quoted and interpreted Newton in the way that became common in the eighteenth century, namely as asserting the physical reality of attraction and of attractive force as inherent to matter, Newton is somewhat less reserved. He first tells Bentley (in his second letter): "You sometimes speak of gravity as essential and inherent to matter. Pray do not ascribe that notion to me, for the cause of gravity is what I do not pretend to know and therefore would take more time to consider of it."

In the third one, he practically comes into the open. Though he does not tell Bentley what he, Newton, believes the force of attraction to be *in rerum*, he tells him that: "It is inconceivable that inanimate brute matter should, without mediation of something else which is not material, operate upon and affect other matter without mutual contact, as it must be if gravitation, in the sense of Epicurus, be essential and inherent in it. And this is one reason why I desired you would not ascribe innate gravity to me. That gravity should be innate, inherent, and essential to matter, so that one body may act upon another at a distance through a *vacuum*, without the mediation of anything else, by and through which their action and force may be conveyed from one to another, is to me so great an absurdity that I believe no man who has in philosophical matters a competent faculty of thinking can ever fall into it. Gravity must be caused by an agent acting constantly according to certain laws, but whether this agent be material or immaterial I have left to the consideration of my readers." As we see, Newton does *not* pretend any longer not to *know* the cause of gravity; he only informs us that he left this question unanswered, leaving it to his readers to find out themselves the solution, namely that the "agent" which "causes" gravity cannot be material, but must be a spirit, that is, either the spirit of nature of his colleague Henry More, or, more simply, God—a solution that, rightly or wrongly, Newton was too cautious to announce himself. But that Dr. Bentley could not—and did not—fail to understand. (pp. 178–179)

The generative grammarian, who formulates grammars to express the mechanical principles of sentence construction is expressing the algebraically formalizable (or deductive-mechanical) properties of language structure—and of *mind*, if we believe that the structure of language is a reflection of the human cognitive and perceptual mechanisms. We base our research on the following working assumption:

(23) Working Assumption. In linguistics, as in physics, we need not have a clear conception of the way in which certain effects are produced in order to be able to study the phenomena and to treat them mathematically.

Stated another way, under this assumption a linguist will seek to formalize the algebraic principles characterizing *how* language operates and not be discouraged if he cannot formalize the principles characterizing *why* language operates as it does.[7] Statement (23) can be regarded any number of ways.

My feeling is that (23) should be regarded as a heuristic device, a methodological assumption which leads a linguist to direct his efforts to the solution of some problems and not others. As a heuristic device it will have utility insofar as it leads us to insightful theories of the organization of language structure. It is not an edict prohibiting specific research; rather it is a practical heuristic which is based on the "feel" of Conant's scientist "for what science can and cannot accomplish." Statement (23) takes into account the economy of research effort, thereby offering a practical guide to ordering our research priorities so we can obtain the maximum return for time and effort invested. Statement (23) reflects the fact that, at our present level of understanding of science, research effort directed to one area of language is more likely to pay off than efforts directed elsewhere.

A misleading interpretation of (23) would be as a metaphysic. A linguist might succumb to the temptation to convert this working assumption into a metaphysical pronouncement about the structure of reality. As Burtt points out, such conversions have happened in the past: "if . . . a man [is] engaged in any important inquiry, he must have a method, and he will be under a strong and constant temptation to make a metaphysics out of his method, that is, to suppose the universe ultimately of such a sort that his method must be appropriate and successful. Some of the consequences of succumbing to such a temptation have been abundantly evident in our discussion of the work of Kepler, Galileo, and Descartes" (1924, p. 229). Whatever metaphysical assumptions eventually become those underlying the study of language, I only hope that they reflect more than the projection onto the world of our methodological assumptions (including working assumptions, etc.). Such a projection is simply the most elementary metaphysics, quite in line with the reflection by an anonymous theologian: "The concepts of religion, if we ardently believe them, become our reality." Restated for science: "The assumptions of our methodology, if we ardently believe them, define our reality." Examination of these issues would take us far afield from the main purpose of this paper.

Alternatively, (23) might be considered to reflect, not a property of the world, but a property of the human capacity to conceptualize the world in intelligible terms. Statement (23) reflects the fact that certain problems may transcend man's intellectual capacities, in particular his "science-forming capacity" (see Stent, 1975, and Chomsky, to appear).

It would be erroneous to amplify (23) into an argument against the study of language in the mechanical view. The admission that certain phenomena might be beyond our present understanding of scientific methods should not lead us to conclude that we cannot form a deductive-mechanical model of language structure. Research has shown that linguistics can develop as a science with goals no lower than (20).

Two radically different reasons may be given as to why problems elude solution. One reason is that the problem transcends the capacity of man's intellectual capacities, the other is that the question in its very asking makes assumptions that render the question meaningless.

Consider this passage by Postal from his talk at the Goals of Linguistic Theory conference:

> the chief—and to my mind most valuable—result of a dozen years or more work on generative grammar is the sharp and steadily deepening demonstration that natural languages are fantastically vast, complex, and mysterious systems whose principles have so far largely eluded specification. It is worth remarking, for example, that after more than a dozen years of generative study of English grammar by dozens and dozens of people, we remain with hardly a single reasonably articulated analysis of any component of the grammar which even approaches relative stability or unchallengeability. Proposal after proposal, from the auxiliary analysis, to selectional features, to noun-phrase conjunction [as in Lakoff and Ross (1970), RCD], to cyclic pronominalization [as in Postal (1966); see Dougherty (1974), RCD], to cross-over constraints, has collapsed or slid into the murk of competing claims and contradictory evidence. Generative transformational work in grammar has thus demonstrated the vastness, intricacy, and underlying obscurity of the system involved, a result which reveals in its light the primitiveness and semi-contentlessness of any conception of grammar worked out so far.
>
> To many this result seems depressing, and its truth is often no doubt resisted on no other ground. In fact, there is no reason to regard it as depressing. It can be taken as a real and important contribution, albeit not one of the sort that was envisaged in the early days of transformational study. Then we naively assumed that it was actually possible at the time to construct generative grammars for human languages. . . . (1969, p. 160)

When we read such passages we should ask if problems elude solution because they transcend man's capacity to understand or because the assumptions upon which research was based rendered meaningless the questions asked. Earlier sections support the position that in the work of Postal, Lakoff, and Ross, research into questions of language structure has been based on an incoherent set of goals, methods, and arguments. Postal starts his second paragraph: "To many this result seems depressing, and its truth is often no doubt resisted on no other grounds." Not a single reference to any researcher is cited—Who are these sentimentalists? Most scientists would "resist the truth" of Postal's assertions by simply pointing out they are false or lacking in motivation.

Generative semantic proposals seem, in general, to fail on at least three counts: First, they exhibit a basic confusion of the typologic and the mechanical views of science. This leads GS researchers to advance arguments (at best, formulated in the typological view) which have little, if any, bearing on generative proposals (formulated in the mechanical view). Second, GS proposals frequently are based on incoherent argumentation—more specifically, Lakoff, Ross, and Postal cite counterexamples to their proposals as support for them (see Dougherty, 1974). Third, GS research does not aim to construct an explanatory theory of language structure or to develop a model meeting the conditions itemized in (9), above. Let us examine this last point.

8. LOGICAL VERSUS RHETORICAL JUSTIFICATION: THEORIES AND BALL-POINT PENS

McCawley (1975) offers some interesting views about the nature of generative semantic research. The views of McCawley are discussed in Dougherty (1975). We can gain some concept of McCawley's notion of science by analyzing his views of scientific revolutions. McCawley concludes his paper with this paragraph:

Dougherty's [1974] statements about revolution and counter-revolution suggest that he has wrongly identified the kind of revolution that Kuhn is concerned with and the kind that Mao is concerned with. A scientific revolution is closer to a technological revolution than to a political revolution. In the technological revolution in which ball point pens have displaced fountain pens, there was no instant consignment of fountain pens to the trash heaps. Rather, a tremendous demand for ball point pens developed and the demand for fountain pens decreased considerably, though to nowhere near zero. This is just like a scientific revolution: the older theory lives on, though with somewhat fewer adherents and a much smaller share of the market for ideas. In asking such questions as (p. 278) "What ever became of those linguists who were thoroughly trained in taxonomic methodology?", Dougherty errs in assuming that they aren't in general just openly continuing to do taxonomic linguistics. The absolute number of taxonomic linguists has probably changed very little in the last fifteen years, though the fraction of linguists doing taxonomic linguistics has decreased drastically due to the drastic increase in the number of people in the field. No colony of displaced persons yearning for their overrun taxonomic homeland need be postulated to explain where they went. A final thought: Was it counterrevolution when some manufacturer of ballpoint pens started manufacturing refills? (p. 155)

McCawley's idea that a scientific revolution is like a technological revolution, while interesting in that it gives us a glimpse of McCawley's understanding of science, has no empirical support. This curious view of scientific revolutions contradicts the rather detailed studies of Kuhn—an author McCawley cites. But more importantly, McCawley's view overlooks the crucial point made by just about every philosopher and historian of science, that in a science, acceptance of a theory is based on its power to explain phenomena and not on mere exigencies of the marketplace.

McCawley offers not a shred of evidence to substantiate his claim that a scientific revolution is like a technological revolution; more specifically, that the replacement of a scientific theory T_1 by another theory T_2 is in any interesting way parallel to the displacement of fountain pens by ball-point pens.

McCawley's view of a scientific revolution as a technological revolution (or more exactly as a replacement of one product by another in the marketplace) agrees in large measure with that of Botha. Botha offers quite extensive evidence to show that many current linguistic proposals lack any logical motivation and are based solely on rhetorical devices. In *Aspects*, a practicing linguist is interested in objectively supported propositions for their own sake. Also, an argument can be valid and offer strong support for a position even if there are few persons capable of understanding it. Botha feels differently: The goal of a scientist is not simply to offer objective, factual motivation for proposals.

Rather, the goal of a scientist is to persuade his colleagues. Developing ideas similar to McCawley's, Botha (1973) states:

> In scientific discourse an argument taken as a whole is put forward by a scholar in order to attain a particular aim: persuasion. The arguing scholar hopes to persuade other scholars to adopt the position or point of view presented in the hypothesized proposition which constitutes the conclusion of the argument. To put it differently, a practising scientist or scholar is on the whole not interested in objectively supported propositions or in acceptable hypotheses merely for their own sake. The practising scientist or scholar wishes, in addition, to *convince* [Botha's emphasis, RCD] his colleagues of the merit of these propositions and hypotheses. For the purpose of convincing his colleagues, the scientist or scholar uses arguments as vehicles of persuasion. (pp. 38–39)

> In empirical science, arguments do not constitute frameworks merely for establishing supported propositions and objectively acceptable hypotheses. Scientists use arguments also for the purpose of "converting" dissenting colleagues to the points of view expressed in these propositions and hypotheses. That is, in empirical science the arguments advanced in scholarly debates have the additional methodological function of being "vehicles of persuasion." The success which an argument achieves in persuading scientists or scholars to adopt the point of view presented in the conclusion of this argument should be judged at a separate level of merit: the *level of persuasive power*. (p. 51)

Botha continues by discussing several ways one might increase the persuasive power of his arguments. He states:

> generally speaking, arguments of well-known and respected scholars in a field will be more persuasive than the arguments of their less well-known colleagues. Consider a second psychological consideration bearing on the persuasive power of an argument. A scholar may increase the persuasive power of his arguments by suggesting (implicitly) that dissenters who refused to accept the conclusion would by such refusal show themselves to be irrational, or behind the times, or would upon such refusal find themselves to be the isolated adherents of a belief which none of their colleagues would seriously entertain. . . . (p. 51)

In view of science offered by McCawley and Botha it is salesmanship, not scholarship, which governs the future of linguistic research.[8]

9. THE LIMIT OF EXPLANATION:
THEORIES AND WORKING ASSUMPTIONS

One of the main problems in generative research is to invent arguments which will show how and why specific data (semantic, phonologic, psycholinguistic, etc.) bear on the empirical adequacy of generative grammars. Research must advance the limits of explanation of TGG into the domain of new, uncharted data.

Any significant theoretical proposal has a certain more or less well-defined limit of explanation. A theory will make certain empirical claims about a certain range of data such that over this range the theory may be verified or refuted by comparing consequences deduced from the theory with the primary (observable) data. There will be data, however, which—although one may feel it is intuitively related to the theory—lies outside of the range of forms described by the theory. The *limit of explanation* for a given theory is the boundary between the forms about which a theory makes refutable claims and the forms about which it does not. Joseph Priestley, one of the discoverers of oxygen, discusses the limits of explanation as a "circle of light".

> The greater is the circle of light, the greater is the boundary of the darkness by which it is confined. But, notwithstanding this, the more light we get, the more thankful we ought to be, for by this means we have the greater range for satisfactory contemplation. In time the bounds of light will be still farther extended; and from the infinity of the divine nature, and the divine works, we may promise ourselves an endless progress in our investigation of them: a prospect truly sublime and glorious. (1781, vol. 2, p. ix)

Outside the circle of light, beyond its limit of explanation, a theory may serve as a working hypothesis. A particular theory is significant not only for the range of forms about which it makes explicit claims which can verify or refute the assumptions of the theory, but also for its utility in leading us to formulate explanatory theories in new areas. Beyond its limit of explanation a theory may suggest groupings of data even if these are not a necessary consequence of the theory's assumptions, and in this sense, a theory has an abductive force in addition to its explanatory power. A "theory" which has nothing but abductive force will be nothing more than a heuristic principle, a working assumption, a methodological assumption, etc. Such heuristics, etc., are frequently more important than our theories since they orient our research, determine what we will accept as an explanation, etc.

Working assumptions, as distinct from explanatory theories, are seldom directly confirmable or refutable. Let us consider a working assumption upon which arguments are frequently constructed.

(24) Working Assumption. All human beings have the same innate language-learning capacity. There is one linguistic theory which specifies the characteristics of all human languages.

If (24) were false, it would be meaningless to search for language universals as discussed by Chomsky (1965). According to Chomsky, language universals have a lower bound (i.e., they must be sufficiently narrow and restrictive to account for the facts of language acquisition based on limits of time, access to data, quality of data, etc.), and they have an upper bound (i.e., they must be sufficiently broad to make available a descriptively adequate grammar for every human language). If (24) were false, we might argue that universals, although they might have a lower bound, have no upper bound. If a language were found which violated a universal, we could contend not that our universal was incorrect but instead that the new language provided evidence for a new species of humanoid. Working assumption (24), which Chomsky accepts, contrasts with the following assumption, which Chomsky rejects:

(25) Working Assumption. There are several subspecies of humanoids. They differ in innate intellectual capacity, specifically in their innate constraints on the form and content of learnable languages.

What empirical evidence bears on the choice between (24) and (25)? Two pieces of evidence select (24) over (25). First, it seems that children are not predisposed to learn one language over another. Second, evidence from the study of genetic mechanisms underlying evolution suggest that (24) is true. Let us examine how evidence from evolution and genetics might support working assumption (24), which underlies Chomsky's argumentation.

Dobzhansky (1970) defines *phenotype* and *genotype,* ideas which are crucial in discussing evolution:

> The concepts of phenotype and genotype were introduced by Johanssen (1909) and they remain basic for clear thinking about genetic and evolutionary problems. They can at present be defined as follows. The phenotype of an individual is what is perceived by observation: the organism's structures and functions—in short, what a living appears to be to our sense organs, unaided or assisted by various devices. The genotype is the sum total of the hereditary materials received by an individual from its parents and other ancestors. The phenotype of an individual changes continuously from birth to death. Barring somatic mutation, the genotype, however, remains stable. This stability is due to the genes reproducing themselves, not to the genes being chemically inert materials or being somehow isolated from the environment. (p. 32)
>
> A phenotype is a biological system constructed by successive interactions of the individual's genotype with the environments in which the development takes place. (p. 36)

Dobzhansky (1964) discusses two types of natural selection: directional selection and stabilizing selection. Consider directional selection:

> Directional natural selection brings innovation. Genes that were once upon a time useful when the species lived in a certain environment may become inferior as the environment changes. Directional selection replaces the old genes with the new ones better suited for new conditions. It was a long-continued directional selection that gradually transformed the genetic endowment of our animal ancestor(s), and built the genetic basis on which human culture arose and developed. It favored the ability to make and use tools, to communicate by means of a symbolic language, to cooperate with one's neighbors in common undertakings, and a host of other human traits and abilities. The selection favored these traits and abilities for one simple reason—their possession conferred on their carriers advantages that enabled them to transmit their genes to the succeeding generations more often than the non-carriers did. (p. 156)

Now consider Dobzhansky's ideas about noninnovative natural selection:

> That natural selection is a common name for several cognate but distinct processes has been realized only within relatively recent years. Schmalhausen (1949) distinguished dynamic (directional) and stabilizing selection. The first changes the adaptive norm of the population; the second tends to keep it constant. A natural population is adapted to a certain range of environments. Environment change is likely to cause a decline in this adaptedness; some formerly favorable genetic variants become disadvantageous and are replaced by new ones. Conversely, in a population that has achieved a high degree of adaptedness in a certain range of environments, the genetic endowment is advantageous, and deviations from it are inopportune. Stabilizing selection eliminates such deviations and promotes, in Schmalhausen's words, "more stable mechanisms of normal morphogenesis."
>
> Waddington (1957) distinguishes two kinds of stablizing selection, normalizing and canalizing. The former protects the adaptive norm by the elimination of harmful mutants, malformations, and weaknesses of various sorts. It was normalizing selection that Blyth wrote about. Canalizing selection, Waddington states, favors "genotypes which control developmental systems which are highly canalized and therefore not very responsive either to abnormalities in the environment or to new gene mutations of a minor character." Canalization refers to the "limited responsiveness of a developing system." Human development is a familiar example. It is so canalized that all human beings are fundamentally similar and recognizably human, despite manifold variations in environments and individual genotypes. Only major mutations and drastic environmental stresses deflect the development from its regular course. . . . (1970, pp. 95-96)

According to Dobzhansky, human development is an example of "canalization." Consider these passages where he elaborates on the process of canalization:

> Canalizing selection (Chapter 4) tends to stabilize the developmental pattern of a species, to make certain traits develop similarly in most environments that this species encounters in its habits. The result is eventually that some traits show little or no variation, being frozen in all representatives of the species. (1970, p. 211)

> canalization . . . may give the same phenotype within the entire range of environments in thich the genotype is viable. Thus, almost all human genotypes ensure the development of a four-chambered heart, a suckling instinct in the infant, a capacity to think in symbols and to learn a language, etc. (1970, p. 167)

Why is it that human beings seem no longer to be undergoing "directional evolution" but tend, as it were, to tread water via "canalizing selection"? Loren Eiseley offers the reason that was early pointed out:

The second stage in human evolution, however—the stage which represents Wallace's original contribution to the subject, and which elicited admiring plaudits from Darwin—involves his recognition of the role of the human brain as a totally new factor in the history of life. Wallace was apparently the first evolutionist to recognize clearly and consciously and with a full grasp of its implications the fact that, with the emergence of that bodily specialization which constitutes the human brain, bodily specialization itself might be said to be outmoded. The evolution of parts, the evolution of the sort of unconscious adaptations which are to be observed in the life cycle of a complicated parasite or the surgical mouth parts of a vampire bat, had been forever surpassed. Nature, instead of delimiting through *parts* a creature confined to some narrow niche of existence, had at last produced an organism potentially capable of the endless inventing and discarding of parts through the medium of a specialized organ whose primary purpose was, paradoxically, the *evasion* of specialization. There had come into existence, Wallace emphasized, a being in whom mind was of vastly greater importance than bodily structure. For the first time there was offered to a complex living creature the possibility of escape from the endless palentological story of a generalized animal becoming increasingly specialized until the destruction of its ecological niche foretells its own extinction. Man has the possibilities within him of remaining in the body he now inhabits while whole faunas rise and change or pass away.... (1961, pp. 306–307)

Dobzhansky elaborates on the point made by Eiseley:

What is most remarkable of all is that, while other organisms become masters of their environments by changing their genes, man does so mostly by changing his culture, which he acquires by learning and transmits by teaching. Indeed, many animals have become adapted to living in cold climates by growing warm fur, by becoming dormant when the weather is cold; man has conquered cold by building fires and wearing warm garments. Adaptation by culture is enormously more rapid and efficient than genetic adaptation; a new thought or a new invention made by one man can become a part of the patrimony of all mankind in a relatively short time. Let us not forget, however, that it is the human genotype that enabled man to invent fire and clothing. Genetic and cultural adaptations are not alternative or mutually exclusive; they are mutually reinforcing. Human genes and human culture are connected by what is known as a circular feedback relationship; in other words, human genes stimulate the development of culture, and the development of culture stimulates genetic changes which facilitate further developments of culture. To say that natural selection has built man's culture is a misleading oversimplification; natural selection has, however, built the genetic endowment that made culture possible. (1964, pp. 145-146)

When Chomsky claims:

I see no reason why cognitive structures should not be investigated rather in the way that physical organs are studied. The natural scientist will be primarily concerned with the basic genetically-determined structure of these organs and their interactions. . . . There is nothing essentially mysterious about the concept of an abstract cognitive structure, created by an innate faculty of mind, represented in some still unknown way in the brain, and entering into the system of capacities and dispositions to act and interpret. . . . Thus, some intellectual achievements, such as language-learning, fall strictly within biologically-determined cognitive capacity. (1975)

He is agreeing essentially point for point with geneticists like Dobzhansky (1964):

Culture is not inherited through genes; it is acquired by learning from other human beings. The ability to learn, and thus to acquire a culture and to become a member of society, is, however, given by the genetic endowment that is mankind's distinctive biological attribute. In a sense, human genes have surrendered their primacy in human evolution to an entirely new, non-biological or superorganic agent, culture. However, it should not be forgotten that this agent is entirely dependent on human genotype; human culture is not possible without human genes. (p. 113)

Human genes enable man more or less easily to acquire a culture, but . . . the genes do not determine what culture he will acquire, just as genes make man able to speak but do not determine what he will say. (pp. 143-144)

10. CONCLUSION

A main way in which science advances is the invention of new argument forms of a previously unknown type which enlarge the limits of explanation by permitting us to see precisely how and why data, which previously was outside the range of theory, can now confirm or refute our theoretical proposals. For example, in pre-Darwinian biology, the plant and animal fossils found in rocks were intuitively felt to have relevance for a biological theory, but no one knew just what their relevance was. With no specific principles to guide them, researchers found one fossil as important or unimportant as the next. Taxonomists collected, labeled, and arranged the fossils in various ways pursuing their typological goal of constructing arguments supporting this or that claim about particular fossils or the general theory of fossils. After Darwin introduced his evolutionary perspective, arguments could be constructed to show the relevance of specific fossils to existing biological forms. Darwin's perspective did not merely order the known fossils, it incorporated a specific form of argumentation which led researchers, via chains of deductive inference, to expect fossils of some types but not others. Darwin's perspective, by making refutable claims about the concept "possible fossil," extended biological theory to include fossil data. If we consider an experiment as a question put to nature, then Darwin's argumentation led to the design of specific experiments. The search for specific fossils of previously unobserved types became a significant part of biological research.[9]

To extend the limits of explanation of TGG to semantic (or psycholinguistic, etc.) data, we need to develop explanatory generative proposals which lead to specific unequivocal claims which can be confirmed or refuted by comparison with semantic data.[10] It is crucial to distinguish a proposal which makes explanatory claims from a proposal which merely makes provocative insinuations about the data. Lovejoy, although discussing a point tangential to ours, presents the point nicely:

> If somebody has a theory that Queen Elisabeth was married to the Duke of Leicester, but makes it a part of the same hypothesis that all possible evidence bearing upon the point has been destroyed, he says what is foolish and unimportant, because by his own admission no one can ever find out whether it is true or not. But he is not saying a thing that has no distinct and intelligible meaning. To maintain then, that a belief which is empirically unverifiable is *ipso facto* meaningless appears not only unwarranted, but absurd. (1913, p. 51)

We can only ask interesting questions about the structure of language internal to a well-defined framework of assumptions. If our framework is ill-defined, we may end up asking questions which are empirically unverifiable but not meaningless. Although our proposals will not be motivated by making empirical claims which may be confirmed or refuted, they may garner interest by insinuating a great deal. Like the analyses discussed earlier, such proposals will be popular with those who think but do not think critically. They will be acceptable to the extent they confirm existing prejudices, satisfy various appetites for sensational scientific discoveries, etc.[11] Proposals which seem to be non-explanatory insinuations about language would include the proposals that quantifiers are higher verbs, that the underlying structure of a sentence is a semantic interpretation, that there are global rules and transderivational constraints, etc. No doubt, some researchers will find it rewarding to contemplate the properties of the conceptually rich systems to which incoherent argumentation may lead, and, no doubt, many hours can be spent toiling to formalize the system. But we must bear in mind that such "insinuation systems" have no discernible descriptive or explanatory utility for characterizing the definitive properties of language and the basic mechanisms of sentence construction.

There are at least three areas in which the student who would be a critic of arguments must focus his attention:

First, he must subject his argumentation to constant self-criticism, remaining constantly aware that his arguments, no less than his theories, are subject to confirmation or disconfirmation in the light of experience. As our goals change through increasing insight into the structure of language, the strength of our arguments may change. Peirce points out tersely the need for constant self-examination: "To be cocksure that one is an infallible reasoner is to furnish conclusive evidence either that one does not reason at all, or that one reasons very badly, since that deluded state of mind prevents the constant self-criticism which is the very life of reasoning" (1966, vol. 2, p. 123).

Second, the student must develop self-sufficiency of the brain. No matter who the teacher is there comes a time when the student confronts the problem unaided. If he has not acquired the methods for dealing with theories and facts, he will flounder. As Poincaré points out: "Method is precisely the selection of facts, and accordingly our first care must be to learn a method" (1956, p. 19). A researcher lacking a sensible method to tell him which facts are important and how and why those facts are important will in all probability collect his data by the pitchfork method. He will likely base his conclusions on a mass of circumstantial evidence welded together more by rhetoric than by logic. Such a concept of research reflects confusion about the nature of scientific activity, the nature of linguistics as a science, the relation of linguists to other sciences, and the concept of explanation in linguistics. We can have no sensible method, and hence can have no meaningful way to select facts, unless we have relatively well-defined, noncontradictory goals. As discussed in sections 3–6, if a linguist is unclear about what constitutes a generative proposal, he cannot possibly have a clear idea as to how to motivate a generative proposal.

Third, and most importantly, the student should acquire a sense of style which is his own interpretation of what Conant calls the scientist's "feel" for what science can and cannot accomplish. Style is the opposite of looseness. Absence of style is redundancy, irrelevance, and confusion. The student of argumentation with a sense of style based on a feel for what science can and cannot accomplish will be able to devise arguments which will directly attain his foreseen end, that is, to decide which of the alternative theories at his disposal provides the most insightful analysis of the principles of sentence construction. Whitehead discusses style as it manifests itself in art, science, logic, etc.:

[As the culmination of a successful education] there should grow the most austere of all mental qualities; I mean the sense for style. It is an aesthetic sense, based on admiration for the direct attainment of a foreseen end, simply and without waste. Style in art, style in literature, style in science, style in logic, style in practical execution have fundamentally the same aesthetic qualities, namely, attainment and restraint. The love of a subject in itself and for itself, where it is not the sleepy pleasure of pacing a mental quarter-deck, is the love of style as manifested in that study.

Here we are brought back to the position from which we started, the utility of education. Style, in its finest sense, is the last acquirement of the educated mind; it is also the most useful. It pervades the whole being. The administrator with a sense for style hates waste; the engineer with a sense for style economises his material; the artisan with a sense for style prefers good work. Style is the ultimate morality of mind.

But above style, and above knowledge, there is something, a vague shape like fate above the Greek gods. That something is Power. But after all, the power of attainment of the desired end is fundamental. The first thing is to get there. Do not bother about your style, but solve your problem, justify the ways of God to man, administer your province, or do whatever else is set before you.

Where, then, does style help? In this, with style the end is attained without side issues, without raising undesirable inflammations. With style you attain your end and nothing but your end. With style the effect of your activity is calculable, and foresight is the last gift of gods to men. With style your power is increased, for your mind is not distracted with irrelevancies, and you are more likely to attain your object. Now Style is the exclusive privilege of the expert. Whoever heard of the style of an amateur painter, of the style of an amateur poet? Style is always the product of specialist study, the peculiar contribution of specialism to culture. (1929, p. 12–13)

A linguist with a "feel" for what science can and cannot accomplish, possessed with a sense of style, and who continuously subjects his reasoning to scrutiny could do much to advance linguistics as a science. Such a linguist would have the potential to invent arguments to bring a closer juxtaposition of theory and data. He would know what justifies his beliefs and just how, why, and to what extent that justification is sufficient. A linguist with a sense of style based on a "feel" for science may often be in error, but he will seldom be in confusion. And this is, in a real sense, the most important thing, for in serious research, truth is more likely to emerge from error than from confusion.

NOTES

1. For discussion of the distinction between "important data" and "interesting data," see Dougherty (1974a).
2. See Delorme and Dougherty (1972) and Dougherty (1973, 1974) for a discussion of the argumentation in Postal's studies of pronominalization.
3. A word of caution: A linguist need specify his model only in as much detail as is necessary to make clear the empirically testable claims of the model. Explicitness has value insofar as it clarifies and articulates our

knowledge and shows what depends on what, but if carried too far, it may become a technical game and consume more energy than it yields insight. For example, it would be of little advantage to catalog the exceptions to our model. Listing exceptions would be useful only insofar as it might suggest or lead to the formulation of new more adequate models. Rigorous quantitative methods are only useful in proportion as they bring about a sharper juxtaposition of fact and theory.

4. C. S. Peirce offers some interesting reflections on this concept of refutability. He claims:

It is a great mistake to suppose that the mind of the active scientist is filled with propositions which, if not proved beyond all reasonable cavil, are at least extremely probable. On the contrary, he entertains hypotheses which are almost wildly incredible, and treats them with respect for the time being. Why does he do this? Simply because any scientific proposition whatever is always liable to be refuted and dropped at short notice. A hypothesis is something which looks as if it might be true and were true, and which is capable of verification or refutation by comparison with facts. The best hypothesis, in the sense of the one most recommending itself to the inquirer, is the one which can be the most readily refuted if it is false. This far outweighs the trifling merit of being likely. For after all, what is a *likely* hypothesis? It is one which falls in with our preconceived ideas. But these may be wrong. Their errors are just what the scientific man is out gunning for more particularly. But if a hypothesis can quickly and easily be cleared away so as to go toward leaving the field free for the main struggle, this is an immense advantage. (1.120)

5. I list only two views: the typologic (taxonomic) and the mechanical (generative). My argument could be sharpened by considering the *three* different sets of goals under discussion. The third view is an incoherent perspective concocted of unit ideas drawn from the taxonomic and generative views.

One might distinguish between the *espoused* goals of GS, such as those stated in Postal (1969), and the *pragmatic* goals, that is, those goals which are the projected consequences of the methods and arguments employed by GS authors. The expoused goals are, at best, in the taxonomic view of language. To find the pragmatic goals, we must ask, What are the projected consequences of research employing the TE argument form? The TE argument form will not yield interesting generative or taxonomic research. This argument form, arising from an ill-defined mix of unit ideas drawn from two well-defined methodological perspectives, provides no *logical* support for a proposal but does offer some *rhetorical* support insofar as it keeps a proposal in the limelight. To some persons these rhetorical considerations count heavily (see Section 8).

Conclusion (17a) follows from considering the pragmatic goals of GS and, to some extent, the espoused goals (see Section 8). That GS authors do not use the theory-comparison method follows from both the espoused and the pragmatic goals.

6. Metaphysics and methodology are intertwined in curious ways. Although there may be difficulty converting a metaphysics into a method of research, there seems to be little difficulty involved in converting a methodology into a metaphysics. I discuss this point later in the text. See also E. A Burtt (1924). One can arrive at remarkable discoveries by mistaking a property of his analysis (working assumptions, methods, etc.) for a property of the data under analysis. See Dougherty (1973), especially pp. 476-479.

7. By italicizing *why*, I mean it as the ultimate *why* and not the *why* which might be rephrased, How do properties of language follow from known properties of the human cognitive capacity, evolution, genetics, etc.? To the extent there is an unclear distinction between the two uses of "why," there is an unclear boundary between science and metaphysics.

Questions like Why does language incorporate the algebraic structures it does?—insofar as they can be rephrased as How do the algebraic structures of language correlate with the known structure of the human cognitive devices, neurology, learning strategies, genetic makeup, etc.?— will be interesting to the scientist to the extent the insights gained investigating such questions are commensurate with the research energy expended.

In saying that linguistics will find its conceptual justification (explanatory adequacy) in studies of nonlanguage phenomena (neurology, etc.), it is not necessarily to be expected that linguistic concepts will be deducible from nonlinguistic concepts. Rather, it may be that the basic conceptual terms (provided by the linguistic theory) in which linguistic explanations (particular grammatical proposals) are formulated will fit into a larger pattern of concepts offered to explain nonlinguistic data. The linguistic concepts will correlate with nonlinguistic concepts under some interpretation.

For example, the particular devices made available by the linguistic theory, the organization of those devices, the constraints on their application, etc., may not be deducible from—but may correlate with— the neurological mechanisms studied by the neurologists in the same way that the Mendelian features governing traits are not deducible from—but correlate with—the behavior of chromosomes as these are studied by the molecular biologists. Dobzhansky (1964) discusses the "mental leap from one field of study to what seemed to be a quite different field" made by Sutton and Boveri when they first formulated their hypothesis that chromosomes are the carriers of genes:

The next breakthrough in genetics was made possible by one of those insights that seem almost trivial after somebody explains them. Indeed, some of the most exciting moments in the life of a scientist come when he suddenly sees things that were before his eyes all the time; it is as though a blindfold falls from one's eyes. However that may be, in 1903, W. S. Sutton, in America, and, independently, Boveri, in Germany, saw that the behavior of genes discovered by Mendel is paralleled by that of chromosomes as seen under the mircroscope. In his work, Mendel probably never saw a chromosome; he inferred the existence of genes from the numerical ratios in which different types of offspring appeared in the progenies of the crosses he made. Genes have not been seen under a microscope even to this day. Sutton and Boveri had to make a mental leap from one field of study to what seemed to be a quite different field. (p. 25)

Let us now accompany Sutton and Boveri on their metaphorical leap from the chromosomes to Mendel's peas. Mendel had discovered that the genes do not blend, but segregate. If two varieties of peas that are crossed differ in that one variety has purple and the other white flowers, then both purple-flowered and white-flowered plants will be found among the hybrids in the second and later generations, and, at that, in predictable proportions. In the process of sex-cell formation in a hybrid, the genes of the purple and of the white parents separate cleanly and pass into different sex cells. They behave as if they were separate physical particles. A hypothesis can then be formulated: the chromosomes are the carriers of the genes. (p. 26)

Dobzhansky notes that the laws of Mendel are not deducible from the achievements of chromosomes and gene chemistry:

There is ... an influential school of thought among scientists which contends that if one concentrates all the attention and all the research support on molecular biology and molecular genetics, then all organismic biology and genetics will somehow explain itself without need of research on the organismic level. I can scarcely imagine a contention more misconceived. The laws of Mendel, of gene segregation and recombination, are not deducible from any of the glorious achievements of chromosome and gene chemistry. And they need not be so deduced; Mendel's laws and much else in biology have been discovered through studies on the organismic level. Biology moves both downward and upward—from the organismic to the molecular and from the molecular to the organismic levels. (p. 83)

The study of transformational generative grammar and the study of neurology, of evolution, etc., can be pursued quite independently. Insofar as each study yields insightful patterns of explanation internal to its confines, the stage will be set for a neurologist-linguist-evolutionist to play the role Sutton and Boveri performed in biology and come up with one of those insights which, as Dobzhansky says, "seem almost trivial after somebody explains them."

8. Theory exposition might be regarded as an optimal marketing strategy if the goal of research is to persuade by devices such as Botha suggests.

9. In general, we might expect that the development of the instruments of research will lead to a more precise model of the phenomena investigated, and conversely, that a more precise model will lead to perfecting the instruments of research. Simultaneously, as our models become more insightful and our methods more attuned to deciding

which of two alternative conceptions provides the most insightful analysis of the phenomena under investigation, we might expect our goals to become higher. This leapfrog relation between theory, methods, and goals is characteristic of science (see Dougherty, 1973, pp. 455–458).

10. Similarly, to extend the limits of explanation to historical data, psycholinguistic data, etc., we need to develop explanatory proposals which can be confirmed or refuted by comparison with empirical data.

11. Some persons think that generative grammar is to be accepted to the extent that generative grammars can solve problems which were considered crucial in the taxonomic framework, in particular, problems of co-occurrence and paraphrase. This is misguided. It is not the goal of generative grammar to solve taxonomic problems. See Dougherty (1974a).

When Chomsky offered a mechanical (generative) view to replace the prevalent typological (taxonomic) view, he simultaneously redefined the class of answerable questions and the important data (see fn. 1).

REFERENCES

Anderson, S. and P. Kiparsky (eds.) (1973) *A Festschrift for Morris Halle.* New York: Holt, Rinehart, and Winston.

Bach, E. and R. T. Harms (eds.) (1968) *Universals in Linguistic Theory.* New York: Holt, Rinehart, and Winston.

Botha, R. P. (1973) *The Justification of Linguistic Hypotheses.* The Hague: Mouton.

Burt, M. K. (1971) *From Deep to Surface Structure.* New York: Harper and Row.

Burtt, E. A. (1924) *The metaphysical Foundations of Modern Science.* New York: Doubleday (Anchor Books).

Chomsky, N. (1957) *Syntactic Structures.* The Hague: Mouton.

_____ (1965) *Aspects of the Theory of Syntax.* Cambridge, Mass.: M.I.T. Press.

_____ (1968) *Language and Mind.* New York: Harcourt Brace Jovanovich.

_____ (1969) "Some empirical issues in the theory of transformational grammar," Talk delivered at Goals of Linguistic Theory conference, University of Texas at Austin; reprinted in Peters (1972).

_____ (1973) "Conditions on transformations," in Anderson and Kiparsky (1973).

_____ (1975) *Reflections on Language.* New York: Random House.

_____, M. Halle and J. Ross (1971) Foreword, in Burt (1971).

Cohen, D. (ed.) (1974) *Explaining Linguistic Phenomena.* Washington, D.C.: Hemisphere.

Conant, J. (ed.) (1948) *Harvard Case Studies in Experimental Science.* Cambridge, Mass.: Harvard University Press.

Delorme, E. and R. C. Dougherty (1972) "Appositive NP constructions: *we, the men; we men; I, a man;* etc." *Foundations of Language* 3:2-29.

Dewey, J. (1916) *Democracy and Education.* New York: The Free Press.

Dik, S. (1968) *Coordination.* Amsterdam: North Holland Publishing Co.

Dobzhansky, T. (1964) *Heredity and the Nature of Man.* New York: New American Library (Signet Science Library Press).

—— (1970) *Genetics and the Evolutionary Process.* New York: Columbia University Press.

Dougherty, R. C. (1970) "Some recent claims on language universals." *Foundations of Language* 6:505-561.

—— (1971) "A grammar of coordinate conjoined structures, Part II." *Language* 47:298-339.

—— (1973) "A survey of linguistic methods and arguments." *Foundations of Language* 10:423-490.

—— (1974) "What explanation is and isn't," in Cohen (1974).

—— (1974a) "Harris and Chomsky at the syntax-semantics boundary," in Hockney (1975).

—— (1974b) "Reflections on the Bloomfieldian counterrevolution," *International Journal of Dravidian Linguistics, IV.2, 249-272.*

—— (to appear *a*). "The logic of linguistic research," *Foundations of Language.*

—— (to appear *b*). "A methodological exorcism of semantic pseudo-problems." *Linguistics.*

Einstein, A. (1927) "Isaac Newton," *Annual Report of the Smithsonian Institution.* Washington, D.C.: Government Printing Office.

Eiseley, L. (1961) *Darwin's Century: Evolution and the Men Who Discovered It.* New York: Doubleday (Anchor Books).

Fillmore, C. (1966) "Toward a modern theory of case"; reprinted in Reibel and Schane (1969), pp. 361-377.

—— (1968) "The case for case," in Bach and Harms (1968).

—— (1969) "On generativity." Talk delivered at Goals of Linguistic Theory conference, University of Texas at Austin; reprinted in Peters (1972).

Gleitman, L. (1965) "Coordinating conjunction in English," *Language* 41:260-293; reprinted in Reibel and Schane (1969).

Hartshorne, C., P. Weiss and A. Burks (eds.) (1966) *The Collected Papers of C. S. Peirce* (8 vols.). Cambridge, Mass.: Harvard University Press.

Harris, Z. (1957) "Co-occurrence and transformation in linguistic structure." *Language* 33:283-340.

—— (1965) "Transformational theory." *Language* 41:363-401.

Hockney, D. (ed.) (1975) *Contemporary Research in Philosophical Logic and Linguistic Semantics.* The Hague: Mouton.

Holton, G. (1973) *Thematic Origins of Scientific Thought.* Cambridge, Mass.: Harvard University Press.

Koyré, A. (1957) *From the Closed World to the Infinite Universe.* Baltimore, Johns Hopkins Press.

Kuhn, T. S. (1957) *The Copernican Revolution.* Cambridge, Mass.: Harvard University Press.

Lakoff, G. (1965) "Irregularity in syntax," doctoral dissertation; reprinted as Lakoff (1970)

_____ (1970) *Irregularity in Syntax.* New York: Holt, Rinehart, and Winston.

_____ and S. Peters (1966) "Phrasal conjunction and symmetric predicates"; reprinted in Reibel and Schane (1969), pp. 113-142.

_____ and J. Ross (1970) "Two kinds of *and.*" *Linguistic Inquiry* 1: 271-272.

Lightfoot, D. (to appear) "The theoretical stakes of subject raising: A review of *On Raising* by Paul M. Postal." *Foundations of Language.*

Lovejoy, A. O. (1913) "Pragmaticism and theology," *The Journal of Theology*; reprinted in Lovejoy (1963).

_____ (1936) *The Great Chain of Being.* New York: Harper & Row (Torchbooks).

_____ (1963) *The Thirteen Pragmatisms and Other Essays.* Baltimore: Johns Hopkins Press.

Maclay, H. (1971) "Overview of linguistics," in Steinberg and Jakobovits (1971), pp. 157-181.

McCawley, J. D. (1975) "Comments on R. C. Dougherty, 'Generative semantic methods'." *International Journal of Dravidian Linguistics.*

Peirce, C. S. (1966) *The Collected Papers of C. S. Peirce* (8 vols.), edited by Charles Hartshorne, Paul Weiss and Arthur Burks. Cambridge, Mass.: Harvard University Press.

Peters, S. (ed.) (1972) *Goals of Linguistic Theory.* Englewood Cliffs, N.J.: Prentice-Hall.

Poincaré, H. (1956) *Science and Method,* translated by Francis Maitland. New York: Dover.

Postal, P. (1966) "On so-called 'Pronouns' in English," in F. Dinneen (ed.), the 19th *Monograph on Languages and Linguistics,* Georgetown University Press, Washington, D.C.; reprinted in Reibel and Schane (1969), pp. 201-224.

_____ (1969) "The best theory," Talk delivered at Goals of linguistic theory conference, University of Texas at Austin; reprinted in Peters (1972).

_____ (1974) *On Raising: One Rule of English Grammar and Its Theoretical Implications.* Cambridge, Mass.: M.I.T. Press.

Priestley, J. (1781) *Natural Philosophy.* London: Wainwright.

Reibel, D. and S. A. Schane (eds.) (1969) *Modern Studies in English.* Englewood Cliffs, N.J.: Prentice-Hall.

Searle, J. (1972) "Chomsky's revolution in linguistics." *New York Review of Books,* June 29, pp. 16-24.

Seuren, P. (ed.) (1974) *Semantic Syntax.* New York: Oxford University Press.

Steinberg, D. D. and L. A. Jakobovits (eds.) (1971) *Semantics: An Interdisciplinary Reader in Philosophy, Linguistics, and Psychology.* Cambridge: At the University Press.

Stent, G. (1975) "Limits to the scientific understanding of man." *Science* 187:1052-1057.

Whitehead, A. N. (1929) *The Aims of Education and Other Essays.* New York: The Free Press.

7

The best argument is in the mind of the beholder

Sanford A. Schane
University of California–San Diego

I

In discussing the nature of linguistic argumentation, I shall argue about arguments within the context of a single central question: If we are confronted with two (or more) competing synchronic analyses, both (or all) of which are compatible with the given data, then which analysis is preferred, appropriate, right? Because I am most familiar with this problem as it pertains to work in phonology, I choose to limit my discussion to this particular domain.

Let us imagine for the moment that we have before us two descriptions covering the same range of linguistic phenomena. The descriptions may follow from either different or the same theoretical assumptions. Where the assumptions differ, then the discussion in general centers around these differences. Many of the arguments of "natural" phonology vis-à-vis standard generative phonology fall into this category—for example, whether or not rules are extrinsically ordered, whether there are rules of absolute neutralization, etc. Here one attempts to adduce evidence in support of particular theoretical assumptions or biases. Alternatively, the competing descriptions may be within the same theoretical framework—for example, both proponents accept the basic assumptions of generative phonology, but the descriptions differ in the choice of underlying representations or of rules. Arguments here may be based on either internal or external evidence (Botha, 1973). The most frequent kind of internal evidence is data not previously considered. One shows how the new data can be explained by the proposed underlying forms or rules. Or else external evidence may be presented—data from historical change, dialect comparisons, acquisitional studies, psycholinguistic experimentation, etc. (To be sure, external evidence is also utilized in cases where the theoretical assumptions differ.) The interpretation of the external data is taken to be in some sense evident. Then the description in question must be compatible with this external evidence.

I shall examine specific instances of competing analyses within different as well as within the same theoretical orientation. I shall look at examples of arguments based on internal as well as external evidence. I hope to demonstrate that each of these argument types has defects. My conclusion will be that, for phonology at least, the so-called "convincing" arguments leave me unconvinced.

Let us begin by considering external justification and, in particular, historical data, if only because evidence drawn from language change has had widespread currency within synchronic phonological argumentation.

II

Generative grammar has inherited the Saussurian dichotomy between diachronic and synchronic description, for after all, as we have heard said time and time again, the normal child has no immediate access to the history of his language. Yet diachronic data have been brought forth in justification of synchronic descriptions, either as confirmatory evidence for a particular analysis or else as a heuristic device in finding the "appropriate" analysis. This type of historical argumentation was particularly prevalent in the early days of generative phonology. Thus, in my original work on French, I noted the similarity between my synchronic rules and certain changes that were attested historically. I remarked that, in spite of this resemblance,

> synchronic rules must be internally motivated and . . . their sole justification cannot be the corresponding diachronic rules, although to be sure, *the latter certainly help to corroborate the validity of the former* [emphasis added, SAS]. In working out an analysis, it is unquestionably an advantage to know the historical developments of the language just as it is advantageous to have access to the standard orthography (for a written language) and to have information on related dialects and languages. . . . Knowing the history of the language allows one to formulate hypotheses concerning the nature of underlying forms and the types of phonological changes still operative in the contemporary language. The confirmation of these hypotheses must then be demonstrated uniquely within the synchronic description. Such internal synchronic justification is indispensable if linguistic descriptions are to have psycholinguistic import and are to characterize what speakers know about their language. (Schane, 1968, pp. 140-141, fn. 29)

To appreciate this particular brand of linguistic argumentation we need to keep clearly in mind one crucial assumption of the generative phonology of the *SPE* vintage: Within a language, underlying representations tend to be relatively stable over a prolonged period of time and from one dialect to the next (Chomsky and Halle, 1968). Instead, it is particular rules and their ordering which vary in time or across space. It is a fairly certain truism that the phonological alternations found in the contemporary language are reflections of sound changes occurring within the history of that language. Now it is the business of generative phonology to account for synchronic phonological alternation and as much as possible, where possible, to derive the various morphemic alternants from a common underlying form. If we couple this task of generative phonology with the assumption regarding the stability of underlying representations, then it should not be surprising that so very often the underlying representations in the contemporary language are nearly identical to earlier attested forms for that language and the synchronic rules needed to convert underlying to derived forms furnish a neat recapitulation of diachronic change. Given this perspective one can see, then, how historical information may be extremely valuable in the pursuit of a synchronic description or even in choosing between two competing descriptions: The analysis which dovetails more closely with the history of the language is the one to be preferred.

As a corollary to historical evidence, data from other dialects or from related languages are sometimes brought forth in support of a particular analysis. Dialect B, for example, may provide more convincing arguments for the choice of a particular underlying representation for Dialect A than can be found within Dialect A itself. The data from Dialect B, in conjunction with the assumption regarding the commonality of underlying forms across dialects, support the choice of an underlying representation for Dialect A.

The coherence of any argument for the justification of a synchronic analysis on the basis of historical or dialectal compatibility has, as we have seen, its foundation in the assumption of the relative immutability of lexical representation. But this assumption about stable underlying forms is just that—an assumption. I know of no independent evidence to suggest, even remotely, that speakers of a language have awareness of the historical, simulated, underlying representations such as are posited by classical generative phonologists. In fact, many of the so-called "natural" phonologists would explicitly deny this fundamental assumption of generative phonology. For them lexical representation is not something relatively constant from parent to child. Rather what happens from generation to generation is that the lexicon undergoes restructuring. In this way underlying forms never have a chance to deviate dramatically from their surface correlates. Grammars turn out to be less abstract than we had hitherto thought. This view, however, is as much an unproven assumption as the one entertained by the generative phonologist. Later I shall examine a more sophisticated type of historical argument advanced by some "naturalists."

In one of his early papers Kiparsky (1968a) made the interesting proposal that linguistic change may provide the needed "window" for indirectly observing linguistic competence. He discussed the situation in English where underlying long vowels are shortened in two principal environments: before at least two consonants (for example, *keep*, *kept*) and in the third syllable from the end of the word (for example, *sane, sanity*). These alternate environments can be collapsed into a single rule by means of the brace notation. It seems that in Old English the process was somewhat more restricted: Shortening took place before at least three—instead of two—consonants (for example, *child, children*) and in the antepenultimate syllable provided there were at least two consonants (for example, *chaste, chastity*). The difference, then, between Old English and Modern English is for the former the extra consonant to the left of the brace

Old English: $V \rightarrow [-\text{long}] \underline{\quad} CC \left\{ \begin{matrix} C \\ \dots V \dots \end{matrix} \right\} V$

Modern English: $V \rightarrow [-\text{long}] \underline{\quad} C \left\{ \begin{matrix} C \\ \dots V \dots \end{matrix} \right\} V$

Since the change in the number of consonants affected both of the contexts for shortening, Kiparsky claimed that such a change validated the brace notation, in that the notation allowed differing environments of a unified process to be collapsed as one rule. Consequently, these historical facts would justify the use of the brace notation in linguistic description, synchronic as well as diachronic.

I do not wish to delve into the question of whether the historical data cited by Kiparsky consitute confirmatory evidence for the brace notation. It is certainly conceivable that some other explanation, such as a theory of syllable timing, could just as satisfactorily accommodate the two cases of vowel shortening. In fact, McCawley (1973) has questioned the use of the brace notation within linguistic description. But what is of interest for our purposes is the general idea of whether diachronic data can be used in arguing for a particular synchronic analysis. However, Kiparsky does not do this; his arguments are intended to support certain theoretical devices to be incorporated within general linguistic theory (Botha, 1973). Diachronic data have been brought forth to support not only notational conventions but other theoretical concepts, such as levels of representation (Kiparsky, 1968b), choice of distinctive features (Kiparsky, 1968a), extrinsic rule ordering (King, 1973), variable rule ordering (Kiparsky, 1968a), constraints on absolute neutralization (Kiparsky, 1968b), and the naturalness of phonological rules (Bach and Harms, 1972; Schane, 1972). These arguments do have a bearing on the particular form in which a synchronic description is couched, but given two possible synchronic analyses, both of which are stated in the "approved" theoretical framework, the historical data provide no reasonable argument for deciding which analysis is more desirable. However, a different line of historical argumentation has emerged precisely for the justification of a particular synchronic description (as well as the theoretical apparatus which goes along with that description).

A synchronic analysis is justified on the basis of the history of the language—but looking forward rather than backward. The argumentation runs as follows: Of several competing descriptions, the one which will explain most insightfully the direction in which the language is *headed* is to be preferred. Vennemann (1973) has employed such a strategy in proposing a concrete solution to Kisseberth's (1969) abstract analysis of Yawelmani, based on Kuroda (1967). There is probably little need to give extensive illustrations of what are by now classic examples. The essential point is that Yawelmani has no surface long high vowels. In the "abstract" solution, however, such vowels are posited in order to account for two types of harmony: "echoing" between the first and second vowel of certain verb stems, and a "rounding" harmony between root and suffix vowels. A rule of absolute neutralization, which lowers the long high vowels to mid ones, is extrinsically ordered after the two harmony processes.

Vennemann, in the framework of his natural generative grammar, allows no rules of absolute neutralization. Consequently, his underlying representations for Yawelmani do not contain long high vowels. The absence of a rule of absolute neutralization is had only at the cost of rendering more complex the two harmony rules, for Vennemann needs to flag with a diacritic those mid vowels which "behave" as though they were high. This diacritic information needs to be built into both harmony rules in addition to the purely phonological environments, which are independently needed for all short vowels and the nonhigh long vowels. To justify this "concrete" analysis Vennemann argues that the "abstract" solution predicts incorrectly possible future changes for Yawelmani. Since rule loss is a recognized type of diachronic change in generative grammar, conceivably, within the "abstract" analysis, the rule of absolute neutralization could be lost, in which case Yawelmani would revert to Pre-Yawelmani and would once again have long high vowels on the surface. In all likelihood this state of affairs is unlikely. Vennemann then states that rule loss within the context of his "concrete" solution predicts a more plausible evolution. Since the additional environments with diacritics add complexity to the vowel harmony rules, it is natural to suppose loss of this excess baggage. As a result harmony would be based on the occurring surface vowels. To support this possibility Vennemann cites data (Newman, 1944) from Chukchansi, a dialect closely related to Yawelmani, where echoing, but not suffix harmony, is based on the "new" long lowered root vowels.

Pre-Yawelmani: ʔili:+hin sudu:k+hun
Yawelmani: ʔile:+hin sudok+hun
Chukchansi: ʔele:+hin sodok+hun

Unfortunately, Vennemann's critique of "abstract" generative phonology is misguided in two respects. First of all, the innovation exemplified in Chukchansi has a straightforward account within the theoretical framework of generative phonology. In Yawelmani both harmony rules must precede the rule of absolute neutralization; in Chukchansi suffix harmony still precedes the rule of absolute neutralization, whereas echoing now follows that rule. That dialects may differ only in rule ordering is, within generative phonology, as much an accepted mechanism of diachronic change as rule loss is. In fact, there is a ready explanation for this development in Chukchansi: Reordering makes the effects of the echoing rule more transparent (Kiparsky, 1971). The second flaw in Vennemann's argument has to do with the "potential" loss of the rule of absolute neutralization. Vennemann should not have even entertained the elimination of this rule (with everything else remaining unchanged), for, as Kiparsky (1968b) pointed out, the effects of absolute neutralization are not reversed. This is not to say that rules of absolute neutralization are never lost, but, I would add, they are lost only if at the same time there is lexical restructuring.

We have been considering future change as a method of argumentation for a particular analysis. The direction in which a language is headed has as "logical" an explanation in one framework as in the other, provided the biases of each theory are accepted. In particular, I am unaware of any natural phonology solution incorporating this line of argumentation, where predictions are made that are not possible within standard generative phonology. For the moment, at least, arguments based on future change are pseudo-arguments at best.

III

Let us turn to other examples of arguments where the choice of one analysis over another may reside entirely in a "theoretical bias." That is, one establishes a certain theoretical constraint, which doubtlessly is esthetically appealing to its proponent, even though the external justification for such a constraint may be totally nonexistent, or at best, meagerly motivated. Confronted, then, with two "plausible" synchronic analyses, the acceptable one is the one following from the theoretical bias. We have already considered an example of a bias in the discussion of Vennemann's "concrete" analysis of Yawelmani. Within that framework a description may not incorporate rules of absolute neutralization. Historical evidence of a sort was then introduced to bolster the bias. I tried to show that the historical material had another possible interpretation, so that these data were neutral as supportive evidence for the bias. Other biases may not even have this degree of external propping.

I shall consider two examples: the claim by Koutsoudas, Sanders, and Noll (1971) of the nonnecessity for extrinsic rule ordering, and Vennemann's (1973) assertion that for morphemes exhibiting phonological alternation the underlying representation of the morpheme must be equivalent to one of the actually occurring allomorphs. If one wanted one would have no difficulty in imagining psycholinguistic support for these biases. One might say, for example, that the intricate ordering of rules required in standard generative phonology would tax the linguistic organization abilities of the language user, or since the child's exposure is to surface forms he has no reason to posit underlying representations more abstract than one of the "audible" alternants. However, because of the present state of the art it is dubious whether psycholinguistic experimentation in the immediate future will acquire the required degree of sophistication needed for such inquiries. The biases, for the moment then, remain as such—biases, and as such must be confronted with data. It is important to emphasize that I am not discrediting the search for linguistic universals. Koutsoudas and company are to be lauded in their concern for uncovering general principles for explaining the organization of grammars. If, indeed, *all* cases of extrinsic rule ordering found in the literature were predictable from general principles, this discovery would be an achievement of no small importance. It would lend strong support to the theoretical apparatus of generative phonology, to the claim that phonological rules are ordered, although the ordering would now be predictable.

The ordering principles proposed by Koutsoudas, Sanders, and Noll (1971) are relatively simple: Rules apply simultaneously; otherwise they apply sequentially whenever applicable. Equivalently, the principles give preference to nonbleeding and to feeding orders. Unfortunately, there are situations not accommodated by this no-ordering hypothesis. An example involves the rules for deriving certain singular and plural nouns in Portuguese. Most noun stems end in a vowel. Should this vowel be *e*, under certain conditions it is deleted word-finally (in the singular). A subsequent rule deletes intervocalic *l* (in the plural).

Generative phonology analysis

	Singular	Plural
	murale#	murale+s#
$e \rightarrow \emptyset \;/\; \rule{0.5em}{0.4pt}\#$	mural#	—
$l \rightarrow \emptyset \;/\; V\rule{0.5em}{0.4pt}V$	—	murae+s#

Koutsoudas, Sanders, and Noll analysis

Singular	Plural
murale#	murale+s#
*mura#	murae+s#

The difficulty resides in the fact that the two rules are in a bleeding relationship. The principles, on the other hand, predict nonbleeding order. This means that both rules can apply simultaneously, and in fact they would in the underlying form of the singular where the *e* is in word-final position and the *l* is situated between two vowels.

Confronted with a situation of this type there are exactly three choices: (a) discard the principle; (b) modify the principle in some way so that the required ordering is accommodated; or (c) keep the principle in its present form but adjust the analysis. The last alternative can be accomplished by changing the underlying representations and/or by modifying the rules. By selecting this alternative, we have two competing analyses: the standard generative one with two extrinsically ordered rules not conforming to the principles, and an analysis with different underlying forms or rules but whose rules conform to the no-ordering hypothesis. Now we need to choose an analysis. If we choose the second analysis because it does not violate our principles for rule ordering, we have become victims of our "bias." It is certainly true that the analysis follows logically from the assumptions, but it is the assumptions themselves which are at issue.

A more blatant example of this type of argumentation is found in Vennemann (1974). The "bias" there is the claim that an abstract representation must be equivalent to one of its allomorphs. However, this constraint, if imposed, allows for no correct underlying representation for certain undeniable instances of phonological alternation. In English there are alternations due to stress placement, such as *telegraph* [télǝgræ̀f], *telegraphy* [tǝlégrǝfiy]. Since each alternant contains one or more schwas, there is no way to predict what "full" vowel(s) will appear in the comparable position(s) of the other alternant. Precisely because no alternant will ever have all of its vowels unreduced, the underlying representation for the stem (i.e., /tele+græf/) has to be an amalgam of both alternants. Yet such counterexamples do not lead Vennemann to abandon his allomorph principle. Rather he proposes that in such situations both allomorphs are to be listed in the lexicon—that is, here is a case of suppletion. In order to save the "original" assumption, a "new" assumption is required. Vennemann has extricated himself by adding "bias" to "bias."

IV

I should now like to consider some competing analyses which, at first sight, may appear to be quite different. However, once the arguments supporting the differences are peeled away, we find that the solutions turn out to be notational variants.

Two different proposed treatments of vowel harmony offer a good example of this type of notational variance. In languages such as Finnish, Turkish, and Hungarian, the vowels of roots and suffixes agree in backness (and sometimes in rounding). One analysis—the assimilation approach—chooses to specify fully the first vowel of the root, whereas subsequent root vowels and all of the suffix vowels are left partially unspecified (i.e., they are not specified for the feature [back]). A phonological rule then assigns to these noninitial vowels a value for backness identical to that of the initial vowel. An alternative analysis—the root-marker approach—was suggested by Lightner (1965). Here *all* vowels—both root and suffix—are unspecified for backness. Instead the root bears an arbitrary diacritic—let us call it [±GRAVE]. Roots (and their suffixes) bearing the diacritic [+GRAVE] will have all of their vowels specified as [+back], whereas those roots marked [−GRAVE] will of course have [−back] vowels.

Assimilation Approach: $V \rightarrow [\alpha\text{back}] / \begin{bmatrix} V \\ \alpha\text{back} \end{bmatrix} (C_0 V)_0 C_0 \underline{\quad}$

Root Marker Approach: $[\alpha\text{GRAVE}] \rightarrow [\alpha\text{back}]$

Lightner defends his analysis with two principal arguments. In classical Mongolian, with which he was concerned, in addition to vowel harmony there was a type of consonant assimilation: The velar stops had postvelar variants when adjacent to back vowels. The root-marker approach attempts to treat the vowel harmony and the consonant assimilation as a single process. However, Zimmer (1967), in his critique of Lightner, maintains that these should be separate rules. Furthermore, Lightner was operating

with the old Jakobsonian features, so that it is no longer
apparent that the present feature system could treat these two
processes as one. Lightner's second point concerns those languages where both prefixes and suffixes harmonize with the
root. He states that the phonological solution requires separate
rules of progressive and regressive assimilation, whereas his
morphological solution obviates the need for such a distinction.
That two rules are required within the assimilation approach
may be indicative of inadequacies in the notational conventions
rather than a reflection of any substantive claims about phonological systems. Zimmer notes, though, that the harmony rule
has a more complicated environment in the assimilation approach than in the root-marker solution. Whatever environmental
complexity shows up in the assimilation rule may once again be
attributable to defects in notation. Furthermore, one should not
overlook the fact that the simplicity of the root-marker rule
depends on the acceptance of the convention that a diacritic
feature of a morpheme is distributed into each of its segments.
The analysis then is based on shaky arguments: choice of a
feature system and correctness of notational conventions. But let
us consider more closely the harmony rule utilized in the
root-marker approach. Since, by convention, the morphological
feature [GRAVE] belongs to every segment, for vowels the rule
essentially replaces every occurrence of $[\alpha \text{ GRAVE}]$ by $[\alpha \text{ back}]$.
Thus, for vowels the phonological feature [back] is in a
one-to-one correspondence with the morphological feature
[GRAVE]. This correspondence would perhaps be more evident
if the arrow in the rule were replaced by an equals sign. What
we have here then is the phonological use of a diacritic feature.

A more interesting example of notational variance is Hale's
(1971) analysis of Maori, as reported by Kiparsky (1971). Native
Maori words end in vowels. However, in the passive and the
gerundive of certain verbs a consonant shows up preceding the
suffixes marking these forms.

Verb	Passive	Gerundive	
awhi	awhitia	awhitanga	'to embrace'
hopu	hopukia	hopukanga	'to catch'
aru	arumia	arumanga	'to follow'
mau	mauria	mauranga	'to carry'

The "preferred" analysis within the standard generative phono-logical framework—what I shall call the phonological solution—would posit underlying suffixes *-ia* and *-anga*, and stems with final consonants that become deleted in word-final position. Hale argues that this "right" solution is wrong for Maori. Instead, he offers a "conjugational class" analysis. The under-lying representation of a stem is identical to its citation form—that is, it ends in a vowel. The inflectional suffixes have several allomorphs: *-tia, -kia, -mia,* etc., and *-tanga, -kanga, -manga,* etc. In the lexicon one needs to indicate for each verb stem which particular allomorph of the suffixes is selected.

Let us attempt to formalize the conjugational class approach. First, it should be noted that for a given verb stem the same consonant generally occurs in both the passive and the ger-undive—that is, *-tia* goes with *-tanga*; *-mia* with *-manga*; etc. Second, the various allomorphs of a suffix do not exhibit total suppletion: Only the initial consonant varies from allomorph to allomorph. Thus, a suffix is composed of two parts: a variable initial consonant and an invariant part following that consonant (*-ia* for the passive, and *-anga* for the gerundive). In the lexicon, then, we need to indicate for each verb stem only the variable consonant. As a notational device I shall note this consonant by placing it in parentheses after its verb stem. For example, a lexical entry such as *hopu(k)* is interpreted to mean that the stem *hopu* takes the consonant *k* with the suffixes *-ia* and *-anga*. We can think of the underlying form of the passive or of the gerundive as consisting of the stem followed by the invariant part of the suffix—for example, *hopu+ia*. An epenthesis rule, in consultation with the lexicon, would insert the appropriate consonant.

Hale states that of the various allomorphs, *-tia* and *-tanga* are basic and should be considered as "unmarked." He cites other data to support this claim: (a) Loan words uniquely take the endings *-tia* and *-tanga*. (b) These endings also occur when a verb is created from some other part of speech. (c) The passive of a derived causative verb is always formed with *-tia*, even though its ordinary passive has an ending beginning with some other consonant—for example, *hopukia* (passive) versus *whakahoputia* (causative passive). (d) Adverbials modifying gerundives exhibit agreement—that is, the adverbial too takes the gerundive ending; for the adverbial the suffix is always *-tanga* even though it might be something else for the verb. (e) The endings *-tia* and *-tanga* may be used whenever one of the "marked" endings is not recalled.

Hale considers these additional facts as strongly supportive of the conjugational class analysis. Kiparsky notes that the passives of derived causatives would be particularly cumbersome to handle within the phonological solution. The difficulties, if any, turn out to be relatively minor. To accommodate these additional data, the phonological solution, like the conjugational class solution, needs to recognize "unmarked" (*-tia* and *-tanga*) and "marked" (*-ia* and *-anga*) forms of the suffixes: Basic verbs take the "marked" endings; other forms (loans, derived verbs, modifying adverbials) take the "unmarked" endings. (In the conjugational class solution basic verbs take either "marked" or "unmarked" endings, and other forms take "unmarked" endings. This distribution of "marked" and "unmarked" could just as easily apply to the phonological analysis.) Once we recognize the "marked" and "unmarked" character of the suffixes within any analysis, Kiparsky's passives of derived causatives become less problematic. Because these forms are derived they take the unmarked suffix *-tia*. Consequently, within the phonological solution, the underlying representation for *whakahoputia*, whose stem is *hopuk*, would be *whaka+hopuk+tia*. The stem-final consonant must be deleted. Since in the phonological solution we already have a rule deleting final consonants we need only generalize the rule: It applies in syllable-final position.

The following table summarizes the relevant features of the phonological and of the conjugational class analyses.

	Phonological solution	Conjugational class solution
1. Lexical entry of stems	hopuk arum	hopu(k) aru(m)
2. Lexical entry of suffixes	(t)ia (t)anga	(t)ia (t)anga
3. Distribution of allomorphs	tia, tanga (unmarked) ia, anga (marked for basic verb stems)	tia, tanga (unmarked) ia, anga (marked for certain basic verb stems)
4. Fate of "unpredictable" consonant	$C \rightarrow \emptyset \ / \ \_\_\_ \$$	$\emptyset \rightarrow C \ / + \_\_\_ V$

The equivalences of the two analyses should be apparent: (a) In the phonological solution certain verb stems terminate in a consonant. In the conjugational class solution all verb stems end in a vowel; additionally there may be a consonant ("conjugation class") marker. In any case a consonant needs to be explicitly indicated in the lexicon, either as an inherent part of the stem or as a separate item eventually to occur with stem and suffix. (b) In both solutions suffixes have two forms: with and without initial *t*. (c) The forms with *t* are the unmarked ones. The marked forms, without *t*, occur, when they occur, only in combination with basic verb stems. Both solutions equally predict that forms with unmarked *t* could replace forms containing some other consonant. In both cases there would be lexical restructuring: change in the final consonant for the phonological analysis, and change in class affiliation for the conjugational class solution. (d) In the phonological solution the stem-final consonant is deleted in syllable-final position, whereas it is retained when followed by a vowel. In the conjugational class solution, in syllable-final position there is no consonant to begin with, but one is inserted preceding a vowel.

The fundamental difference between the two solutions centers around the "marked" situation—whether the "unpredictable" consonant belongs to the stem or to the suffix. If we consider just internal linguistic arguments there is no reason to prefer one analysis to the other. Both solutions accommodate the data. Both solutions are more or less of equal formal complexity. Perhaps there are external arguments in support of one of the analyses. Hale, for example, notes that Maori children, after being taught some basic principles of linguistic analysis, consider the consonant as a part of the suffix in their segmentation of the passive and of the gerundive forms. However, these children were literate in their language and this morphemic analysis agrees with the traditional way of looking at the problem. One cannot discount the powerful influence of orthography and of school-taught grammar. The presence or absence of a consonant in Maori is reminiscent of French liaison—exemplified by such well-known examples as *petit ami* versus *peti(t) garçon*—where a similar alternation occurs. It would not surprise me to discover that French children, exposed to some basic linguistic principles, might decide that a word such as *peti(t)* terminates in a *t*. This treatment would then appear to support the phonological solution. But I think that the real reason behind such an analysis lies in the children's knowledge of conventional French orthography. For the moment at least, the external evidence seems uncertain.

V

An introductory book on the nature of science states that "science studies certain relations between particular events" (Campbell, 1973, p. 37.). Theories are explanations of these relations between events. Modern linguistics, unlike other disciplines, has imposed an additional requirement on its theories—that they be psychologically "real" models of the way in which speakers intuitively organize "relations between linguistic events." Arguments dealing with external evidence are often arguments attempting to validate the "psychologically correct" grammar. Yet given the nature of the external data presently utilized within phonology, they are of little value in arguing for a particular analysis since opposing analyses, whether based on same or different theories, can be shown to be compatible with these data.

There is no denial that the data of linguistics, unlike, say, physics, are peculiarly human. But because we know so little about how speakers acquire and organize linguistic knowledge, it may be unrealistic, or at least premature, to believe that our theories do, or should, mirror faithfully speakers' organization of linguistic events. On this issue I have to agree with Stockwell's statement pertaining to syntax: "Since we don't know much of anything substantial about how speakers store their extensive knowledge of their languages, or how they retrieve it and put it to use in forming sentences, we are free to build formal models with *no notion of process whatever* built into them. They provide analogs to the *content* of what speakers know, but not analogs to the *storage or processing* of that content" (Stockwell, 1976, chap. 5).

This is not to say that the search for "psychologically real" grammars is not a worthwhile pursuit. It would be no small achievement to have a glimpse at the organization of speakers' internalized grammars. But because present knowledge in this area is so meager, one cannot realistically make claims for a particular analysis by appealing to what speakers do. It is meaningless, for example, to reject Chomsky and Halle's (1968) analysis of English on the grounds that their underlying forms and rules would be incredibly difficult for the young language learner, since such an argument is founded on an unfounded assumption about language learners. Instead, I prefer to see an alternative description with hard-core data. Ross's (1972) re-analysis of English stress is a good example of this. Proposals can be made to stand or fall by confronting them with crucial data. I do not mean merely looking at selected isolated ex-amples, but rather embarking upon full-fledged descriptions of languages. What I am advocating then is more concern for descriptive linguistics. It has become fashionable to argue theo-retical points or to base an analysis on highly limited data from a limited few exotic languages, among which must be Nupe and Yawelmani. (This paper is no exception.) For example, a proposal about rule ordering should be confronted with all the rules of the language, and not with just two or, at most, three of them. I believe that some, but certainly not all, of the current controversies in phonology might be settled if there were more interest in detailed description.

Since theories and analyses are the creations of humans, a "human" element enters into an evaluation. An analysis should be *intellectually satisfying* in that it offers some explanation as to why the language works the way it does. Consider the two analyses of Yawelmani to which we referred earlier. The "ab-stract" analysis posits underlying high vowels, needed for certain harmony rules, which are subsequently lowered to mids. The "concrete" solution has only mid vowels in underlying repre-sentation, but those mids with the behavior of high vowels are marked with a special diacritic for triggering the harmony rules. I happen to prefer the "abstract" solution, for it offers, to me, a satisfying explanation for the harmony processes: The "funny" mid vowels *are*, in some deeper sense, the "missing" high ones. But this is my own preference; consequently, it is an esthetic judgment. This observation brings me then to an important point—namely, that most of the arguments in phonology today reduce to arguments over esthetic judgments. The various ex-amples of competing analyses cited previously lend credence to this view. The proponent of a competing analysis, in justification of his solution, bases his arguments on internal or external evidence. In each case I attempted to show that the argument turned out to be invalid—because the opposing analysis could make the same claims or because the two analyses were notational variants or because of biases. Due to the nature of the internal or the external evidence at hand, there is no "logical" reason to prefer one analysis to the other. It is for this reason that the choice may be entirely an esthetic one. Furthermore, I do not think that phonology is unique here. Many of the controversies within syntax also strike me as controversies over esthetic judgments. Although there may be many types of arguments around, I conclude that there are few good ones and even fewer convincing ones. For the moment, the best argument, like beauty, is in the mind of the beholder.

REFERENCES

Bach, E. and R. T. Harms (1972) "How do languages get crazy rules?," in Robert P. Stockwell and Ronald K. S. Macaulay (eds.), *Linguistic Change and Generative Theory*. Bloomington: Indiana University Press.

Botha, R. P. (1973) *The Justification of Linguistic Hypotheses*. The Hague: Mouton.

Campbell, N. (1973) *What Is Science?* New York: Dover.

Chomsky, N. and M. Halle (1968) *The Sound Pattern of English*. New York: Harper and Row. Abbreviated as *SPE* in this chapter.

Hale, K. (1971) "Deep-surface canonical disparities in relation to analysis and change: An Australian example." Unpublished.

King, R. D. (1973) "In defense of extrinsic ordering." Indiana University Linguistics Club, Bloomington.

Kiparsky, P. (1968a) "Linguistic universals and linguistic change," in Emmon Bach and Robert T. Harms (eds.), *Universals in Linguistic Theory*. New York: Holt, Rinehart and Winston.

_____ (1968b) "How abstract is phonology?," Indiana University Linguistics Club, Bloomington.

_____ (1971) "Historical linguistics," in William Orr Dingwall (ed.), *A Survey of Linguistic Science*. Linguistics Program, University of Maryland.

Kisseberth, C. W. (1969) "On the abstractness of phonology: The evidence from Yawelmani." *Papers in Linguistics* 1:248-282.

Koutsoudas, A., G. Sanders and C. Noll (1971) "On the application of phonological rules." Indiana University Linguistics Club, Bloomington.

Kuroda, S.-Y. (1967) *Yawelmani Phonology*. Cambridge, Mass. M. I. T. Press.

Lightner, T. (1965) "On the description of vowel and consonant harmony." *Word* 21:127–134.

McCawley, J. D. (1973) "On the role of notation in generative phonology," in Maurice Gross, Morris Halle and Marcel-Paul Schützenberger (eds.), *The Formal Analysis of Natural Languages*. The Hague: Mouton.

Newman, S. S. (1944) *Yokuts Language of California*. Viking Fund Publications in Anthropology, 2. New York.

Ross, J. R. (1972) "A reanalysis of English word stress (Part I)," in Michael K. Brame (ed.), *Contributions to Generative Phonology*. Austin: University of Texas Press.

Schane, S. A. (1968) *French Phonology and Morphology*. Cambridge, Mass.: M. I. T. Press.

_____ (1972) "Natural rules in phonology," in Robert P. Stockwell and Ronald K. S. Macaulay (eds.), *Linguistic Change and Generative Theory*, Bloomington: Indiana University Press.

Stockwell, R. P. (1976) *Foundations of Syntactic Theory*. Englewood Cliffs, N.J.: Prentice-Hall.

Vennemann, T. (1973) "Phonological concreteness in natural generative grammar," in R. Shuy and C. J. Bailey (eds.), *Toward Tomorrow's Linguistics*. Washington, D.C.: Georgetown University Press (1973).

_____ (1974) "Words and syllables in natural generative grammar," in Anthony Bruck, Robert A. Fox and Michael W. La Galy (eds.), *Papers from the Parasession on Natural Phonology: April 18, 1974*. Chicago: Chicago Linguistic Society.

Zimmer, K. E. (1967) "A Note on Vowel Harmony." *IJAL* 33:166–171.

8
Performance models and the generative-interpretive debate

Ashley J. Hastings
Andreas Koutsoudas
University of Wisconsin-Milwaukee

I. INTRODUCTION

Few controversies in contemporary linguistic theory have engendered as much argumentation as the debate between the generative semanticists and interpretive semanticists. A wide range of arguments, many of them intricate and ingenious, have been employed by the proponents of these competing theoretical viewpoints; a large number of semantic and syntactic phenomena have been explored to considerable depth in the search for new, more forceful arguments. Yet the issue remains unresolved. Some linguists are committed to the generative semantics approach, some to the interpretive; others regard the two theories as notational variants; and still others doubt that they are notational variants but are not committed to either approach. It is not surprising, therefore, that the generative-interpretive debate is frequently cited as a particularly interesting and difficult case study in the analysis of linguistic argumentation.

Botha (1973) has performed a careful dissection of linguistic argument forms, devoting much of his analysis to the generative-interpretive debate. He concludes that "the primary cause of the strikingly inconclusive state of these controversies lies in the fact that the logic of justification of transformational grammar lacks both appropriate conditions of evidence and clear, well-understood standards of acceptability" (p. 327).[1] While we find Botha's treatment of this question interesting and insightful, we try to show here that, even if the opposing sides in the generative-interpretive debate were in full agreement with respect to conditions of evidence and standards of acceptability, the kind of argumentation which has been used in this debate would still fail to lead to any conclusion. This, we argue, is because the grounds on which the debate has been waged are inappropriate to the basic issue which divides the two theoretical viewpoints. More specifically: while the main point at dispute between generative semanticists and interpretive semanticists has to do with the *form* of linguistic competence, the arguments which have been used to contest this issue have been concerned with the *content* of linguistic competence. We suggest that only strong mentalist[2] arguments are in principle capable of resolving the generative-interpretive debate. We try to show that one such argument, based on the types of performance models which are compatible with grammars of different forms, makes it appear unlikely that interpretive semantics, to the extent that it differs from generative semantics, is a plausible model of linguistic competence.

II. AN OVERVIEW OF THE
GENERATIVE-INTERPRETIVE DEBATE

In this section, we set forth what appear to be the main points at issue between generative semantics and interpretive semantics,[3] review briefly the types of arguments which have been employed in this controversy, and show why these arguments are inherently incapable of deciding the main issues.

1. In both generative semantics and interpretive semantics, the goal of linguistic theory is taken to be the specification of

the class of possible grammars of human languages, where a grammar is a set of rules which relate semantic representations and phonetic representations. Both theories recognize a phonological component which mediates between phonetic representations and surface structures, and another component or components which mediate between surface structures and semantic representations. It is with respect to this latter set of rules that the two theories differ.

The central position of generative semantics is stated succintly by Lakoff (1971, p. 232):

> The generative semantics position is, in essence, that syntax and semantics cannot be separated and that the role of transformations, and of derivational constraints in general, is to relate semantic representations and surface structure.

This contrasts with the interpretive semantics position, as stated by Jackendoff (1972, p. 23):

> In addition to transformations, there are all the different kinds of semantic rules operating at different levels of the derivation.

Jackendoff presents a diagram (1972, p. 4) of an interpretive semantics grammar in which a transformational component and a semantic component are shown as distinct parts of the grammar. Comparing these alternatives, we see that generative semantics regards the rules that relate semantic representations and surface structures as a single component in which no distinction is made between syntactic and semantic rules, while interpretive semantics distinguishes between a semantic and a syntactic component.

Another point of contrast between the two theories is found in their respective positions on lexical insertion. According to Lakoff (1971, p. 233), generative semantics assumes that "a lexical transformation associated with a lexical item I maps a phrase-maker P containing a substructure Q which contains no lexical item into a phrase-marker P′ formed by superimposing I over Q." As we understand Lakoff's terminology, Q is a subtree containing only semantic information; I contains phonological information along with, presumably, syntactic information (syntactic features). A generative semantics lexical insertion rule, then, has the following form (where SI = semantic information, PI = phonological information, and SF = syntactic features):

$$[SI] \longrightarrow [PI, SF]$$

The interpretive semantics position, according to Jackendoff (1972, p. 21), is that "lexical insertion rules insert lexical items freely under category symbols. ..." A lexical item is a set of semantic, phonological, and syntactic properties (Jackendoff, 1972, pp. 37–38). An interpretive semantics lexical insertion rule, then, has the following form (where CS = category symbol):

$$[CS] \longrightarrow [SI, PI, SF]$$

Thus the two theories differ in the form of their lexical insertion rules.

A third difference between generative semantics and interpretive semantics is that the latter, but not the former, has a component of rules (phrase structure rules) which, together with the lexical insertion rules, specify an infinite set of structures (deep structures) which are more abstract than surface structures but less abstract than semantic representations (Jackendoff, 1972, pp. 4–5). While generative semantics could in principle define a level of representation corresponding to deep structure (Lakoff, 1971, p. 238), this would not require a phrase structure component. In order to be "generative," of course, a theory must have some way of specifying an infinite number of structures (Chomsky, 1965, pp. 15–16); this function is performed in the generative semantics theory by a set of rules which specify the class of well-formed semantic representations (McCawley, 1968, p. 165).

In the above cursory comparison of generative semantics and interpretive semantics, we set forth what we feel to be the principal differences between them.[4] More detailed aspects of the two theories are brought out, where relevant, in the subsequent sections.

2. We now consider critically some arguments representative of those used in the generative–interpretive debate. All of the

arguments examined are advanced by supporters of the interpretive semantics position (Chomsky and Jackendoff). We wish to emphasize that this is *not* because we regard the argumentation of these individuals, or of interpretive semanticists in general, to be in any way superior or inferior to that of generative semanticists. We selected these arguments for discussion because we believe them to be among the most widely known and frequently cited arguments in the generative-interpretive debate. It should become clear, in what follows, that our criticisms of these arguments would be equally appropriate to any comparable arguments which have been or could be advanced by supporters of generative semantics.

The arguments we examine fall into these three categories, each of which we consider in turn:

Arguments based on descriptive adequacy

Arguments based on generality and explanatory adequacy

Arguments based on theoretical power

Some Arguments Based on Descriptive Adequacy

A. Jackendoff (1972, pp. 109–110) argues that any theory which derives pronouns transformationally (as generative semantics does) must resort to "drastic" measures to account for sentences with crossing coreference, such as

The man who deserves it will get the prize he wants.

because, assuming that the underlying source of a pronoun is a fully specified noun phrase identical with its antecedent, such a sentence must have an infinite underlying (semantic) representation:

The man [who deserves the prize [which the man [who ...] wants]$_j$]$_i$ will get the prize [which the man [who deserves the prize [which ...]$_i$ wants]$_j$]

Interpretive semantics avoids this problem, Jackendoff argues, because it generates pronouns directly in deep structure and establishes coreference by means of an interpretive rule. The semantic representation of such a sentence would simply include the pronouns (or rather their semantic representation) along with a table of coreference indicating that they are coreferential with their respective antecedents.

However, this argument does not succeed in demonstrating the superiority of interpretive semantics. This is because the assumption of the interpretive semantics framework is neither sufficient nor necessary to avoid the problem of infinite semantic representations. It is not *sufficient* because an additional assumption is required, namely, that the semantic representation of a pronoun is not an exact duplicate of the semantic representation of its antecedent. This is explicitly noted by Jackendoff (1972, pp. 110):

> Furthermore, in the process of semantic interpretation, a pronoun need not be replaced with a duplicate of the noun phrase with which it is coreferential (which would again bring up the problem of recursion). . . .

The interpretive semantics framework is not *necessary* to solve this problem, either. Once it is granted that the semantic representation of a pronoun need not be identical to the semantic representation of its antecedent, the transformational analysis of pronouns can be preserved by deriving pronouns from fully specified noun phrases which are not distinct from their antecedents. (Karttunen, 1971, and Kuroda, 1971, develop a solution along these lines.) The semantic representation of the sentence given above would then be like

The man [who deserves the prize$_j$]$_i$ will get the prize [which the man$_i$ wants]$_j$

It seems to us, then, that Jackendoff's argument fails to show that interpretive semantics is superior to generative semantics. We wish to emphasize, though, that this is not because of any deficiency in Jackendoff's prosecution of the argument. The argument is simply inappropriate to the issue at hand. This is because, as we have seen, the crucial step in solving the problem of crossing coreference is the assumption that the semantic representation of a pronoun need not be completely identical to the semantic representation of its antecedent. This is a specific assumption about the *content* of grammars. It has nothing to do with questions concerning the *form* of grammars, that is, whether there is a distinct semantic component, whether there is a phrase structure component, etc. Since the defining characteristics of generative semantics and interpretive semantics are the respective assumptions they make concerning the *form* of grammars, it follows that the argument we have just examined is irrelevant in deciding between the two theories.

B. Chomsky (1972c, pp. 85–88) presents an argument to show that there are facts which cannot be accounted for in the generative semantics framework but which pose no problem for a theory which generates deep structures via a phrase structure component. (While Chomsky had the "standard" theory in mind, interpretive semantics is equivalent in this respect.) The outline of this argument is as follows:

1. The expressions (a), (b), and (c) [Chomsky's (33), (34), (35)] have the same semantic representation.
   (a) John's uncle
   (b) the person who is the brother of John's mother or father or the husband of the sister of John's mother or father
   (c) the person who is the son of one of John's grandparents or the husband of a daughter of one of John's grandparents, but is not his father
2. The sentences S_a, S_b, and S_c, formed by inserting (a), (b), and (c) into (d) [Chomsky's (36)], are not paraphrases and therefore have different semantic representations.
   (d) Bill realized that the bank robber was ___.
3. The semantic representation of (d) is the same in S_a, S_b, and S_c.
4. Assuming points (1)–(3), generative semantics is faced with a contradiction, since (1) and (3) imply that S_a, S_b, and S_c have the same semantic representation, while (2) denies this.
5. In the standard theory, (a), (b), and (c) "would derive from three different deep structures, all mapped onto the same semantic representation" (p. 86).
6. "it is necessary to define *realize* in such a way that the meaning assigned to 'NP realizes that p' depends not only on

the semantic interpretation of p but also on the deep structure of p" (p. 86).

7. "In the standard theory, the contradiction does not arise. The analogues of [(1)–(3)] are simultaneously satisfied by: (i) rules which assign the same semantic representation to [(a), (b), and (c)]; (ii) rules which make reference to the deep structure of the item appearing in the context of [(d)] in determining the meaning. Condition [(3)] then poses no problem" (p. 87).

It is worth noting that the standard-theory "analogues" of (1)–(3) have "K-initial structure" in the place of "semantic representation."[5] (Obviously, no semantic representation in any theory can satisfy contradictory requirements.)

In order to criticize Chomsky's argument, we must first get a clear understanding of what he is proposing as a standard-theory analysis of S_a, S_b, and S_c. He clearly assumes that the semantic representations of (a), (b), and (c) are identical, and that the semantic representations of S_a, S_b, and S_c are different. It must be the case, then, either that the semantic representation of (d) is different in the three sentences, or that there is some *other* way in which the semantic representations of S_a, S_b, and S_c differ. Whichever is the case, let us assume that the semantic representations of S_a, S_b, and S_c contain, respectively, some features D_a, D_b, and D_c which distinguish them. Chomsky furthermore assumes that there are semantic rules which assign D_a, D_b, or D_c to the semantic representation of the sentences in question, depending on whether (a), (b), or (c) appears in the context of (d) in deep structure. These rules must apparently refer to the particular syntactic and lexical forms of (a), (b), and (c). They are triggered by certain properties of *realize*.

We can now construct a generative semantics solution which is no more or less tentative than Chomsky's proposal. Let us assume that (a), (b), and (c) have identical semantic representations, and that the semantic representations of S_a, S_b, and S_c differ with respect to D_a, D_b, and D_c. Let us assume further that the semantic representation of *realize* triggers certain rules which map the semantic representation of (a, b, c) onto the syntactic and lexical forms (a), (b), and (c) in the environment of D_a, D_b, or D_c, respectively. In outlining this solution, it is

not necessary to resort to phrase structure rules, a semantic/
syntactic dichotomy, or any other feature which distinguishes
the standard theory or interpretive semantics from generative
semantics.

It seems to us, therefore, that Chomsky's argument shows
nothing at all about the relative merits of generative semantics as
opposed to the standard theory or interpretive semantics. This is
because the argument leads—at most—to conclusions about the
content of the grammar of English: there must be certain rules
which correlate certain aspects of semantic representation with
certain syntactic and lexical structures, etc. No conclusions
follow as to what *form* the grammar must have.

Some Arguments Based on Generality and Explanatory Adequacy

C. Jackendoff (1972, pp. 110-111) offers this argument:

There are many noun phrases such as *the bum, the bastard,* and *the poor guy* that can be used coreferentially with another noun phrase if they are reduced in stress. These "pronominal epithets" can occur in some subset of the environments in which pronominalization is possible, and they function semantically more or less as specialized pronouns. We would obviously be missing a generalization if we did not handle them by a rule of the same kind as pronominalization, hopefully a rule that could collapse with pronominalization.

In a transformational framework [e.g., generative semantics—AJH/AK], however, the generalization cannot be captured. The pronominalization transformation changes NPs into pronouns. In a consistent treatment, in certain contexts an NP could be turned into a pronominal epithet instead. But then which pronominal epithet would the NP be changed into? The meaning is obviously changed if we substitute an epithet for a pronoun or one epithet for another.

In an interpretive framework, we can mark epithets as special lexical items which may function as pronouns in certain contexts of the pronominalization rule, adding their lexical meaning to the intended attributes of the person they refer to. Thus no change need be made in the nature of the interpretive theory in order to include these cases.

Jackendoff is quite correct in pointing out that it is not possible
to change a noun phrase into an epithet without changing the
meaning. In the generative semantics framework, just as in any

other theory, semantic representation is by definition a representation of meaning; therefore, a generative semantics solution to this problem must take it as given that the full semantic content of an epithet is present at the beginning of the derivation. Since, as Jackendoff notes, "epithets add their lexical meaning to the intended attributes of the person they refer to," the most natural assumption is that the semantic representation of an epithet contains *all* the intended attributes of the person referred to. For example, in the sentence

Joe is broke, but I won't lend the bum a cent.

the semantic representation of *the bum* would be, in abbreviated format,

$$\begin{bmatrix} [\text{JOE}] \\ [\text{BUM}] \end{bmatrix}$$

where JOE is the set of attributes of *Joe* and BUM is the set of attributes of the epithet *bum*. Assuming, with Jackendoff (1972, p. 117), that the pronominalization rule in a transformational (e.g., generative semantics) account adds the feature +PRO in certain environments to a noun phrase which is identical with another, it must be stipulated that epithetic semantic material does not count against identity. (That epithets have a special semantic property is demonstrated by the existence of two readings for sentences like *Algernon is a bastard*, where *bastard* is an epithet on only one reading.) Epithets can then be lexically marked as capable of functioning as pronouns. Thus, just as [JOE, +PRO] is lexicalized as *he*, [[JOE], +PRO, [BUM]] is lexicalized as *bum*. If the conditions for pronominalization are not met, we presumably derive sentences like *That bum Joe is asking for a loan*.

It seems, then, that the generalization noted by Jackendoff can be captured in either theory. In pointing out that epithets should be marked in a special way, Jackendoff has made a contribution to our understanding of the *content* of a general account of pronouns and epithets. However, nothing at all follows from this with respect to the *form* of grammar.

D. A very interesting argument against generative semantics

(and in favor of a theory like interpretive semantics) grows out of Chomsky's well-known work on nominalization (1970; see Chomsky, 1972b). The argument is set forth succinctly in Chomsky (1972d, pp. 158–161). We quote the key points:[6]

> derived nominals correspond only to forms that exist prior to syntactically motivated transformations.
>
> the patterns in question must exist independently for noun phrases, quite apart from these nominalizations. . . .
>
> derived nominals have the internal structure of noun phrases. . . .
>
> derived nominals do not contain elements that are unique to verb phrases and never appear in other noun phrases, specifically, aspect.
>
> In all these respects derived nominals differ from gerundive nominals. . . . These are not subject to the . . . variation of meaning that is characteristic of derived nominals. . . . As far as form is concerned, gerundive nominals correspond not only to base structures but to derived structures as well . . .; they do not correspond in form to independently existing noun phrases; . . . they do not have the internal structure of noun phrases . . .; and they may contain aspect. . . .

Chomsky's explanation for these differences between gerundive and derived nominals is that gerundive nominals are transformationally derived, while "derived" nominals are generated directly in the base, with certain lexical items capable of appearing in more than one syntactic category. Thus, for example, the gerundive nominal *John's proving the theorem* is derived from the corresponding sentence, but the derived nominal *John's proof of the theorem* is a deep structure noun phrase; *prove/proof* is a lexical item which can appear as either a verb or a noun. Since generative semantics would claim that both kinds of nominals are derived from their semantic representations, Chomsky says, no explanation for the facts mentioned above is possible in a generative semantics account.

However, it is not at all obvious to us that a parallel explanation cannot be achieved within the generative semantics approach. Such an explanation would be forthcoming if it were the case that nouns like *proof* are not transformationally derived from their corresponding verbs and that, more generally, nominalizations like *John's proof of the theorem* are not derived from corresponding sentences but rather arise in the same way as other noun phrases. It seems to us that such an account is possible in the generative semantics framework. Let us assume, first, that the lexical categories Noun, Verb, etc., are not present in semantic representations. This assumption is motivated by the frequently made observation that syntactic categories do not appear to have any systematic semantic import. An approximation of the semantic representation of *John's proof of the theorem* or *John's proving the theorem* would be JOHN PROVE THEOREM with, presumably, the thematic (case) functions of JOHN and THEOREM specified. Assuming, with Chomsky, that PROVE can appear as either a noun or a verb, and that there is no transformation which changes verbs into nouns, the only way *John's proof of the theorem* can be derived is by directly inserting the noun *proof* rather than the verb *prove*. Since the resulting noun phrase would never have been a sentence, it would not be able to undergo any transformation restricted to sentences. Since only verb phrases contain aspect, the presence of aspect in a semantic structure (e.g., JOHN $\begin{smallmatrix} \text{PROVE} \\ \text{[+PERF]} \end{smallmatrix}$ THEOREM) would be a sufficient condition on which to base a restriction prohibiting the insertion of a noun in such cases; thus, no nominal like *John's proof of the theorem* could contain aspect. Being noun phrases, derived nominals would be subject to general rules applicable to noun phrases, such as the rules inserting *'s* and *of* (Jackendoff, 1974), and would thus have the structure of noun phrases. In the case of noun–verb pairs with idiosyncratic semantic correspondence, the semantic representation would determine whether the noun or the verb was to be inserted; thus the meaning of sentences and their corresponding "derived" nominals would be related as closely or as remotely as the meanings of the noun–verb pairs involved, while gerundive nominals, being transformationally derived from sentences, would be directly related in meaning to the corresponding sentences.

It seems to us, then, that the discrepancies between gerundive and derived nominals can be explained in a generative semantics framework, provided that the transformational analysis of derived nominals is abandoned. In his work on nominalization, Chomsky has proposed important innovations with respect to the content of grammars, but it is far from clear that any conclusions can be drawn from this concerning the form of grammars.

Some Arguments Based on Theoretical Power

B. Jackendoff (1972, p. 12) presents the following argument:

> In the standard theory of pronominalization, ... it is claimed that pronouns are transformationally reduced forms of fully specified NPs. Transformations producing pronouns must ... verify that a potential pronoun is coreferential with its antecedent. Therefore this theory must specify that coreferentiality of two NPs is a possible condition on transformations. What is not explained is why only pronominalization-like rules ever make use of this kind of condition. Why, for example, is there no rule that moves an NP if it is coreferential with an NP elsewhere in the sentence? In the interpretive theory of pronominalization ..., where pronouns are generated by the base and semantic rules determine their antecedents, there is no need for transformations ever to refer to coreference conditions. Hence we can deprive transformations of the ability to refer to coreference and construct a weaker theory in which a movement rule dependent on coreference cannot be stated.

This argument is of course relevant to generative semantics, since in this theory it is generally assumed that transformations must be able to refer to coreference. Given this, it is indeed remarkable that no movement rule depends on coreference. We would be astonished, for example, to find a dialect of English in which Dative Shift could apply only if the indirect object were coreferential with another noun phrase.

However, it is possible to turn this argument around. In the interpretive theory, semantic rules must predict that certain noun phrases are coreferential. Therefore, this theory must specify that coreferentiality of two noun phrases is a possible consequence of semantic rules. What is not explained is why only pronominalization-like rules ever have this consequence. Why, for example, is there no semantic rule that marks two noun phrases as coreferential just in case one of them is in a particular position resulting from a movement rule (e.g., the post-Dative Shift indirect object position)? This would be analogous to placing coreference conditions on a movement rule, in a generative semantics grammar. We suspect that it would not be difficult to impose an appropriate constraint on semantic coreference rules; such a constraint might stipulate that the structural descriptions of coreference rules must mention NP_1, $\frac{NP_2}{[+PRO]}$, and perhaps certain precedence and dominance relations, but nothing else. Clearly, though, the mere assumption of the interpretive theory of pronominalization is *not sufficient* to eliminate the superfluous descriptive power that Jackendoff wants to eliminate; a rather specific constraint on coreference rules is also required. The interpretive theory is *not necessary* in this regard, either, because an equivalent constraint can be imposed in generative semantics: only pronominalization-type rules can depend on coreference. The only conclusion which follows from Jackendoff's argument, then, is that the content of grammars must be constrained in a particular way. This argument has no bearing on the form of grammars; it does not force us to decide between the transformational and interpretive approaches to pronominalization, or between generative semantics and interpretive semantics in general.

F. Finally, we discuss an entire class of arguments, of which the preceding one is a special case. These arguments arise from the fact that interpretive semantics has a greater amount of theoretical machinery than does generative semantics. The keynote is stated by Chomsky (1972d, p. 127):

> If enrichment of theoretical apparatus and elaboration of conceptual structure will restrict the class of possible grammars and the class of sets of derivations generated by admissible grammars, then it will be a step forward (assuming it to be consistent with the requirement of descriptive adequacy).

Placing this squarely in the present context, the general argument is that if the multiplicity of rule-types postulated in interpretive semantics leads to a more restricted class of grammars (which still contains the grammars of all possible languages), then interpretive semantics is to be preferred.

But it is clear that just positing a greater number of rule-types is not sufficient to achieve the desired restriction on the class of grammars. In fact, if these rule-types are not severely constrained, the class of grammars is even *less* restricted, as we can see from these remarks by Jackendoff (1972, p. 23):

> [In generative semantics], there is only one way in which similarity in meaning or co-occurrence restrictions between two constructions can be captured: a transformation. In a theory permitting a number of different kinds of rules, such as the theory to be explored here [interpretive semantics—AJH/AK], there are many ways of capturing generalizations. . . .
>
> With all these different kinds of rules at our disposal, several very different analyses will often come to mind for the same phenomenon. How do we decide which account is to be preferred? . . . [T]he decision will be made on the basis of how the rules interact with each other most naturally and how appropriate the power already proposed for a particular type of rule is for something new.

While this last statement might seem to imply that it is the skill and experience of the analyst, rather than the theoretical apparatus, which will ultimately restrict the class of grammars, it is clear that this is not what Jackendoff means. He intends for the theory itself to exclude a large number of conceivable grammars by imposing heavy constraints on the power of each type of rule (Jackendoff 1972, pp. 379 ff.). These constraints would include precise limitations on the power of functional structure rules, modal structure rules, coreference rules, and focus and presupposition rules, all of which make up the semantic component. There are also heavy constraints on the several types of transformations: insertion, deletion, and movement rules. Jackendoff sums up the situation (1972, p. 384):

> We see, then, that the research on English grammar presented here tends toward a picture of universal grammar as a relatively rigid, highly structured affair, with fewer options for the language learner than the variety of rule types seems initially to indicate.

In our view, this work by Jackendoff does indeed make an impressive contribution toward the goal of constraining linguistic theory, in that he has set forth a number of concrete examples of the kinds of constraints needed. However, it seems to us that, once again, we have no basis for concluding that interpretive semantics is superior to generative semantics, because the proposed constraints have to do with the content, not the form, of grammars. By this we mean that the formal properties of interpretive semantics are neither sufficient nor necessary to achieve the desired restrictions on the power of linguistic theory.

We have already seen that the particular formal characteristics of interpretive semantics are not sufficient to restrict the theory. Nothing is gained merely by assuming, for example, that there are distinct syntactic and semantic components, since without imposing constraints on the various rule-types, even more grammars are possible than in a theory with only transformations. But as far as we can see, the formal assumptions of interpretive semantics are not necessary, either, because none of the constraints Jackendoff proposes depend in any way on the semantic–syntactic dichotomy. Consider first the constraints on the semantic component. Jackendoff (1972, p. 380) states that "each subcomponent in English consists of a highly restricted type of rule," and goes on to characterize the restrictions on each type. For example, "any device used to mark focus and presupposition, be it stress, syntactic position, or a focus morpheme, will be interpreted at the surface structure. . . ." Nothing in the substance of this restriction relies on the assumption that focus and presupposition rules are semantic rather than syntactic rules, as we can see by paraphrasing the restriction in a generative semantics framework: rules referring to focus and presupposition have their effect at surface structure, whether their outputs involve stress, syntactic position, or a focus morpheme. In either version, the domain of the constraint is specified in terms of the theory-independent notions of "focus," "presupposition," and "surface structure"; there is no need to say anything about the notion "semantic rule."

The notion "syntactic rule" is also unnecessary for stating constraints on grammars. For example, Jackendoff (1972, pp. 382–383) says that lowering transformations can be prohibited in his theory; they are replaced by semantic rules. Now, it is certainly true that a theory with no restrictions on lowering transformations would be too powerful. Such transformations have been motivated by a rather small set of phenomena, usually involving aspects of semantic structure like the scope of quantifiers, which on the semantic level may be "higher" than (i.e., outside of) the clause in which they appear in surface structure.

But no restriction in theoretical power is achieved by merely transferring this power from the syntactic component to the semantic component. The semantic rules which in Jackendoff's theory replace lowering transformations must be restricted in such a way that they have no superfluous power; they must not be defined so loosely that they could, for example, assign a "higher" position in semantic structure to any arbitrary element. No doubt it is possible to formulate the required condition on semantic rules: scope-assignment rules may refer only to quantifiers, negation, etc. But it is obvious that this condition can be paraphrased in generative semantics terms: lowering rules may refer only to quantifiers, negation, etc. There is no need here to refer to the notions "syntactic rule" or "semantic rule."

There is every reason to conclude, then, that the particular theoretical apparatus of interpretive semantics is simply irrelevant to the task of restricting the class of possible grammars. While it is true, of course, that an elaborate conceptual structure is required in order to define what kinds of rules are allowed, this structure involves concepts like "coreference," "focus," "scope," etc., which are common to both generative and interpretive semantics. Nothing appears to be gained (or lost) by proposing a basic formal distinction between semantic and syntactic rules. Arguments based on theoretical power can lead to conclusions about what constraints are required on the content of grammars; but these arguments will not help settle formal questions such as those dividing generative and interpretive semantics.

3. It seems to us, then, that the wrong kinds of arguments have been used in the generative–interpretive debate. While the difference between generative and interpretive semantics lies in the form, or organization, which they stipulate for grammars, the arguments which we have examined all deal with the content, or substance, of grammars. Such arguments may force us to accept certain proposals concerning what grammars should or should not contain; but these proposals, as we have seen, can be accommodated within the organizational framework of either generative or interpretive semantics, with no difference in the descriptive, explanatory, or theory-restrictive consequences.

III. AN ARGUMENT BASED ON PERFORMANCE THEORY

1. J. D. Ringen (1975, pp. 9 ff.) points out that within the mentalist view of the subject matter of linguistics, there are two main positions: strong mentalism and weak mentalism. All mentalists agree that a grammar is intended to characterize the linguistic knowledge (competence) which underlies the use of language. But strong mentalists hold that a grammar should characterize the form as well as the substance (content) of linguistic competence, while weak mentalists require only that a grammar characterize the substance of competence. A strong mentalist making a claim about the form of grammars asserts the psychological reality of some formal feature of grammars. A weak mentalist making a claim about the form of grammars is not asserting anything about the psychological reality of any formal feature of grammars, but is (at most) asserting that grammars must possess some formal feature in order to correctly characterize the substance of linguistic competence. A strong mentalist claim about the form of grammars could be falsified by showing that the formal feature in question could not correspond to any psychologically real formal feature of competence. Evidence of this kind would have no bearing, however, on a weak mentalist claim about the form of grammars; such a claim could be falsified only by showing that grammars possessing the formal feature in question do not correctly characterize the substance of linguistic competence (because they are descriptively or explanatorily inadequate, or because they are not sufficiently restricted in power).

The generative-interpretive debate concerns the form of grammars. In section II, we examined some typical arguments from this debate and found that they did not actually bear on the formal issues that divide generative and interpretive semanticists. Since all the arguments we examined presented evidence of the weak mentalist type, their failure suggests that the generative-interpretive debate is not a weak mentalist controversy. It is worthwhile, then, to reconsider the debate from the strong mentalist point of view—that is, to regard generative semantics and interpretive semantics as making conflicting claims about the actual form of linguistic competence. This will, of course, require us to abandon the weak mentalist argumentation, which has heretofore been employed in the debate, and turn instead to strong mentalist argumentation.[7]

According to Ringen (1975, p. 13), "adopting a strong mentalist view would require a serious alliance with psychology and a serious concern with the construction and evaluation of theories of linguistic performance." It appears to us that arguments based on performance-model considerations can, in principle, resolve the generative–interpretive debate. Before proceeding to a demonstration of this, let us consider the conceptual foundations which would underlie such arguments.

2. A model of linguistic performance is an attempt to characterize the actual psychological processes involved in producing and comprehending utterances. In production, the input to the model is the semantic content which a speaker wishes to express, and the output is a specification of motor commands to the organs of articulation. In comprehension, the input is an acoustic waveform, and the output is a semantic content. For many purposes, it is convenient to ignore the differences between articulation and phonetic perception; we can then simply characterize the output of production, and the input to comprehension, as a phonetic representation. The goal of performance theory, then, is to characterize the processes by which speakers and hearers associate semantic and phonetic representations.

Since all normal human beings produce and comprehend utterances, it is reasonable to assume that the essential principles underlying these processes do not differ from individual to individual or from language to language. That is, the goal of performance theory is surely to find a *general* answer to the question, "How do people produce and comprehend utterances?" In this respect, a model of linguistic performance is conceptually parallel to models of memory retrieval, pattern recognition, and other such processes, which are formulated and tested by cognitive psychologists. These models aim at generality, in the sense that they are intended to characterize the respective processes independently of any particular memories, patterns, and so forth. It is quite true, of course, that different individuals will recall different things and recognize different patterns. It is not within the province of process models to account for such differences; rather, they are to be accounted for by the fact that different individuals, through their particular experiences, acquire different bodies of knowledge (cognitive structures) with which general cognitive processes interact. In the case of language, the fact that different individuals speak and understand different languages is not to be accounted for by formulating different performance models, but by assuming that there are different cognitive structures which interact with the general processes of producing and comprehending utterances. To a strong mentalist linguist, a grammar is simply a model of such a cognitive structure. From this perspective, it is a point of definition that grammars are employed in performance. Thus, as Fodor, Bever, and Garrett (1974, p. 21) put it, "the central question for psycholinguistics is: How does the speaker-hearer employ the knowledge of his language represented by a grammar to effect the encoding and decoding of speech?"

If strong mentalists are committed to the goal of discovering the actual form, as well as the content, of the cognitive structures called grammars, they cannot be indifferent to the interaction between grammar and performance. In the investigation of any complex form of behavior, the nature of the relevant cognitive processes and the forms of the cognitive structures with which they interact are assumed to have reciprocal implications. For example, one cannot formulate a model of the process of recall without being concerned with the form in which memories are stored, and vice versa. Some psychologists view memory as a file of traces of prior experience and view recall as a process of associating these traces with eliciting stimuli; others regard memory as a schema of dominant elements and regard recall as a process which reconstructs prior experience from the stored elements (Manis, 1971, p. 35). Clearly, there is a necessary relationship of compatibility between process and form: memories consisting only of schemata of dominant elements would be inadequate in terms of the association process, while memories consisting of traces of entire experiences would be redundant in terms of the reconstruction process. Similarly, the form of grammars and the nature of the performance processes which utilize them are intimately related matters and must be investigated concurrently. As an illustration, Clark and Haviland (1974, pp. 120–121), discussing the Complex NP Constraint as formulated by Ross (1967), show that the form of this constraint is compatible with only one of several conceivable models of the comprehension process; other comprehension models would require the constraint to be formulated in different ways. Thus, "the decision of which formulation of the constraint does fit into the process will require the use and testing of process models within linguistics."

By attending to the interaction between grammar and performance, it should be possible to investigate questions which go far beyond the formulation of particular constraints or rules. Bearing in mind that a theory of grammar, from the strong mentalist point of view, is a theory of the cognitive structures which are employed in linguistic performance, it is appropriate to ask the following: (1) What kind of performance model would be compatible with a given theory of grammar?[8] (2) What empirical predictions are made by such a performance model? (3) Are these predictions correct? If it should turn out that a particular theory of grammar is compatible only with a particular kind of performance model and the empirical predictions made by this kind of performance model are incorrect, we would have a strong mentalist argument against the associated theory of grammar. In the remainder of this paper, we present an argument of this type—a strong mentalist argument against interpretive semantics.

3. First let us consider the compatibility of the "analysis-by-synthesis" (ABS) model of performance, suggested in Katz and Postal (1964), with generative and interpretive theories of grammar.

In ABS, a sentence is comprehended in the following way. The input sentence is stored, and the grammar is used to generate (synthesize) candidate strings for matching with the input. Once a match has been achieved, the semantic interpretation of the generated string is determined, which completes the process of comprehension. The production of a sentence is carried out in a similar manner. The meaning which is to be expressed is stored, and the grammar generates candidate strings which then undergo semantic interpretation; once a match with the stored meaning has been achieved, the sentence is produced.

It is easy to see that generative semantics is incompatible with ABS. Since the synthesis of candidate strings is supposed to be carried out without any reference to meaning, any grammar employed in an ABS model must have a means of specifying an infinite set of abstract syntactic structures; this is precisely the function of the phrase structure rules of interpretive semantics, which generative semantics lacks. Furthermore, the generation of candidate strings will involve the insertion of lexical items, again without reference to meaning; but the lexical insertion rules in generative semantics are stated in terms of the correspondence between the meaning and the form of lexical items and are thus inappropriate to the ABS model. Finally, ABS requires the separate functioning of syntactic and semantic rules, implying a division of the grammar into the corresponding components; again, generative semantics is inappropriate, because it does not distinguish between syntactic and semantic rules. In short, ABS requires access to a grammar organized in a particular way, and generative semantics grammars are manifestly *not* organized in that way. If, then, ABS should turn out to be the most plausible performance model, generative semantics would be correspondingly implausible as a model of competence.

Interpretive semantics, unlike generative semantics, is quite compatible with ABS. As we have seen, ABS requires grammars which have the means to specify an infinite set of syntactic structures filled with lexical items, without reference to meaning; it also requires that the rules for semantic interpretation be employed exclusively during a particular stage in the production and comprehension processes. The phrase structure rules, lexical insertion rules, and distinct semantic component of interpretive semantics are therefore *necessary*, from the viewpoint of an ABS model.

Furthermore, it seems to us that ABS is the *only* performance model which makes any motivated use of the phrase structure component, lexical insertion rules, and semantic–syntactic distinction found in interpretive semantics. To see this, let us consider how a non-ABS performance model would employ an interpretive semantics grammar. In the production process, the input to the model is a semantic representation. If there is no synthesis of candidate strings for interpretation and matching with the input, then the only other logically possible assumption is that the syntactic and lexical properties of the sentence which is to be produced are determined with reference to the semantic input, in accordance with the rules of the grammar.

Thus, with respect to lexical content, the production process involves consulting the grammar to determine the phonological shapes and syntactic properties of the lexical items which correspond to the semantic properties of the input. In interpretive semantics, these correspondences are stated within the lexical entries themselves (see Section II.1). Since all the information needed to determine the lexical content of a sentence is given in the lexical entries, there does not appear to be any need for the interpretive semantics lexical insertion rules, which insert lexical items freely under category symbols. In other words, these lexical insertion rules would never be consulted, in a non-ABS production model.

Another part of the production process is to determine the grammatical relations which correspond to the functional structure (thematic relations) of the semantic input. In interpretive semantics, there are functional structure rules which state these correspondences (Jackendoff, 1972, p. 378). By consulting these rules, together with the lexical entries, a non-ABS production model would be able to determine the appropriate abstract (deep) syntactic structure corresponding to a semantic input. Since this would be done without consulting the phrase structure rules, the phrase structure component of interpretive semantics seems to have no role to play in a non-ABS production model.

Furthermore, in a non-ABS production model, various aspects of the surface structure would be determined by consulting the surface interpretation rules, which state correspondences between certain features of semantic structure and certain features of surface structure, and by consulting the transformations, which relate abstract syntactic structures to surface structures. Notice that in these phases of the production process, as well as in the others discussed above, there is no need to refer to the distinction between syntactic and semantic rules. The type of rule which is consulted at each stage is determined intrinsically: at the first stage, when nothing has yet been determined concerning the sentence to be produced, the only rules which are relevant are those which refer to the semantic level; after the abstract syntactic structure has been determined, the transformations are relevant, since they refer to that level. Nothing in the non-ABS production of a sentence would depend on the notion that some rules are syntactic while others are semantic.

It appears to us, then, that interpretive semantics is logically incompatible with a non-ABS production model, in that interpretive semantics claims that grammars have certain formal properties which have no motivation from the non-ABS point of view. As for a non-ABS comprehension model, the situation is the same. The abstract grammatical relations of a sentence would have to be determined by consulting the transformations; the complete semantic interpretation would be determined by consulting the surface interpretation rules, lexical entries, and functional structure rules. As in production, there would be no part of this process in which the phrase structure component or the lexical insertion rules would have to be consulted, and the type of rule used at each stage would be intrinsically determined, with no special significance attached to the semantic-syntactic distinction.

Generative semantics grammars, on the other hand, would be entirely appropriate for use by a non-ABS performance model. The various types of rules which such a model would have to consult all have their analogues in generative semantics; furthermore, generative semantics lacks the additional apparatus which we have seen to be superfluous from the viewpoint of a non-ABS model.

If generative semantics is incompatible with ABS, while interpretive semantics is compatible *only* with ABS—as we have tried to show—then the generative–interpretive debate, as a strong mentalist issue, hinges on the question of whether or not ABS is accepted as the most plausible model of linguistic performance. We now discuss some rather compelling reasons for concluding that ABS is not, in fact, a plausible performance model.

4. The main drawback of ABS is pointed out by Greene (1972, p. 143):

[T]he whole analysis-by-synthesis notion is in itself highly counter-intuitive. The idea that a person arrives at a match either for "what he wants to say" or for a sequence of incoming sounds by allowing his knowledge of syntactic rules to start generating strings at random would obviously be wildly uneconomical. When one thinks of all the possible words that might be inserted from the lexicon, it would clearly take an unmanageable amount of time before the correct matching string happened to be produced.

Fodor, Bever, and Garrett (1974, p. 317), citing Miller's calculation that the number of twenty-word sentences in English is of the order of the number of seconds in the lifetime of the universe, state that "it is obviously impossible that the recognition of any given twenty-word sentence involves searching a space of that many derivations." They conclude that "some heuristics will need to be employed to drastically reduce the size of the space to be searched."

What would such heuristics be like? Consider the question of how lexical items are comprehended. In ABS, lexical items are inserted randomly during the synthesis process, then compared with the input; once a phonological match is found, the semantic properties of the inserted lexical item are incorporated in the interpretation of the sentence. Clearly, this implies that the comprehension of a lexical item takes a random amount of time—an implication which, as far as we know, is empirically unsupported.[9] A heuristic for eliminating the random search through the lexicon is clearly called for. The only conceivable form for this heuristic to take would be something like: search the lexicon for lexical items whose phonological properties agree with the input, then read their semantic properties into the interpretation of the sentence. But this is entirely analogous to simply consulting the lexicon, as would be done in a non-ABS model. Adopting this heuristic thus amounts to abandoning part of the synthesis process—namely, lexical insertion. To take another example: in producing a sentence, ABS assumes that the grammatical relations necessary to encode the functional structure of the input would be determined by randomly synthesizing abstract syntactic structures (via the phrase structure rules), interpreting them, and comparing the result with the input. To eliminate the implausible randomness of this procedure, we would need a heuristic which could constrain the synthesis process in such a way that it would produce only a syntactic structure which embodied the correct grammatical relations,

given the functional structure of the input. But this is tanta-
mount to consulting the functional structure rules, as would be
done in a non-ABS model. There would then be no need to
synthesize anything via the phrase structure component.

We have seen that ABS is empirically inadequate unless
heuristics are added to the model. Adding these heuristics,
however, renders the synthesis process redundant, and results in
a non-ABS model. As Fodor, Bever, and Garrett put it (1974, p.
393); "[As] these heuristics become more sophisticated, the
importance of the synthesis loop becomes less clear. With
production as with recognition, the limit of such elaborations on
ABS models is a straight-through heuristic system."[10]

From these considerations, we conclude that ABS is not a
plausible model of performance and that interpretive semantics,
being compatible only with ABS, is consequently an implausible
model of grammar. Generative semantics therefore appears to be
preferable, since it differs from interpretive semantics in precisely those formal characteristics which led us to associate the
latter with ABS.

IV. SUMMARY AND CONCLUSIONS

We have tried to make the following points:

1. Generative semantics and interpretive semantics make different claims about the form of grammars; thus, they differ on
   the level of strong mentalism.
2. Nevertheless, the generative–interpretive debate has consisted
   of weak mentalist arguments dealing with the content of
   grammars. The debate has therefore been inconclusive.
3. Performance model considerations are relevant to strong
   mentalist arguments about the form of grammars.
4. Interpretive semantics is compatible only with analysis-by-
   synthesis (ABS), while generative semantics is compatible
   with non-ABS performance models.
5. ABS is empirically inadequate; its inadequacies cannot be
   remedied without converting it into a non-ABS model.
6. Therefore, from the strong mentalist viewpoint, performance-
   model considerations resolve the generative–interpretive
   debate in favor of generative semantics.

We would also like to point out several conclusions which do *not* follow from the arguments we have set forth:

1. It has not been shown that generative semantics, as it stands, is compatible with an adequate performance model. No adequate performance model has yet been developed, to our knowledge. The strongest conclusion that can be drawn from our argument is that, whatever theory of grammar may ultimately be found compatible with an adequate performance model, it will resemble generative semantics rather than interpretive semantics, with respect to the formal properties outlined in Section II.1.
2. The possibility of strong mentalist arguments in favor of interpretive semantics has not been precluded. It is conceivable that grammars are *acquired* in a way more compatible with interpretive semantics, even though they are *employed* in a way more compatible with generative semantics.
3. It has not been shown that interpretive semantics is an inadequate theory for the exploration of weak mentalist questions, or that weak mentalist investigations are of no value. To the contrary, such work as Jackendoff's (1972) demonstrates that interesting and important contributions can be made within the interpretive semantics framework.

Finally, let us recall that our purpose has not been to settle the generative-interpretive debate but rather to show that strong mentalist argumentation will be necessary if it is to be settled. We would further suggest that this approach will be required for the resolution of many other serious disputes in linguistic theory.

NOTES

1. The lack of "appropriate conditions of evidence" and "clear, well-understood standards of acceptability" renders linguistic controversies inconclusive because linguists frequently reject the evidence on which other linguists' arguments are based and/or disagree as to what constitutes independent motivation, explanation, and so forth. See Botha (1973) for discussion.
2. Strong and weak mentalism are distinguished by the degree of psychological reality which they impute to grammars. A strong mentalist

position is that a grammar should represent the form as well as the content of a speaker's linguistic knowledge, while a weak mentalist position is that a grammar should represent the content, but not necessarily the form, of linguistic knowledge (Ringen, 1975, p. 10). The relevance of these concepts to our discussion is made clear in Section III.

3. Neither generative semantics nor interpretive semantics is a monolithic theory; nevertheless, it is possible to identify crucial points which are diagnostic of each. In comparing the two theories, we rely primarily on the formulations in Lakoff, 1971 (generative semantics) and Jackendoff, 1972 (interpretive semantics).

4. The two theories have been contrasted in various other ways, but these are not relevant to our concerns. For example, Katz and Bever (1974) argue that generative semanticists are "attacking" the distinction between grammaticality and ungrammaticality; but it is clear from their discussion that this attack cannot be regarded as an automatic consequence of the formal assumptions of generative semantics, and there is no apparent reason why interpretive semanticists could not mount a parallel attack, if they should choose to do so.

5. The K-initial structure in the standard theory is defined as the deep structure minus lexical items (Chomsky, 1972c, p. 65).

6. We omit here one of Chomsky's points: that derived nominals "fall under a simple phrase structure schema that applies as well to verb and adjective phrases." This statement is difficult to evaluate, in view of the fact that this schema depends on two positional categories— complement and specifier—which appear to be abbreviations for various types of constituents rather than constituents in their own right, and whose precise natures vary according to the lexical category of the head of the phrase. It is thus not clear what is claimed by the schema, which seems equivalent to a partial conflation of several distinct phrase structure rules. See Jackendoff (1974) for an illuminating discussion of these questions.

7. We wish to thank Jon Ringen for discussing with us the concepts of strong and weak mentalism. However, we alone are responsible for the way in which these terms are construed and applied in this chapter.

8. That is, given a particular theory specifying the formal properties of grammars, what kind of performance model would require that grammars be organized in the specified way?

9. The ABS procedure for comprehending lexical items also seems to imply that the phonological and semantic identification of a lexical item is a unitary event (since a lexical item, i.e., a semantic-phonological correspondence, is supposedly identified as a whole only when a match has been found between the phonological properties of a lexical item in a synthesized string and the phonological properties of a corresponding portion of the input). There is evidence, however, that phonological identification and semantic identification are separate events, with phonological identification occurring prior to semantic

identification: it has been found in word-association experiments that subjects can respond to a stimulus word with a phonological association more quickly than with a semantic association (Clark, 1970, pp. 272–273).

10. As another example of the problems which accompany attempts to enrich ABS by adding heuristics, consider the following heuristic proposed by Katz and Postal (1964, p. 167). Since it is obviously impossible that the comprehension of a sentence involves a completely random search through the infinite set of well-formed syntactic strings, it is suggested that only those strings which are equal in length to the input would be synthesized. But the entire input must be available before this heuristic can be employed. This would seem to predict that the comprehension of a sentence cannot begin until the entire sentence has been heard, which is clearly false. The heuristic might be refined in such a way that synthesis begins as soon as input begins to be received, with the length of the synthesized strings keeping pace with the length of the input. This would effectively put the synthesis process under the control of the input rather than of the grammar. Combining this with other necessary heuristics which utilize various other properties of the input (e.g., phonological properties) to constrain synthesis, the synthesis process seems to amount to nothing more than a transcription of the results of the heuristics. As far as we can see, this would be equivalent to a non-ABS system.

REFERENCES

Botha, R. P. (1973) *The Justification of Linguistic Hypotheses.* The Hague: Mouton.

Chomsky, N. (1965) *Aspects of the Theory of Syntax.* Cambridge, Mass.: M.I.T. Press.

_____ (1972a) *Studies on Semantics in Generative Grammar.* The Hague: Mouton.

_____ (1972b) "Remarks on nominalization," in N. Chomsky (1972a), pp. 11–61.

_____ (1972c) "Deep structure, surface structure, and semantic interpretation," in N. Chomsky (1972a), pp. 62–119.

_____ (1972d) "Some empirical issues in the theory of transformational grammar," in N. Chomsky (1972a), pp. 120–202.

Clark, H. H. (1970) "Word associations and linguistic theory," in J. Lyons (ed.), *New Horizons in Linguistics,* pp. 271–286. Baltimore: Penguin.

_____, and S. E. Haviland (1974) "Psychological processes as linguistic explanation," in D. Cohen (ed.), *Explaining Linguistic Phenomena,* pp. 91–124. Washington, D.C.: Hemisphere.

Fodor, J. A., T. G. Bever and M. F. Garrett (1974) *The Psychology of Language.* New York: McGraw-Hill.

Greene, J. (1972) *Psycholinguistics.* Baltimore: Penguin.

Jackendoff, R. S. (1972) *Semantic Interpretation in Generative Grammar.* Cambridge, Mass.: M.I.T. Press.

_____ (1974) "Introduction to the $\overline{\text{X}}$ convention." Bloomington: Indiana University Linguistics Club mimeograph.

Karttunen, L. (1971) "Definite descriptions with crossing coreference." *Foundations of Language* 7:157–182.

Katz, J. J., and T. G. Bever (1974) "The fall and rise of empiricism." Bloomington: Indiana University Linguistics Club mimeograph.

_____ and P. M. Postal (1964) *An Integrated Theory of Linguistic Descriptions.* Cambridge, Mass.: M.I.T. Press.

Kuroda, S.-Y. (1971) "Two remarks on pronominalization." *Foundations of Language* 7:183–198.

Lakoff, G. (1971) "On generative semantics," in D. D. Steinberg and L. Jakobovits (eds.), *Semantics: An Interdisciplinary Reader in Philosophy, Linguistics, and Psychology*, pp. 232–296. New York: Cambridge University Press.

Manis, M. (1971) *An Introduction to Cognitive Psychology.* Belmont, Calif.: Brooks/Cole.

McCawley, J. D. (1968) "The role of semantics in a grammar," in E. Bach and R. H. Harms (eds.), *Universals in Linguistic Theory*, pp. 125–170. New York: Holt, Rinehart & Winston.

Ringen, J. D. (1975) "Linguistic facts: A study of the empirical scientific status of transformational generative grammars," in D. Cohen and J. R. Wirth (eds.), *Testing Linguistic Hypotheses*, pp. 1–42. Washington, D.C.: Hemisphere.

Ross, J. R. (1967) "Constraints on variables in syntax." Doctoral dissertation, Cambridge, Mass.: M.I.T. Bloomington: Indiana University Linguistics Club mimeograph (1968).

9
What the theorist saw

Myrna Gopnik
McGill University

I. INTRODUCTION

In this chapter I would like to look at some different ways in which empirical research about language is carried out and to suggest a way in which these different approaches may be related. In particular I would like to look at the way empirical evidence from fields allied to linguistics, for example, sociolinguistics, psycholinguistics, and computational linguistics, interacts with the work in what we may call "pure" linguistics.[1] For convenience and brevity I will draw most of my examples from sociolinguistics, but the analysis is equally applicable to other allied fields.

The work going on in linguistics today is not all being done in terms of one unified theory of language. There is a great diversity in the kinds of assumptions and evidence which different workers in the discipline feel are relevant to their work. If the work in linguistics is not unified by a single theory, then we can ask what kind of unity it does have. In a sense this

217

is a question about the sociology of knowledge more than about the logical structure of knowledge. The two concepts, however, are not entirely separable. For example, Kuhn in his *The Structure of Scientific Revolutions* (1962) investigates some of the ways the social organization of scientific communities interacts with the change and growth of theories; and Popper (1963), in his concern with the growth of knowledge by means of conjectures and refutations, deals with the ways in which different theories interact to produce new theories. What I want to do in this chapter is look at the ways some of these interactions take place in linguistics. Obviously not all the factors which go into such interrelationships can be discussed in one chapter. The particular focus of this chapter will be how different theories are delimited by the kinds of simplifications of data which they find appropriate and necessary. In addition to this, I will look at the ways in which various differences of this kind can affect the growth of a theory of language.

II. SOME REFLECTIONS ON THE PRESENT STATE

A theory is a well-defined formal object[2] that exhibits particular properties in the way statements within it are constructed and related, and the way these statements relate to states in the world. A discipline, like linguistics, is not a formal object in the same sense as a theory is. It is not delimited by the formal properties of the statements made within it, but rather by the set of empirical objects with which it concerns itself.[3] What unites people within a particular discipline is the identity or at least partial overlap of the empirical phenomena they are trying to explain. In those cases where a single theory is universally accepted by all the members of a discipline this distinction between a study of the set of rules accounting for the phenomena and the empirical phenomena itself is often blurred. For example, the discipline of genetics has become synonymous with descriptions in terms of DNA and RNA. In subatomic physics, however, this is not the case. The discipline is defined by an interest in accounting for a constantly growing and baffling set of phenomena that regularly spawns new parameters and new theories to go with them.

Linguistics seems at the moment to be somewhere in between. The problem is not so much the discovery of new data, as it is in subatomic physics, but rather the reanalysis of well-known data in terms of a complete and coherent theory. There is little agreement at the moment in the discipline as to whether or not such a theory exists. Proponents of transformational generative grammar (TGG) behave as if such a disciplinary matrix does exist. They match Kuhn's[4] description of intraparadigmatic behavior by having well-defined small and specific problems to solve and well-defined modes of argument and explanation in which to couch their answers. They form a cohesive group and refer to other work within the paradigm.

However, though workers within this disciplinary matrix have great confidence in their theory, and their work within it, it is by no means a universally accepted theory. Botha, for example, seriously questions the validity of the modes of argument and explanation which are employed. After listing a number of specific problems, he concludes:

> It is evident that unless the negative metascientific properties of transformationalist acceptability standards are dealt with as outlined above, the chances that crucial intra-paradigmatic controversies will be settled in a rational manner at the level of acceptability will remain remote. In particular, it is unclear how the generative semantics vs. interpretive semantics controversy could be settled in a reasoned manner at this level if the acceptability standards whose key concepts/distinctions are "empirical" vs. "notational", "restricted descriptive latitude", "conceptual homogeneity", and "independent motivation" were to retain their unfavourable metascientific characteristics. (1973, p. 323)

Derwing objects to the theory on these and other grounds. In *Transformational Grammar as a Theory of Language Acquisition*, he questions both the methodological and the empirical soundness of the theory:

> Chomsky is not only unable to justify this notion of linguistic "competence" as the "psychological" interpretation belatedly attached to his formal notion of a generative grammar; he is also unable to justify the choice of one version of such a model over any other. This problem has arisen, I have argued, primarily because competence models have been so constructed that only data related

to the introspective reports of speakers have any direct bearing on them. And this situation, in turn, has arisen from Chomsky's own basic unwillingness to break away from the Bloomfieldian tradition, which dealt only in facts related to the speech output and refused to take into account evidence from the domain of psychology. The linguists' tenacious attachment to "competence" models of the Chomskyan sort can therefore best be explained in terms of a long-standing (and still continuing) search for a useful descriptive system for the facts of speech and no more than this. But if the Chomskyan dream of explaining language use is ever to be realized, we linguists are eventually going to have to learn to play some new tunes. As Hill has said, Chomsky's task is indeed a "dazzling" one, yet "at present one can only say that its very recognition is the chief step so far taken towards achieving it." (1973)

Besides these explicit metatheoretic objections to the theory of transformational grammar there is abundant evidence of tacit nonacceptance of it in the actual work linguists do. For example, if we look at the journal *Language* we see that very much of the work being done is not on the kinds of problems and solutions delimited by this disciplinary matrix.

Of course TGG is not the only disciplinary matrix at the moment in linguistics. There are other more or less well-defined groups working within linguistics—from Harris' transformational group to Lamb's stratificational group. No one of these paradigms, however, has universal or even widespread acceptance. Once we realize that this paradigmatic diversity exists we are naturally lead to ask how these different paradigms interact.

If these modes of interaction can be made explicit, then certain aspects of interparadigmatic conflict[5] may be clarified. In particular, we can hope that once the grounds of these conflicts are made explicit, then the ways in which the conflicts can be resolved will become clearer.

III. METATHEORETIC FRAMEWORK

In order to discuss the ways in which various current theories about language are related it is necessary first to develop a set of concepts about theories and theory building in general. There is a vast body of work in the philosophy of science which is pertinent to this problem, but, of course, I cannot go over all that here. I will therefore try to restrict this section of the paper to a brief and simple statement of the fundamental concepts which I need to discuss some of the ways in which different linguistic theories are related. This, of course, necessitates over-simplifying or neglecting entirely serious problems in the philosophy of science, but that seems unavoidable.

The problem of integrating several different kinds of data in order to provide an explanation for some phenomenon is not peculiar to linguistics. It is a problem for all empirical inquiry. What I would like to do in this part of the paper is to provide a model for empirical inquiry which would account for different kinds of data and would show how these different kinds of data are related to each other. In particular, what I would like to discuss is how every theory separates data into three different classes and, further, how these different classes of data function quite differently in the construction of an explanation. The model I will present works for all empirical explanations—linguistics as well as physics. I hope that viewing the construction of theories of linguistics by means of this analysis will make clear and explicit the way in which sociolinguistic theories, for example, interact with "pure" linguistic theories.

IV. DIFFERENTIATING AMONG DATA
OF DIFFERENT KINDS

The first thing to get clear is why and how data about a particular event are divided into different classes. As a first approximation let's say that the aim of any empirical theorist is to be able to explain a given set of events by means of an explicit set of rules (laws). As Nagel puts it:

It is the desire for explanations which are at once systematic and controllable by factual evidence that generates science; and it is the organization and classification of knowledge on the basis of explanatory principles that is the distinctive goal of the sciences. More specifically, the sciences seek to discover and to formulate in general terms the conditions under which events of various sorts occur, the statements of such determining conditions being the explanations of the corresponding happenings. This goal can be achieved only by distinguishing or isolating certain properties in the subject matter studied and by ascertaining the repeatable patterns of dependence in which these properties stand to one another. In consequence, when the inquiry is successful, propositions that hitherto appeared to be quite unrelated are exhibited as linked to each other in determinate ways by virtue of their place in a system of explanations. (1961, p. 4)

The first problem we face is that the world doesn't present itself in neatly parceled-out objects; the question is how we distinguish and isolate the properties of the phenomenon which we are looking at. Language, as most other empirical phenomena, is first of all continuous in time. In order to study any empirical object, we must first of all isolate separate phenomena from this continuous stream. Temporal continuity is usually resolvable by some arbitrary boundaries being established. The more difficult problem, however, is to decide which aspects of the object thus isolated are important to the explanation of the object, which are inconsequential, and which are totally extraneous. There is, of course, no *principled* way to select the important aspects as opposed to the unimportant aspects of an object. Choices of this kind are an essential first step in any investigation, but rules for the selection of the important aspects of an event cannot be constructed. The choices are a result of the intuition and experience of the investigator.[6]

All theories about language must isolate certain aspects of linguistic objects to pay attention to and must ignore other aspects as unimportant. Theories of language, of course, can differ from one another in which aspects they choose to look at and which they choose to ignore. But the story is more complex than a simple dichotomy between important and unimportant aspects. In empirical theories the various aspects of a complex event are usually divided into at least three classes:

1. Those aspects of the event which are crucial to the explanation of the event
2. Those aspects of the event which may have some role in the explanation of the event but which have only a peripheral effect
3. Those aspects of the event which have no role at all in the explanation of the event

For a linguistic object an example of the first class might be the actual sequence of sounds, an example of the second class might be the place of residence of the speaker, an example of the third class might be the weight of the speaker.[7]

This three-way division is purely a theoretical construct; there is nothing in the nature of the data itself that suggests the boundaries between the different classes. Moreover, the division between class 2 parameters and class 3 parameters is very fuzzy. It might be more accurate to think of class 2 and class three parameters as a single class in which kinds of data are ranked as to the extent of their effect on the phenomena to be described. For the purposes of the proposed model this difference in formulation makes no difference, and since it is more convenient to refer to two discrete classes we shall use the first formulation.

The starting point for the construction of any theory is determining the aspects of the object which are felt by the investigator to be crucial to the explanation/description of the object. It is these aspects which become the formal parameters upon which the rules of the theory are defined. Another way of looking at this is to say that the first stage in the construction of any empirical theory is to abstract from the data a set of objects idealized in a particular way. The theory must be constructed so that it accounts for the relationships among such idealized objects by means of explicit rules. Of course, not all the properties of the object need be accounted for by the rules. In particular, there will be a class of effects caused by class 2 parameters which will be ignored. To be judged successful, the theory must account for all and only properties of the object caused by class 1 parameters.[8]

For the purpose of constructing a theory the experimenter must specify the idealization of the data he is going to account for. This step specifies the parameters which will occur in his rules. But, in fact, when he specifies the idealization he is going to account for he usually does much more. The statement of the idealization not only specifies which parameters are going to be considered but also usually lists some aspects of the event which will not be accounted for. These aspects are what we have called class 2 parameters, data which have only a marginal effect on the phenomena under examination. For example, in *Aspects*

Chomsky specifies the idealization which he will be working under by saying:

> Linguistic theory is concerned primarily with an ideal speaker-listener, in a completely homogeneous speech-community, who knows its language perfectly and is unaffected by such grammatically irrelevant conditions as memory limitations, distractions, shifts of attention and interest, and errors (random or characteristic) in applying his knowledge of the language in actual performance. This seems to me to have been the position of the founders of modern general linguistics, and no cogent reason for modifying it has been offered. To study actual linguistic performance, we must consider the interaction of a variety of factors, of which the underlying competence of the speaker-hearer is only one. In this respect, study of language is no different from empirical investigation of other complex phenomena. (1965, pp. 3–4)

What Chomsky is doing here is listing those aspects of the data which he is not going to worry about. He will not have parameters in his rules which range over such variables as memory limitations or nonhomogeneous speech communities. On the other hand it is clear that he believes that these parameters have an effect on the data. As he says,

> Only under the idealization set forth in the preceding paragraph is performance a direct reflection of competence. In actual fact, it obviously could not directly reflect competence. A record of natural speech will show numerous false starts, deviations from rules, changes of plan in mid-course, and so on. (1965, p. 4)

In this context "performance" is described as "the actual use of language in concrete situations." That is, it is the full range of unidealized data which confronts the linguist. Of course, it is not really accurate to say that the data is totally unidealized. Any description of the data of experience must necessarily use some abstract categories, and these categories are necessarily theoretical entities, not perceptual entities. Therefore, every description has some level of idealization. Popper, for example, in discussing the empirical basis of science points out that

> We can utter no scientific statement that does not go far beyond what can be known with certainty "on the basis of immediate experience." (This fact may be referred to as the "transcendence inherent in any description.") Every description uses universal names

(or symbols, or ideas); every statement has the character of a theory, of a hypothesis. The statement, "Here is a glass of water" cannot be verified by any observational experience. The reason is that the universals which appear in it cannot be correlated with any specific sense-experience. (An "immediate experience" is only once "immediately given"; it is unique.) By the word "glass," for example, we denote physical bodies which exhibit a certain law-like behaviour, and the same holds for the word "water." Universals cannot be reduced to classes of experiences; they cannot be "constituted." (1968, pp. 94–95)

In the description which Chomsky gives of "performance" in the passage from *Aspects,* we find theoretical terms like "language" and "concrete situation"; so, in fact, some idealization of the data is assumed. It is important to see that no linguistic theory can deal directly with the empirical data. All descriptive statements are idealizations at some level or other. The point of this chapter is to see how these levels interact.

It's not at all clear from the way Chomsky uses "performance" here just what level of idealization is intended. I think it is safe to assume that all of the aspects of the data which he lists specifically as "grammatically irrelevant" are to be accounted for under "performance." But whether the idealization that performance is to account for is *defined* by this list or whether it is just a kind of wastebasket for anything anyone wants to put in it is unclear. What is clear is that a theory of performance will have rules which range over different parameters than those which occur in the rules Chomsky is interested in constructing. Furthermore, Chomsky suggests that some of the parameters which will occur in such a theory are memory limitations, nonhomogeneous speech communities, etc. In terms of the distinctions made earlier in this chapter, a theory of performance will range over what is for Chomsky class 2 parameters.

Competence, on the other hand, will have class 1 parameters. That is, competence is to be accounted for by rules over parameters which are "grammatically relevant." Deciding which parameters are in fact grammatically relevant is not done by any formal set of criteria. It is done by hunches and intuitions. Chomsky says that competence is "the speaker-hearer's knowledge of his language" (1965, p. 4). It is this "competence" which the linguist must account for. "Competence" in this context can be interpreted in at least two ways:

1. As a definition. That is, "competence" and "the speaker-hearer's knowledge of his language" are definitionally equivalent. Therefore, when the rules over the class 1 parameters are developed, they will account for competence and thereby for its definitional equivalent, the speaker-hearer's knowledge of his language.
2. As an empirical hypothesis. Competence in this case is the set of rules over class 1 parameters (or maybe the output of these rules; this distinction seems unclear in Chomsky here). In this case the speaker-hearer's knowledge of his language is not definitionally equivalent to competence but is rather accounted for by some other set of rules over some other set of empirically determined parameters. The hypothesis in this case is that these two empirically independently determined concepts will turn out to be equivalent in some way.

For the purposes of this chapter, to see how theories of language are interrelated, the distinction between these two interpretations is important and will be discussed in a later section.

In order to develop a model for the interaction of various linguistic theories, what is important at this point is to see that someone constructing any empirical theory must arbitrarily choose some parameters as relevant for accounting for the phenomena in question. Other parameters are dismissed as irrelevant. But these irrelevant parameters are not in fact totally irrelevant. They are not the factors which are presumed to have *no* effect on the phenomena. They are the parameters which are presumed to have *some* effect, though not a crucial effect.

Of course, one of the ways science changes significantly is when parameters shift from one class to another. A nice example of this, perhaps apocryphal, is the experimenter who moved from Columbia to the University of Chicago taking all his experimental worms with him. Unfortunately, they wouldn't behave in Chicago the way they did in New York. What he found out was that what he thought was a class 3 parameter was really a class 1 parameter. The worms were sensitive to the magnetic field of the earth, a parameter which the experimenter had assumed to be totally irrelevant. This change of a class 3 parameter to a class 1 parameter only locally changed biological theory. However, revolutionary changes in scientific theories have also come about through such changes. The change from Newtonian to Einsteinian physics is certainly the most notable of such cases. For Newton the behavior of physical systems could be accounted for independently of any parameters about the observer system; for Einstein parameters about the observer system were crucially necessary in order to account for physical systems.[9] In linguistics the change from structuralist theories to transformational generative theories involved, among other things, such a shift in parameters. The parameters in the structuralist rules ranged over certain kinds of directly observable, empirically given linguistic sequences; the parameters in the rules of the transformationalist were in addition allowed to range over abstract categories of nondirectly observable entities.[10]

While this historical effect of the status of parameters is very interesting in itself, I am more concerned in this particular chapter with a view of the relationship of various contemporaneous linguistic theories. In order to understand the interaction among various theories, the picture of how an individual theory chooses among parameters which has been developed so far in this chapter must be supplemented with a broader picture of the kinds of explanations and levels of empirical verification which such theories provide.

V. LEVELS OF VERIFICATION

Every scientific theory must, at some point, match the descriptions which are generated by its rules to some empirically determined objects. If the descriptions match the empirical objects then, informally speaking,[11] the theory is partially confirmed. If, on the other hand, the descriptions do not match the empirical objects, then the theory is falsified. This mechanism of testing hypotheses embodied in rules against some empirically given data is the essential step in any scientific theory. In discussing the problems of verification/falsification,

Scheffler says:

> Accounts which are cognitively significant may be worth entertaining and worth examining for truth on their merits, for they are, in fact, either true or false. Empirically significant accounts, in particular, fall in the province of empirical science, for they are not only in fact true or false, but their truth or falsehood is not decidable by reference to their forms or meanings alone; observation is required in addition. On the other hand, accounts which are not analytically true or false, and also not empirically significant, are surely not worth entertaining in science. For, being neither true nor false, they are surely not true, and so cannot possibly serve as explanations at all. (1963, p. 128)

A theory with simple, elegant, and interesting rules which are not testable is not a scientific theory. It may be a superbly worked-out formal system, but it is not a scientific theory.

While it may be reasonably straightforward to state that a theory must be testable and tested, it is not easy to describe how decisions of such tests are to be determined. If you remember that the rules of any theory are defined on idealized objects, the problem becomes clear. The descriptions generated by the rules are descriptions of idealized objects. However, idealized objects are not given empirically. They are theoretical constructs. What are given empirically are real objects. One of the problems of testing is to decide when a description of an idealized object matches a real object. This obviously is no easy or straightforward task.

Moreover, the methods by which such tests should be made is itself dependent on the theory involved. There are at least three different ways in which characteristics of the theory affect the kinds of tests which it is subjected to. In the first place the choice of class 1 parameters selects the aspects of empirical data which must be subjected to tests. In addition to this effect of theoretical choices focusing on particular aspects of the empirical data, theoretical assumptions also affect the kinds of tests which are appropriate. For example, Chomsky assumes that judgments of grammaticality are part of the overt knowledge of the speaker, therefore for him direct interrogation about grammaticality is an appropriate testing methodology. On the other hand, Labov in discussing the relationship between his work on hypercorrection in New York and Gumperz' work in Norway, says:

> The values that are covert in Norway are overt here, and vice versa. We must assume that people in New York City want to talk as they do, yet this fact is not at all obvious in any overt response that you can draw from interview subjects. I think that we can tap the more covert subjective responses by different types of subjective response tests by using various ingenious devices. We can, for example, investigate the possibility that a social value of masculinity is attributed to the casual style of working class speech in New York City. (1966, p. 108)

The third way in which theoretical assumptions affect tests of that theory is that the number and extent of the expected effects of class 2 parameters determines how close an empirical fit is required for a test to count as a positive instance. In other words every prediction based on a set of rules on idealized objects will have a certain degree of empirical "give." The prediction will be considered accurate if it falls within a given range. The degree of this looseness of fit will depend, at least in part,[12] on the kind and number of peripheral effects (class 2 parameters) which are being ignored. If a large number of peripheral effects are being ignored for the sake of the idealization, then a prediction which even loosely fits the empirical data will be counted as a positive confirming instance for the theory. The difference between the predicted values and the actually occurring values will be attributed to the effect of the class 2 parameters. In physics, for example, deviations from expected predictions about moving bodies are attributed to parameters like air resistance, which are ignored in the formulation of the rules which apply to bodies moving in a vacuum. For example, very early on Galileo in *Dialogues Concerning Two New Sciences* observed:

> Thus if we consider only the resistance which the air offers to the motions studied by us, we shall see that it disturbs them all and disturbs them in an infinite variety of ways corresponding to the infinite variety in the form, weight, and velocity of the projectiles. . . . Of these properties of weight, of velocity and also of form, infinite in number, it is not possible to give any exact description; hence, in order to handle this matter in a scientific way, it is necessary to cut loose from these difficulties; and having discovered

and demonstrated the theorems, in the case of no resistance, to use
them and apply them with such limitations as experience will teach.
(Kahl, 1963, p. 66)

If the empirical fit is too loose to be attributed to the
postulated class 2 parameters, then either the rules within the
theory must be wrong and the empirical data in question must
be regarded as a falsifying instance[13] or there must be another
class 2 parameter which has an effect on the data and which has
not been taken into account by the theory. Labov, for example,
uses this second kind of argument in evaluating some of his data
about hypercorrection in New York:

> The usefulness of the Index of Linguistic Insecurity is that it gives us
> an independent measure of the same kind of behavior: to recognition
> of a standard of correctness different from one's own speech. The
> value of this index was shown quite clearly in the case of one man, a
> plumber ... the plumber that I mentioned didn't show this kind of
> behavior, and so it is possible that his index score shouldn't be
> lumped together with those of most lower middle class subjects. I
> may have two separate kinds of behavior classed as one. (1966, p.
> 109)

VI. TYPES OF DIFFERENCES AMONG THEORIES

If we just consider those few metatheoretic distinctions made
above, we can characterize at least two different ways in which
theories of language can differ.[14] In the first case they can select
altogether different class 1 parameters. In this case the variables
which occur in the rules one constructed to explain linguistic
phenomena will be different. Of course, there will usually be
some overlap in the parameters chosen by various theories of
linguistics. However, in this first case to be discussed there is
some significant difference in the set of class 1 parameters
chosen by one theory as opposed to the set chosen by another
theory.

·   In the second case the set of class 1 parameters of one theory
is a proper subset of the set of class 1 parameters of another
theory. The usual way in which this relationship works is that
one theory derives a set of rules based on a certain set of

parameters. A second theory accepts these rules and then extends the theory by writing rules on the class 2 parameters of the first theory. That is, the second theory tries to account for the effects of parameters which the first theory dismissed as having only peripheral effects. In physics, for example, a theory which accounted for friction and air resistance would be such a theory.

Let's look first at theories which differ in their choice of class 1 parameters. There are very many theories at the moment in present-day linguistics which differ in the kinds of parameters which they feel are necessary to an adequate description of language. For example, for Hymes the social setting of language is not incidental to the description of language. For him parameters concerning the social relationships between the speaker and hearer are necessary for the rules which purport to describe language. As we have seen earlier in this chapter such variables are not dealt with in Chomsky's theory. Any empirical linguistic object which Chomsky looks at must, of course, include social facts about the speaker and hearer, but his theory does not include them as class 1 parameters. Chomsky says explicitly that his account of linguistic objects will be neutral with respect to the difference between the speaker and the hearer.

> To avoid what has been a continuing misunderstanding, it is perhaps worth while to reiterate that a generative grammar is not a model for a speaker or a hearer. It attempts to characterize in the most neutral possible terms the knowledge of the language that provides the basis for actual use of language by a speaker-hearer. (1965, p. 9)

When he says that he is going to account for the use of language by a speaker-hearer, he is explicitly eliminating the possibility of rules ranging over variables having to do with the relationship between speakers and hearers as separate theoretical categories because within his theory they are grouped in a single unified category. Chomsky's theory therefore explicitly excludes as variables a set of parameters which Hymes wants to use to write his rules. This conflict between the appropriate parameters for a theory is put perhaps most strongly when Chomsky declares:

> Linguistic theory is concerned primarily with an ideal speaker-listener, in a completely homogeneous speech-community. (1965, p. 3)

and Labov responds:

> Linguistic theory can no more ignore the social behavior of speakers
> of a language than chemical theory can ignore the observed properties
> of the elements. (1971, p. 213)

The fact that such differences exist, while interesting in itself, is of less concern than the question about what effect such differences have on the growth of knowledge about language. The resolution of these differences among theories of language is one way in which the knowledge about language can be increased. In order to reconcile or resolve such differences we first have to see how they function.

While there may be no set of principles for choosing class 1 parameters from the empirical data itself, once these parameters have been chosen their role in the construction and confirmation of the theory within which they function may be very different. In particular the choice of class 1 parameters can be seen as a kind of tentative hypothesis about the variables which can account for the properties of language or the choice can be regarded as a definition of the essential nature of language. Earlier in this chapter in a different context we discussed a similar ambiguity in Chomsky's use of "competence." This difference in the status of the class 1 parameters makes a significant difference in the ways theories which differ in the choice of class 1 parameters can interact.

Let's try to make this difference in status as clear as possible. The data about language does not present itself to the linguist in terms of parameters. The linguist chooses particular parameters, which he then uses to explain the data. This explanation will be a set of rules which accounts for variation in the data in a principled way. The choice of parameters cannot be formally derived from the data itself. However, this choice is not wholly arbitrary. On the one hand the linguist may see these choices as a kind of informed first guess as to which parameters will turn out to be necessary and sufficient for explaining linguistic phenomena. If the original assignment of class 1 parameters is viewed in this way, then evidence confirming or disconfirming the output of the rules on these parameters can easily be incorporated into the theory. If a chosen parameter does not function in rules which describe linguistic phenomena then it may be discarded; if a new parameter, not chosen originally, can be incorporated in a rule which describes linguistic phenomena then it may be added. Since any particular choice of class 1 parameters is only a tentative hypothesis about what will be necessary for a complete account of language, a change in parameters is easily incorporated into the theory.

On the other hand the original choice of class 1 parameters may be viewed not as a tentative hypothesis about parameters necessary for accounting for empirical data but rather as a statement of the essential characteristics of language. In this view the parameters are chosen because they reveal the *real* nature of language. Other parameters may superficially affect language, but they do not change what is really going on in language itself. Chomsky clearly sees the universal grammar as made up of the essential properties of language. For example in *Aspects* in a discussion of the inadequacies of previous grammars, he says:

> An essential property of language is that it provides the means of expressing indefinitely many thoughts and for reacting appropriately in an indefinite range of new situations. The grammar of a particular language, then, is to be supplemented by a universal grammar that accommodates the creative aspect of language use and expresses the deep-seated regularities which, being universal, are omitted from the grammar itself. Therefore it is quite proper for a grammar to discuss only exceptions and irregularities in any detail. It is only when supplemented by a universal grammar that the grammar of a language provides a full account of the speaker-hearer's competence. (1965, p. 6)

For Chomsky the essential properties of language are to be accounted for in the universal grammar. The properties of the universal grammar are necessarily found in generative grammars of particular languages. As he puts it:

> The study of linguistic universals is the study of the properties of any generative grammar for a natural language. Particular assumptions about linguistic universals may pertain to either the syntactic, semantic, or phonological component, or to interrelations among the three components. (1965, p. 28)

For Chomsky the universal grammar reflects the essential properties of language. These properties are ncessarily those which occur in the grammars of particular languages. If we recast this in the terminology of this chapter we would say that the universal grammar specifies the parameters which have to be used to account for empirical data about particular languages. Furthermore, these parameters, for Chomsky, captured the essential nature of language.

If this essentialist view is held toward the choice of class 1 parameters, then the difference between two theories which differ in the choice of class 1 parameters is incorrigible. Even if there is empirical evidence which indicates that a new parameter successfully accounts for linguistic variation, it need not, indeed it cannot, be incorporated into the theory. By definition the new parameter is accounting for a variation which is not essential for language. For example, Chomsky recognizes that Bever can successfully account for adjective order by using psychological parameters pertaining to heuristic strategies. The rules of TGG cannot account for adjective order. Chomsky says, however, that this does not mean that parameters on heuristic strategies should be added to the kinds of parameters linguistic rules can operate on. What it means is that a phenomenon (adjective order) that originally looked like it was explainable in terms of linguistic rules turns out to be explainable by non-linguistic rules. In other words, we were wrong about the nature of the phenomenon and not wrong about the nature of linguistic rules. A theory can be an adequate theory of language and not account for adjective order because adjective order is not really a linguistic phenomenon.[15]

It is clear that if two theories differ in the class 1 parameters which they choose and if, further, they hold essentialist interpretations of these choices, then there is no empirical evidence which can reconcile these theories. The investigation of parameters which are not part of the chosen set of class 1 parameters is considered to be misguided and uninteresting because it is not concerned with the essential characteristics of language. As we have pointed out earlier in this chapter, the choice of class 1 parameters indicates that kind of data which should be looked at. In the case of essentialist theories with different class 1 parameters, the phenomena investigated by the other group will be considered to be simply nonlinguistic phenomena and therefore, in principle, can have no effect on real linguistic theory.

The essentialist position claims that it knows what the nature of language is and therefore empirical phenomena which are accounted for by parameters not within the theory of language are simply not linguistic phenomena. The opposite is true of the view which holds that the choice of class 1 parameters is a tentative hypothesis to account for linguistic phenomena. In this case the claim is that the investigator knows what linguistic phenomena are and that the rules formulated on the class 1 parameters can be tested against this class of phenomena. Parameters must be chosen so that they account for all linguistic phenomena. If some linguistic phenomena is accounted for by parameters which are not yet in the theory, then they must be added to the theory. In the same way parameters in the theory which do not account for linguistic phenomena must be discarded.

If two theories differ in their choice of class 1 parameters from this point of view, they can be reconciled by looking at patterns of empirical confirmation. The usual case is where data which appears random within one theory is shown to be predictable within another theory. In linguistics today one-way random variation is expressed is via optional rules. An optional rule is a way of expressing the fact that two linguistic forms occur and that the occurrence of one or the other cannot be predicted. Within the theory the forms occur randomly. If linguistic phenomena which appear to be random in one theory can be predicted reliably within a different theory having different parameters, then these parameters should be added to the first theory so that its parameters will be sufficient to account for all variation.

Let us consider an example of this pattern of prediction from parameters. If we want to represent the pronunciation of /r/ in New York City within a transformational generative grammar we can do it in two different ways. We might represent each word having both an *r* and *r*-less pronunciation by two different underlying forms, one with an /r/ and one without an /r/. The speaker could optionally choose either underlying form and, following phonological rules, end up with corresponding *r* or r-less surface form. Or alternatively, we might choose one single underlying form[16] and then have an optional phonological rule which either deleted the /r/ in the case where the r variety was the underlying form or inserted the /r/ in the case where the r-less variety was the underlying form. We can, therefore, represent this situation by having either an optional choice between two different underlying forms or by having an optional rule which the speaker might or might not choose to use. In either case which choice the speaker makes is not determined, and therefore the resulting pattern of forms with and without the /r/ is random from the point of view of this theory.

If however we look at the same set of empirical events (i.e., the utterance of a given set of words by speakers in New York City) and add markers of social class to the set of class 1 parameters, then the events which look random from the point of view of TGG becomes predictable from the point of view of this new theory. Labov describes the relationship between social class and the pronunciation of /r/ by saying:

> It was found that the speech of most individuals did not form a coherent and rational system, but was marked by numerous oscillations, contradictions and alternations which were inexplicable in terms of a single idiolect. For this reason, previous investigators had described large parts of the linguistic behavior of New Yorkers as being a product of pure chance, "thoroughly haphazard." But when the speech of any one person in any given context was charted against the over-all pattern of social and stylistic variation of the community, his linguistic behavior was seen to be highly determined and highly structured. . . . We see that only one class group shows any degree of r-pronunciation in casual speech; that is, in every-day life, r−1 functions as a prestige marker of the highest ranking status group. The lower middle class shows only the same negligible amount of r-pronunciation as the working class and lower formal styles, the lower middle class shows a rapid increase in the values of /r/, until at Styles D and D', it surpasses the usage of the upper middle class. This cross-over pattern appears to be a deviation from the regularity of the structure shown by the other classes. To describe this phenomenon, the term HYPERCORRECTION will be used, since the lower middle class speakers go beyond the highest status group in their tendency to use the forms considered correct and appropriate for formal styles. (1966, pp. 85, 88)

Two theories which differ in class 1 parameters and hold the hypothetical interpretation of these parameters can interact by providing empirical evidence which follow this pattern. If the random data of one theory can be accounted for by rules on different parameters within another theory, then the two theories may be combined to form a new theory with broader explanatory power.[17]

The pattern described above is not the only pattern which would lead one theory to adopt the parameters of another theory. The second case we will consider is the case where a phenomenon which looks predictable within one theory can be shown to be random or have a different distribution within another theory. The usual cause of this is that the regularity is an artifact of the method of investigation and not of the phenomenon itself. As we said much earlier in this chapter, the method of investigation is influenced by the way in which the parameters are assumed to interact. However, in some cases the method of investigation *creates* regularity in the data rather than *tests* for such regularity.

An example of such a situation is the use of the linguist as an informant. In order to be able to use the linguist as an informant parameters such as the education of the speaker must not be class 1 parameters. That is, it must be assumed within the theory that education about language will not affect judgments of grammaticality. Under this assumption it is to be expected that judgments of linguists about grammaticality are representative of such grammaticality judgments in the population as a whole, because there is no parameter which distinguishes between linguists and everybody else. If such an assumption is wrong and if, as seems likely,[18] the linguist's education about language affects his judgments of grammaticality, then grammaticality judgments which are agreed on by linguists may be a result of their role as linguists rather than a result of regularities in the language.

The pattern of empirical evidence which argues for the inclusion of a new parameter into the theory of language in this case is the demonstration that the perceived regularity can be shown to be a result of the class chosen for investigation, and further that the assumption that this class was representative of some larger class can be shown to be false by means of the parameter in question.

Up until now we have been considering theories which differ in their choice of class 1 parameters. We have seen that these differences are often irreconcilable. There are other cases where certain patterns of evidence could argue for the inclusion of a new parameter in a theory. The problem is that the evidence in linguistics is rarely so conclusive and comprehensive that an alternate interpretation is not possible. Therefore, even in those cases where persuasion by means of empirical evidence is possible, it is often not practically feasible.

There is, as I have mentioned earlier in this section, another way in which theories may be related with respect to their choice of parameters. One theory may accept the rules written on the class 1 parameters of another theory and see its job as writing rules for some of the class 2 parameters of this other theory. In this way some of the class 2 parameters of one theory may become the class 1 parameters of another theory. These two theories share a large number of class 1 parameters and differ in that some class 2 parameters of one theory are class 1 parameters for the other theory.

There are many examples of this kind of relationship among scientific theories. For example, general genetic theory assumes the rules to be operating over unspecifiedly large populations. The genetic patterns arrived at by such studies do not always match the patterns observed in real populations. Therefore, theories have been developed which keep all of the rules of general genetics but investigate how such rules operate in a slightly different idealization in which populations are small. In physics, of course, technology has demanded that Galileo's idealization be expanded to include rules which cover air resistance and the shape of objects. Very often this investigation of class 2 parameters affects the earlier theory. The new investigation may provide insights about errors in the earlier rules or in the methodology of gathering evidence or in the assumptions about the way the parameters were related. In this way, while the investigation of class 2 parameters may start out to be a complementary activity to the investigation of class 1 parameters, the integration of the knowledge gained by this investigation into the earlier theory may require major changes in that theory. There are many examples of theories in linguistics which have this relationship.

For example, TGG has had this relationship with many theories investigating its class 2 parameters. As we have seen, TGG calls these parameters performance constraints. Chomsky, characteristically, believes that the only fruitful way a theory can be built to investigate these parameters is in the way we have just been discussing. That is, a theory which accounts for performance constraints must incorporate the rules on the class 1 parameters of TGG. In *Aspects* he considers the possibility of the investigation of rules written on the class 2 parameters based on psychological data.

> To my knowledge, the only concrete results that have been achieved and the only clear suggestions that have been put forth concerning the theory of performance, outside of phonetics, have come from studies of performance models that incorporate generative grammars of specific kinds—that is, from studies that have been based on assumptions about underlying competence. In particular, there are some suggestive observations concerning limitations on performance imposed by organization of memory and bounds on memory, and concerning the exploitation of grammatical devices to form deviant sentences of various types. (1965, p. 10)

He does not, in this section, consider an investigation of the class 2 parameters on sociological data, but presumably he would hold the same position toward those. What we would like to show is that the sociolinguistics of the Labovian school can be viewed as having this relationship to TGG.

The first question I would like to look at is the effects of such a relationship between theories on the empirical confirmation of the theories. As we have seen in the first section of this paper, the closeness of the empirical "fit" is partially dependent on the kind and number of class 2 parameters which are being ignored for the sake of the idealization. The difference between the values predicted by the rules of the theory and the actual empirically occurring values can be accounted for in three ways: either the difference is a result of the effects of class 2 parameters, or the difference is a result of measurement error, or the difference indicates that the rules of the theory are wrong. If the difference is due to the effect of class 2 parameters, then rules on these parameters should improve the closeness of fit of the empirical predictions. Writing rules on class 2 parameters can confirm a theory in two different ways. In the first place if rules on class 2 parameters do, in fact, improve the closeness of fit, then the original hypothesis that these parameters had some effect on the phenomena in question would be confirmed. It could of course turn out that a class 2 parameter which had been hypothesized to have an effect on the empirical data in fact had no such effect.[19] If, however, rules on class 2 parameters can be written, then the hypothesis is confirmed, and further, the functioning of this parameter is explicitly accounted for by a set of rules.

The conflict between the two theories arises about the significance of the findings and the place in the theory of these now-rule-governed class 2 parameters. Should they have the same importance in a new theory as all of the other class 1 parameters since they now function as variables in a set of rules, or should they still have a separate status as peripheral rules not really belonging to the major theory? If the second alternative is chosen, then these parameters are not a proper part of the account of the nature of the phenomena in question but rather are accounts of the *limitations which experience teaches us*. From this point of view the improvement in the closeness of fit of empirical prediction provided by these new rules does not raise the level of confirmation of the central theory itself. It only affects a subsidiary hypothesis about what kinds of parameters would account for the differences between predicted values and actual empirical values. While the fact that such rules can be written might in itself be interesting, they could in no way affect the central theory which, in principle, sees these parameters as essentially peripheral.

If the first alternative is chosen, then a new theory must be constructed in which the old class 2 parameters become class 1 parameters and in which the aspects of the phenomena which they account for are now seen as important for a complete account of the phenomena.

It is clear that Chomsky sees work on performance constraints (class 2 parameters) as subsidiary to the central theory. He says, for example: "The only studies of performance, outside of phonetics, are those carried out as a by-product of work in generative grammar (1965, p. 15). Labov, on the other hand, devotes almost all of his paper "The Study of Language in its

Social Context" to arguing that parameters about social data must be included in a theory of language and further that this theory of language should include the work done in TGG.

At the beginning of his paper Labov tries to put his work in perspective both with respect to its place in a general theory of language and with respect to its place in the history of linguistics. He says:

> This paper will deal with the study of language structure and evolution within the social context of the speech community. . . . If there were no need to contrast this work with the study of language out of its social context, I would prefer to say that this was simply linguistics. It is therefore relevant to ask why there should be any need for a new approach to linguistics with a broader social base. It seems natural enough that the basic data for any form of general linguistics would be language as it is used by native speakers communicating with each other in every-day life. Before proceeding, it will be helpful to see just why this has not been the case. (1971, p. 153)

Thus, he clearly claims that sociolinguistic variables must be included in a theory of language, as was not done in the past.

When we look at the kinds of rules which Labov uses to represent the individual instances of linguistic variation, it is clear that they are based on the descriptive formalisms developed within TGG, for example, distinctive features and transformations. Labov, in his article devoted to an argument against Chomsky's methodology, asserts explicitly that generative grammar should remain part of a theory of language. As he puts it:

> The limiting of our field of inquiry has certainly been helpful in the development of generative grammar—the working out of abstract models based upon our intuitive judgments of sentences. We cannot afford any backward steps: anyone who would go further in the study of language must certainly be able to work at this level of abstraction. (1971, p. 156).

Three things seem clear from Labov's point of view: first, that any theory of language must include parameters that range over social contexts; second, that the abstract linguistic analyses developed by TGG should be preserved; and third, that the study of these social contexts demands changes in testing procedures.

The first two of these points confirm the view that Labov sees his theory as requiring that some of Chomsky's class 2 parameters be incorporated into a new theory as class 1 parameters. If such new class 1 parameters were in fact added to the theory, then it is to be expected, as I have pointed out earlier, that they have an effect on the nature of the tests to which the theory might be subjected. For example, Labov questions the use of linguistic intuitions about acceptability[20] as a valid methodology for confirming linguistic hypotheses. He points out that Chomsky's original assumption that the great majority of the intuitive judgments of native speakers would be clear and unambiguous and only a few doubtful cases would remain which could then be decided by the theory itself has not worked out that way. Doubtful judgments abound even at points crucial to questions of grammatical theory. He asserts that "The two assumptions of the homogeneity and accessibility of language which led to this situation are seriously brought into question by this development" (1971, p. 160). After presenting the results of tests of intuitive judgments run on native speakers, Labov concludes:

> There is no evidence that consistent and homogeneous judgments can be obtained from native speakers on such crucial matters. . . . It is now evident that the search for homogeneity in intuitive judgments is a failure. Once this result is accepted, the strongest motivation for confining linguistic analysis to such judgments disappears. In many ways, intuition is less regular and more difficult to interpret, than what speakers actually say. If we are to make good use of speakers' statements about language, we must interpret them in the light of unconscious, unreflecting productions. Without such control, one is left with very dubious data indeed—with no clear relation to the communicative process we recognize as language itself. (1971, p. 162)

It has been claimed in this paper that changing class 2 parameters to class 1 parameters improves the closeness of empirical fit of the theory. Labov asserts that by following his program we not only would now look at "the basic data for any form of general linguistics [which is] language as it is used by native speakers communicating with each other in every-day life" (1971, p. 153), but also we would be able to have real empirical tests of linguistic hypotheses. For Labov the closeness of fit required by TGG is too loose to decide whether any set of empirical evidence is or is not a confirming instance:

> As a theory of language this approach is seriously defective, since it offers us no means of discovering whether our model is right or wrong. Originally, the generative grammar was constructed to produce all the acceptable sentences of the language and none of the unacceptable ones. But if we now compare the model with what speakers say, we cannot draw any decisive conclusions from the way it matches or fails to match the data. (1971, pp. 162–163)

He claims, however, that if we expand the theory by adding parameters on the social context, then linguistic hypotheses can be confirmed or disconfirmed by empirical evidence. In the discussion of "Hypercorrection as a Factor of Linguistic Change," he says:

> A great many discussions of linguistic structure have led to moot alternatives, and some writers have come to expect such impasses as a matter of principle. Others feel that the resolution of alternative theories must lie in arguments from simplicity, or symmetry, or other such abstract considerations, rather than conformity with empirical evidence. The point of view which lies behind the work reported here is that two theories are not different in any meaningful way if they both conform equally to the observable evidence. Sociolinguistic study provides us with a rich new vein of evidence that helps us to resolve disputes which would otherwise remain moot and meaningless. Suppose, for example, that a phonological analysis proposed a triangular system of this type:
>
> A
>
> B   C
>
> It might be argued that this is merely an arrangement of symbols on paper, and that we might equally well have a system in which A and B are parallel, and where C is the only low vowel. The distribution of variants within B and C should be helpful in resolving this question. If we find, for example, that the distributions of non-cognitive variants of the phonemes B and C are both concentrated at a higher point for the younger generation, as compared to the older generation (or for ethnic group Z as opposed to ethnic group Y), we have empirical evidence for the structural parallelism of B and C. (1966, p. 103)

From a more general point of view he concludes "The Study of Language in its Social Context" with the same point:

> The penalties for ignoring data from the speech community are a growing sense of frustration, a proliferation of moot questions, and a conviction that linguistics is a game in which each theorist chooses the solution that fits his taste or intuition. I do not believe that we need at this point a new "theory of language"; rather, we need a new way of doing linguistics that will yield decisive solutions. By enlarging our view of language, we encounter the possibility of being right: of finding answers that are supported by an unlimited number of reproducible measurements, in which the inevitable bias of the observer is cancelled out by the convergence of many approaches. . . . Within the framework provided, the solutions offered to the problems of consonant cluster simplification, copula deletion, and negative concord represent abstract relations of linguistic elements that are deeply embedded in the data. It is reasonable to believe that they are more than constructions of the analyst—that they are properties of language itself. The state of linguistics is indeed promising if we can assert this about any single result of our research. (1971, p. 213)

Labov is the major theorist of the position that TGG must be supplemented by rules on social context variables in order to both account for important aspects of linguistic data and to provide a closer empirical fit for confirmation of linguistic hypotheses. However, this position is echoed by other linguists. For Cedergren and Sankoff variable rules are an improvement over optional rules because they account for more details of the empirical data. In "Variable Rules: Performance as a Statistical Reflection of Competence," they say, for example:

> The notion of optionality fails to capture the nature of the systematic variation which exists even on the level of the grammar of a single individual. It does not permit the incorporation of relativity or covariation between the presence of certain features in the linguistic environment of a rule and the frequency of operation of the rule. The label "optional" fails to convey any information as to how the elements of the structural description of a rule favor or constrain its operation. Rather, use of this label implies that all such information is foreign to the COMPETENCE of the native speaker. . . . The analysis of speech behavior has repeatedly revealed that the possibilities represented by abstract optional rules are distributed in a reproducible and well-patterned way in a given speaker and in a given

speech community. Although performance may be considered only an approximate reflection of competence—because of statistical fluctuations in rule execution frequencies, and interference from physiological factors, memory limitations, and errors—it is difficult to escape the conclusion that those aspects of performance that are found to be thoroughly systematic in an individual and throughout a community are reflections of linguistic competence. (1974, pp. 333-334)

Though they want to use variable rules because such rules account for systematic variation, Cedergren and Sankoff see this work as a continuation of TGG. In the abstract of their paper, they describe their work by saying:

Competence is modeled in conventional generative terms, except that optional rules are assigned application probabilities as functions of the structure of the input strings, possibly depending on the extra-linguistic environment as well. (1974, p. 333)

Thus they see their work, at least in part, as a way of improving the empirical predictions of TGG by supplementing it by rules on variables of the social context.

VII. CONCLUSION

What I have tried to show in this paper is that the different positions taken by various theories of language cannot be resolved by empirical evidence alone. By looking at these conflicting theories from the point of view of the philosophy of science, we can see that many of the conflicts grow out of problems which are widespread in the construction of any empirical scientific theory. If we understand how theories can interact and how the idealization of the data affects this interaction, then we can see more clearly just where and how empirical evidence can affect theories of language. As we have seen, differences which grow out of essentialist beliefs about the nature of language are, in principle, not amenable to change by empirical evidence. However, other kinds of differences between theories can be affected by empirical evidence. I have tried to indicate here the patterns of evidence and their relation to levels of confirmation which would allow for the interaction of different theories. If we understand the ways in which some interaction can take place, then perhaps we can arrive at a broader and better-confirmed theory of language.

NOTES

1. The distinction which I am making here is similar to the distinction which Botha makes between internal and external evidence in chaps. 4 and 5 of *The Justification of Linguistic Hypothesis* (1973). He provides a good analysis of the kinds of rules which must be written to allow external hypotheses. My concerns here are somewhat different than his. I am concerned with showing that these distinctions depend on the particular kinds of idealizations of data which are established within the theory in question.

2. This is, of course, a simplification. Philosophers of science differ in many respects over what a scientific theory is. For the purposes of the distinction we want to make here this characterization is adequate.

3. Kuhn in the postscript to *The Structure of Scientific Revolutions* discusses at length the kinds of things which unite a group of workers into what he calls a "disciplinary matrix." This is a refinement of some of the range of meaning which ambiguous term *paradigm* had in the original version of the work.

4. In the chapter "The Nature of Normal Science" in *The Structure of Scientific Revolutions,* Kuhn provides a detailed description with copious examples from the history of science of intraparadigmatic assumptions and behavior.

5. In this chapter I am concerned with *inter*paradigmatic conflicts. For a very complete analysis of *intra*paradigmatic conflict within transformational generative grammar, see Botha (1973).

6. Though no formal rules for such choices can be construed, such activity is clearly not random. There may be heuristic devices which assist such choices; however, the rules for such choices are not part of the philosophy of science but rather are the provenance of the psychology of creativity.

7. In mechanics, for example, we might have class 1 = mass, class 2 = air resistance, class 3 = color of object.

8. This, of course, should not be viewed as a static situation. Theories are constantly being revised, and one of the ways this revision takes place is that parameters which are hypothesized to be class 1 parameters turn out to have only a minimal effect and therefore become class 2 parameters and vice versa.

9. This change will be fully documented in a three-volume history of relativity which Kuhn is now writing.

10. An interesting question, though not one which I will pursue here, is the empirical status of such entities.

11. The problem of what we mean when we say that a theory is confirmed is a knotty question in the philosophy of science. For example, the relationships among such concepts as verification, falsification, confirmation, probability, truth and falsity is complex, to say the least. I am side-stepping these problems here, but for one view of the way these concepts interact, see Popper's *The Logic of Scientific Discovery* (1968).

12. Another way in which such looseness of fit may be introduced is by the inaccuracy of the measuring instruments themselves. It is not always easy, however, to decide when the error is a measurement error and when it is due to assumptions of the theory itself.

13. While it is perfectly clear what we mean by a falsifying instance, it is not always clear how to decide when we have one. This point is an interesting point of conflict between Kuhn and Popper. For Popper the aim of a scientist should be to come up with a falsifying instance to his hypothesis because verifying instances do not add to our knowledge about the hypothesis in question. Kuhn argues that, while falsifying instances may in principle be possible, in practice they never occur within a theory. Possible falsifying instances within a theory are seen as unsolved problems. It is only when a new theory is accepted which solves these problems that they are seen as falsifying instances of the old theory.

14. Theories, of course, can differ in many ways. For example, they may differ in the kinds of formalisms which they use; however, I will not discuss these kinds of differences here.

15. Chomsky took this position in a seminar he gave at McGill in 1974.

16. The criteria one uses for choosing the underlying form is itself of theoretical interest. The meaning of such criteria as "naturalness," "ease of articulation," and "simplicity" is problematic, but we do not have time to consider these problems here.

17. There are many constraints on how theories can be put together to form a new theory. For example, in order for the results of two different theories to be conjoined to form a new theory, they must have compatible formalisms and methodological assumptions.

18. There is ample evidence that expectations affect perception. That is, if a framework is constructed that leads the subject to expect a certain outcome, then he may read that outcome into the data which is presented to him whether it is there or not. He will tend to see in the data what he expects to see. It would be very strange if linguists were immune to this mechanism. One would expect that their beliefs about what sentences *should* occur would influence their judgment of what sentences *do* occur.

19. This is obviously an informal conclusion because there is no way that the fact that no rule has been found can be interpreted to mean that no rule exists.

20. There is a terminological problem here. The intuitions which Labov is questioning here are, in Chomsky's terms, judgments of grammaticality, not acceptability. Chomsky asserts that there is a clear distinction between these terms and that "the notion of 'acceptable' is not to be confused with 'grammatical." (1965, p. 11).

REFERENCES

Botha, R. (1970) *The Methodological Status of Grammatical Argumentation.* The Hague: Mouton.

_____ (1973) *The Justification of Linguistic Hypotheses.* The Hague: Mouton.

Bright, W. (ed.) (1971) *Sociolinguistics.* The Hague: Mouton.

Cedergren, H. and D. Sankoff (1974) "Variable rules: Performance as a statistical reflection of competence." *Language*

Chomsky, N. (1965) *Aspects of the Theory of Syntax.* Cambridge, Mass.: M.I.T. Press.

_____ (1971) *Problems of Knowledge and Freedom.* New York: Random House.

_____ (1972) *Language and Mind.* New York: Harcourt Brace Jovanovich.

Derwing, B. (1973) *Transformational Grammar as a Theory of Language Acquisition.* Cambridge: At the University Press.

Fishman, J. (1971) *Advances in the Sociology of Language.* The Hague: Mouton.

Hymes, D. (1962) "The ethnography of speaking," in J. Fishman (ed.), *Readings in the Sociology of Language.* The Hague: Mouton.

Kahl, R. (ed.) (1963) *Studies in Explanation.* Englewood Cliffs, N.J.: Prentice-Hall.

Kuhn, T. (1962) *The Structure of Scientific Revolutions.* Chicago: University of Chicago Press.

Labov, W. (1966) "Hypercorrection by the lower middle class as a factor in linguistic change," in Bright (1971).

_____ (1971) "The study of language in its social context," in Fishman (1971).

Nagel, E. (1961) *The Structure of Science.* New York: Harcourt Brace Jovanovich.

_____, P. Suppes and A. Tarski (eds.) (1962) *Logic, Methodology and Philosophy of Science.* Stanford, Calif.: Stanford University Press.

Popper, J. (1963) *Conjectures and Refutations, The Growth of Scientific Knowledge.* London: Routledge & Kegan Paul.

_____ (1968) *The Logic of Scientific Discovery.* New York: Harper & Row.

Scheffler, I. (1963) *The Anatomy of Inquiry.* New York: Knopf.

10
Black English deep structure

Marvin D. Loflin
University of Nevada–Las Vegas

In this chapter I argue for an analysis of Black American English which leads to the conclusion that the grammars of Black American English (BAE) and Standard American English (SAE) have different deep structures. In particular, I argue for the claim that the BAE auxiliary system contains a specific set of deep structure constituents; since these constituents do not appear in any known analyses of SAE, it must be concluded that the grammars of BAE and SAE have different deep structures. If this is so, it follows that it is either false that all dialects of a language have the same deep structure or it is true that BAE is not a dialect of English; that is, it is a separate language.

The argument that the deep structure of BAE is different from that of SAE is based on an analysis of BAE auxiliaries which is in turn based on well-known methodological testing procedures in linguistics. In using such methodology, this study is differentiated from previous studies of BAE. Indeed, the testing and argument methodologies used in the analysis of BAE presented here must be the kind used in any future analyses of BAE, if those analyses are to be taken seriously.

In this discussion it is assumed that tests in general are operations specified for performance upon a definable object domain and that linguistic tests are operations specified for performance upon definable linguistic symbol strings.

Given that operations on an object domain are possible and that the selected operations demonstrate crucially that the objects upon which the operations are performed have properties and relations of certain kinds, tests as taxonomic procedures involve at least the following:

(i)   Isolation of a candidate object set;
(ii) Definition of the relevant operation or operations; and
(iii) Performance of the operation(s) on the candidate object in order to subclassify them and determine whether or not they possess the structures and relations presupposed by the tests.

Data objects representing unclear cases are subjected to the test and, depending on the results, pronounced in or out of the type defined by the test. An example of a linguistic test used as a taxonomic procedure is to be found in Lakoff and Ross (1966). They proposed a *do so* test which operated on definable symbol strings composed of two or more sentences and joined with "and" or "but." For example, consider the following sentence from Lakoff and Ross:

(1)   Harry forged a check, but Bill could never bring himself to forge a check.

If we assume that substitution is an operation and that (1) constitutes an instance of an object from an object data domain (specifically, it is two sentences joined by *but*) and that anything for which *do so* can be substituted in (1) is a verb phrase, we can systematically test for verb phraseness by substituting *do so* for all possible substrings of symbols in (1). For example, if we substitute *do so* for substrings in sentence (1), one acceptable result is (2). Thus,

(2)   Harry forged a check, but Bill could never bring himself to do so.

is a sentence resulting from the application of the *do so* test. Lakoff and Ross state that

> "do so" may be substituted only for a verb phrase containing a nonstative verb. Thus (8) cannot be derived from the structure underlying (7).
>
> (7)   Bill knew the answer, and Harry knew the answer too.
> (8)   *Bill knew the answer, and Harry did so too.

(Lakoff and Ross, 1966)

The intent is clear; Lakoff and Ross wish to subclassify verb phrases into different types in the context of a specifiable object domain, and they propose to do so using a *do so* test. Certain things are true of the Lakoff and Ross *do so* exercise; in particular, it meets all the conditions of a taxonomic test as set forth above. Specifically, symbol strings are designated that belong to the defined data domain, an operation is defined (or one that can be reduced to more primitive operations), and that operation is performed on unclear cases in order to subclassify them and determine whether or not they possess the structures and relations presupposed by the tests.

It is our contention that all theory construction in linguistics proceeds by means of these kinds of tests. Such tests are used to taxonomize and to set the limits of permissible generalization as defined by the operation or procedure. The goal of devising a test in theory construction is to find operations for ungeneralized-upon objects.

The activity of postulating interesting generalizations presupposes the selection of an object domain and the definition of operations that can be performed on the objects specified in the domain. We shall now use tests in analyzing the auxiliary structure of Black American English.

The data domain is a set of natural language sentences. Each natural language sentence is composed of constituent sentences. The sentences in the set have been placed in the set because they meet at least two conditions: (a) they were obtained from what were presumed to be speakers of Black American English; and (b) they are compound or complex or compound-complex sentences (see the Appendix). Our goal is to generalize on the auxiliary structure of BAE by specifying a set of operations that would appear to be performable on BAE auxiliary forms.

The test for interesting generalization is whether or not auxiliary forms cooccur across sentence boundaries. Any cooccurrence is presumed to be nonrandom and a reflection of meaning relationships at some level. For example, if two sentences are combinable by the operator *OR*, then their auxiliary structures are more related than if they are not combinable by the operator *OR*; the test for postulatable relationship then is susceptibility to *OR* combination. This is natural language *OR* use, not logical *OR* use. The goal is to define an operation which articulates an agreement or cooccurrence relationship between auxiliary forms and captures generalizations that coincide with BAE native speaker intuition. Since we are interested in finding a way to generalize on auxiliary structure, we have to ask, what operations (as captured by rules) can be performed on auxiliary structures and what is the data domain within which the postulated operations are applicable? For purposes of this inquiry exercise, our tests will be auxiliary agreement rules, that is, operations performable upon the data domain of multi-sentence sequences containing two auxiliary forms and joined by combining relationships of different kinds. More specifically, we plan to determine what kinds of generalizations are revealed by an operation of auxiliary agreement. The data domain to be tested is a set of BAE sentences that are combined by *OR*, *AND*, *BUT*, REL, and COMP. In effect, we are postulating a data domain, and hypothesizing that there is an agreement operation which can be specified for substrings of the data domain. Further, we wish to maintain that just as the Passive rule constitutes a test for NP-ness (that is, if and only if movement in passivation, then and only then an NP; or, if and only if susceptible to *do so* substitution, then and only then a verb phrase of type x); so also, if and only if cooccurrent with a range of auxiliary forms y, then and only then an auxiliary form of type x.

OR COMBINATIONS

In all the *OR* conjoinings in the data the deleted verb is assumed to have the same auxiliary structure as the undeleted verb. Five different auxiliary forms were found in the *OR*-conjoined sentence data:

find
got
been moppin
was makin
be

Using these data as evidence (see Data Set #1 in the Appendix), it must be acknowledged that *OR* conjoinings are highly constrained in the natural language sample usage. First, there are no sentences combined with *OR* which are totally dissimilar; second, all verbs in *OR* conjoinings are identical; third, all auxiliaries in *OR* conjoinings are identical; and fourth, in every *OR* combination one of the verbs and its associated auxiliary is reduced.

The only auxiliary form excluded from the data is *is* − V + *in*. It is presumed that this exclusion is an accident of the data and that the grammatical rules which state the cooccurrence relations obtaining between auxiliary forms across *OR* boundaries should embody the following hypothesis:

(3) Only sentences may be conjoined with *OR* which contain *identical* auxiliary forms.

Rule #1 Agreement Hypothesis #1:
** *OR* Auxiliary Agreement**

$$W - Aux - X - OR - Y - Aux_d - Z \Rightarrow$$
$$W - Aux - X - OR - Y - Aux - Z$$

Having proposed an *OR* agreement rule, we taxonomized auxiliary forms in *OR*-conjoined sentences by whether or not they met the conditions specified by the operations presupposed by the rule. We are seeking to generalize on auxiliary forms and are using agreement relations as the framework within which to seek generalizations; any new *OR* data which meets the conditions of being uttered by a native speaker of Black American English would force a reconceptualization of the *OR* Auxiliary Agreement rule. New data would change the details of the conceptualization, not the taxonomizing procedure for arriving at the conceptualization. In other words, the rule is changed to reflect what is discovered as a result of operating on objects that satisfy the conditions of the data domain.

This hypothesis suggests that in sentences disjunctively combined with *OR* what is predicated of time in those sentences must be identical. Because of the restricted nature of these facts many interesting issues are raised. For example, how do negatives enter into *OR* conjoinings? Are there alternate forms involving *either*, and are there other types of *OR* reductions and substitutions?

Whatever might serve as disconfirming evidence for an expanded data set, the hypotheses derived from these data can be disconfirmed by any combination of sentences conjoined by *OR* such that the auxiliary forms of the two sentences are different. However, unless it can be demonstrated that all possible combinations are realizable in natural language use, the procedure proposed here as a criterion for hypothesis formation will stand.

For the sake of convenience in the presentation of the remaining data and subsequent discussion, auxiliary forms will be labeled and abbreviated in the following way:

Data Set #2   Auxiliary Data Array

eat + $\emptyset$	= Generic	= GEN
eat + *ED*	= Perfective	= PERF
BEEN + eat + *IN*	= Indefinite past	= INDEFPAS
WAS + eat + *IN*	= Definite past	= DFPS
BE + eat + *IN*	= Atemporal	= A-TEMP
IS + eat + *IN*	= Present	= PRES

Further, let us assume, as an initial auxiliary hypothesis, that these forms are unstructured in the category subcomponent of a grammar and that the following rule reflects this:

Rule #2   Auxiliary Hypothesis #1

$$\text{Aux} \rightarrow \left\{ \begin{array}{l} \text{GEN} \\ \text{PERF} \\ \text{INDEFPAS} \\ \text{DFPS} \\ \text{A-TEMP} \\ \text{PRES} \end{array} \right\}$$

AND COMBINATIONS

The *AND* data which follows differs from the *OR* data in several ways: (a) there are many more auxiliary combinations possible; (b) in general, there are more accompanying pro-form substitutions; and (c) there is less meaning congruence between the *AND*-conjoined sentences than between the *OR*-conjoined sentences.

In these data (see Data Set #3), we find the following patterns:

Data Summary #1

GEN *AND* GEN
GEN *AND* PERF
GEN *AND* DFPS
GEN *AND* A-TEMP
*GEN *AND* PRES
*GEN *AND* INDEFPAS

In sentences conjoined by *AND*, the auxiliary forms PRES and INDEFPAS never cooccur with GEN, and the forms GEN, PERF, DFPS, and A-TEMP may.

Rule #3   Agreement Hypothesis #2:
      AND Auxiliary Agreement (GEN)

$$\text{W} - \text{GEN} - \text{X} - AND - \text{Y} - \text{Aux}_\text{d} - \text{Z} \Rightarrow$$

$$\text{W} - \text{GEN} - \text{X} - AND - \text{Y} - \left\{ \begin{array}{l} \text{GEN} \\ \text{PERF} \\ \text{DFPS} \\ \text{A-TEMP} \end{array} \right\} - \text{Z}$$

It would take any combination of sentences conjoined by
AND such that the auxiliary forms of the two sentences would
be GEN combined with PRES or INDEFPAS to disconfirm this
hypothesis. Further, given a sentence on the left containing a
GEN auxiliary, what must be true of the auxiliary in the
sentence on the right? Simply, it must be one of four forms—
GEN, PERF, DFPS, or A-TEMP. Thus, if we generate two-
sentence sequences and provide the second sentence with an
auxiliary dummy symbol, it is possible to substitute (that is,
perform the operation of substitution) the coocuring auxiliary
forms in the second sentence for the auxiliary dummy symbol.

Based on data from the *AND*-GEN corpus, we venture to
reformulate our auxiliary hypothesis:

Rule #4   Auxiliary Hypothesis #2

$$\text{Aux} \longrightarrow \left\{ \begin{array}{l} \text{PRES} \\ \text{INDEFPAS} \\ \text{NONINDEFPAS} \end{array} \right\}$$

$$\text{NONINDEFPAS} \longrightarrow \left\{ \begin{array}{l} \text{GEN} \\ \text{PERF} \\ \text{DFPS} \\ \text{A-TEMP} \end{array} \right\}$$

Now it is possible to reformulate Agreement Hypothesis #2:

Rule #5   Agreement Hypothesis #2a: *AND*
Auxiliary Agreement (GEN) Revised

$$W - \text{GEN} - X - AND - Y - \text{Aux}_d - Z \Rightarrow$$

$$W - \text{GEN} - X - AND - Y - \text{NONINDEFPAS} - Z$$

The category NONINDEFPAS is postulated in the category
subcomponent in order to provide a more general symbol in the
transformational rule. Notice that if the goal is to generalize on
auxiliary forms, and if one takes as facts the cooccurrence of

auxiliary forms in *AND*-combined sentences (that is, the data domain is the set of *AND*-combined sentences), and one assumes that warrant for a generalization is a generalized use in an operation (in this case, substitution for specifying agreement), and that generalized symbol constructs represent at least one form of interesting generalization, then the agreement operation reflected in Rule #5 (where the construct NONINDEFPAS is used to generalize on the set GEN, PERF, DFPS, A-TEMP) is a test as defined and used in this paper. To argue for use in a rule is to argue for a deep structure construct. NONINDEFPAS is used in a rule; it, therefore, is a deep structure construct. Unless a grammar of Standard American English contains this construct, it must be presumed to have a different deep structure.

In the next data set (see Data Set #4 in the Appendix), we find the following patterns:

Data Summary #2

PERF *AND* PERF
PERF *AND* GEN
PERF *AND* DFPS
*PERF *AND* PRES
*PERF *AND* INDEFPAS
*PERF *AND* A-TEMP

In sentences conjoined by *AND*, the auxiliary forms PRES, INDEFPAS, and A-TEMP never cooccur with PERF while PERF, GEN, and DFPS may.

Rule #6   Agreement Hypothesis #3: *AND*
**   Auxiliary Agreement (PERF)**

$$W - PERF - X - AND - Y - Aux_d - Z \Rightarrow$$

$$W - PERF - X - AND - Y - \begin{Bmatrix} PERF \\ GEN \\ DFPS \end{Bmatrix} - Z$$

The evidence needed to disconfirm this hypothesis is any combination of sentences conjoined by *AND* such that the auxiliary forms of the two sentences are PERF *AND* PRES or INDEFPAS or A-TEMP. Based on data from the *AND*–PERF corpus (Data Set #4), we venture to reformulate our auxiliary hypothesis.

Rule #7   Auxiliary Hypothesis #3

$$\text{Aux} \longrightarrow \left\{ \begin{array}{l} \text{PRES} \\ \text{INDEFPAS} \\ \text{NONINDEFPAS} \end{array} \right\}$$

$$\text{NONINDEFPAS} \longrightarrow \left\{ \begin{array}{l} \text{A-TEMP} \\ \text{TEMP} \end{array} \right\}$$

$$\text{TEMP} \longrightarrow \left\{ \begin{array}{l} \text{GEN} \\ \text{PERF} \\ \text{DFPS} \end{array} \right\}$$

And, this in turn makes it possible to reformulate Agreement Hypothesis #3.

Rule #8   Agreement Hypothesis #3a:
**   *AND* Auxiliary Agreement**
**   (PERF) Revised**

$$W - \text{PERF} - X - AND - Y - \text{Aux}_d - Z \Rightarrow$$

$$W - \text{PERF} - X - AND - Y - \text{TEMP} - Z$$

Once again, we postulate a symbol, in this case TEMP, in order to use that symbol in an operation of substitution in an agreement rule in order to generalize on relations between auxiliary forms across sentence boundaries. And, once again, usability in a rule is an argument for deep structure status. TEMP is usable in a rule; hence, it is a deep structure entity. And, again, unless the grammar of Standard English contains the same construct, it must be assumed that Black and Standard English possess different deep structures. In these data (see Data Set #5), we find the following patterns:

Data Summary #3

> DFPS *AND* DFPS
> DFPS *AND* GEN
> DFPS *AND* PERF
> *DFPS *AND* PRES
> *DFPS *AND* INDEFPAS
> *DFPS *AND* A-TEMP

In sentences conjoined by *AND*, auxiliary forms PRES, INDEFPAS, and A-TEMP never cooccur with DFPS while DFPS, GEN, and PERF do.

Rule #9   Agreement Hypothesis #4: *AND*
Auxiliary Agreement (DFPS)

$$W - DFPS - X - AND - Y - Aux_d - Z \Rightarrow$$

$$W - DFPS - X - AND - Y - \begin{Bmatrix} DFPS \\ GEN \\ PERF \end{Bmatrix} - Z$$

In line with Auxiliary Hypothesis #3, it is possible to reformulate Agreement Hypothesis #4 as:

Rule #10   Agreement Hypothesis #4a:
AND Auxiliary Agreement
(DFPS) Revised

$$W - DFPS - X - AND - Y - Aux_d - Z \Rightarrow$$

$$W - DFPS - X - AND - Y - TEMP - Z$$

Evidence required to disconfirm Hypothesis #4a would be any combination of sentences conjoined by *AND* such that the auxiliary forms of the two sentences are DFPS *AND* PRES or INDEFPAS or A-TEMP.

Based on data from our DFPS corpus, we see that we have no need for reformulate our auxiliary hypothesis. In fact, although each reformulation of our auxiliary hypothesis has given us more general symbols for use in our agreement rules, until this point we had no independent syntactic motivation for our hypothesis. However, now the hypothesis formulated to account for the PERF corpus is independently motivated by the DFPS corpus.

In these data (see Data Set #6), A-TEMP, PRES, INDEFPAS, and GEN do not cooccur with A-TEMP. Thus, we find the following patterns:

Data Summary #4

A-TEMP *AND* DFPS
A-TEMP *AND* PERF
*A-TEMP *AND* A-TEMP
*A-TEMP *AND* PRES
*A-TEMP *AND* INDEFPAS
*A-TEMP *AND* GEN

In sentences conjoined by *AND*, the auxiliary forms A-TEMP, PRES, INDEPAS, and GEN never cooccur with A-TEMP while DFPS and PERF do.

Rule #11   Agreement Hypothesis #5:
AND Auxiliary Agreement (A-TEMP)

$$W - \text{A-TEMP} - X - AND - Y - \text{Aux}_d - Z \Rightarrow$$

$$W - \text{A-TEMP} - X - AND - Y - \left\{ \begin{array}{c} \text{DFPS} \\ \text{PERF} \end{array} \right\} - Z$$

Evidence required to disconfirm Hypothesis #5 would be any combination of sentences conjoined by *AND* such that the auxiliary forms of the two sentences are A-TEMP *AND* A-TEMP or PRES or INDEFPAS or GEN.

Based on data from the *AND*– A-TEMP corpus, once again we venture to reformulate our auxiliary hypothesis.

Rule #12   Auxiliary Hypothesis #4

$$\text{Aux} \longrightarrow \left\{ \begin{array}{l} \text{PRES} \\ \text{INDEFPAS} \\ \text{NONINDEFPAS} \end{array} \right\}$$

$$\text{NONINDEFPAS} \longrightarrow \begin{array}{l} \text{A-TEMP} \\ \text{TEMP} \end{array}$$

$$\text{TEMP} \longrightarrow \begin{array}{l} \text{GEN} \\ \text{DEFPAS} \end{array}$$

$$\text{DEFPAS} \longrightarrow \begin{array}{l} \text{PERF} \\ \text{DFPS} \end{array}$$

Rule #13   Agreement Hypothesis #5a:
**   *AND* Auxiliary Agreement**
**   (A-TEMP) Revised**

$$\text{W} - \text{A-TEMP} - \text{X} - AND - \text{Y} - \text{Aux}_\text{d} - \text{Z} \Rightarrow$$
$$\text{W} - \text{A-TEMP} - \text{X} - AND - \text{Y} - \text{DEFPAS} - \text{Z}$$

BUT COMBINATIONS

In these data (see Data Set #7), we find the following patterns:

Data Summary #5

GEN *BUT* GEN
GEN *BUT* PERF
*GEN *BUT* DFPS
*GEN *BUT* A-TEMP
*GEN *BUT* INDEFPAS
*GEN *BUT* PRES

In sentences conjoined by *BUT*, the forms DFPS, A-TEMP, INDEFPAS, and PRES never cooccur with GEN, while GEN and PERF do.

Rule #14   Agreement Hypothesis #6: *BUT*
**   Auxiliary Agreement (GEN)**

$$\text{W} - \text{GEN} - \text{X} - BUT - \text{Y} - \text{Aux}_\text{d} - \text{Z} \Rightarrow$$

$$\text{W} - \text{GEN} - \text{X} - BUT - \text{Y} - \left\{ \begin{array}{l} \text{GEN} \\ \text{PERF} \end{array} \right\} - \text{Z}$$

Evidence required to disconfirm Hypothesis #6 would be any combination of GEN with DFPS or A-TEMP or INDEFPAS or PRES.

Given the present formulation of the auxiliary hypothesis, there is no way to satisfy both the *BUT*-GEN corpus and the *AND*-A-TEMP corpus. That is, if we examine Auxiliary Hypothesis #4, we note that the DEFPAS category rewrites as DFPS or PERF. This means that DFPS and PERF are in the grammatical category DEFPAS. However, the *BUT*-GEN data suggests that GEN and PERF should be in a different grammatical category, a fact requiring a reformulation of the auxiliary hypothesis which would contradict the formulation postulated to satisfy the category needs of DFPS and PERF in the *AND*-TEMP corpus.

What we have here is a cross-classification problem which might best be resolved by abandoning the category approach and adopting a syntactic feature system such as the one proposed to handle cross-classification in noun phrases (Chomsky, 1965).

Other possibilities also exist. For example, we might find independent motivation for one or the other of the hypotheses; such motivation would sway the description to favor the appropriate analysis. A third alternative is to find additional cooccurrence relations such that the conflict is removed because the evidence increases the class of cooccurring objects and makes it similar to one of the other categories. It should be noted, however, that regardless of whether the correct analysis is in terms of features or nodes, the properties which the features or nodes represent are deep structure properties of BAE.

In these data (see Data Set #8), we find:

Data Summary #6

PERF *BUT* PERF
PERF *BUT* DFPS
PERF *BUT* GEN
*PERF *BUT* A-TEMP
*PERF *BUT* PRES
*PERF *BUT* INDEFPAS

PERF occurs only with PERF, DFPS, and GEN. It does not

occur with A-TEMP, PRES, or INDEFPAS. Thus, evidence required to disconfirm Hypothesis #7 would be conjoined sentences in which PERF combines with A-TEMP, PRES, or INDEFPAS.

Rule #15 Agreement Hypothesis #7: *BUT*
Auxiliary Agreement (PERF)

$$W - PERF - X - BUT - Y - Aux_d - Z \Rightarrow$$

$$W - PERF - X - BUT - Y - \begin{Bmatrix} PERF \\ DFPS \\ GEN \end{Bmatrix} - Z$$

And, it is possible to reformulate Agreement Hypothesis #7 to make use of categories provided by Auxiliary Hypothesis #3 (Rule #7):

Rule #16 Agreement Hypothesis #7a:
BUT Auxiliary Agreement
(PERF) Revised

$$W - PERF - X - BUT - Y - Aux_d - Z \Rightarrow$$
$$W - PERF - X - BUT - Y - TEMP - Z$$

We now see that Auxiliary Hypothesis #3 wherein a category, TEMP, is postulated not only describes the facts of the *AND-PERF* corpus, and the *AND*-DFPS corpus but also the *BUT-PERF* corpus. Thus, Auxiliary Hypothesis #3 is independently motivated by three different corpora. Not only is Auxiliary Hypothesis #3 justified through the independent motivation described, but it also captures generalizations in its provision of input categories for transformational rules. In the presentation, each successive reformulation of the auxiliary hypothesis provided structure which increased the possibility for generality in the transformational rules. Aside from the possibility of describing the auxiliary using features, a task which should be explored, we have demonstrated that categories in the category formulation in Auxiliary Hypothesis #4 are independently justified. This independent motivation argues for the correctness of the rules. As used here, to provide independent motivation is to demonstrate that generalizations holding for more narrow domains of data also hold for more extended data domains.

SUMMARY OF RULES

(1)   Auxiliary Hypothesis for Black American English

$$\text{Aux} \longrightarrow \begin{Bmatrix} \text{PRES} \\ \text{INDEFPAS} \\ \text{NONINDEFPAS} \end{Bmatrix}$$

$$\text{NONINDEFPAS} \longrightarrow \begin{Bmatrix} \text{A-TEMP} \\ \text{TEMP} \end{Bmatrix}$$

$$\text{TEMP} \longrightarrow \begin{Bmatrix} \text{GEN} \\ \text{DEFPAS} \end{Bmatrix}$$

$$\text{DEFPAS} \longrightarrow \begin{Bmatrix} \text{PERF} \\ \text{DFPS} \end{Bmatrix}$$

(2)   Auxiliary Cooccurrences in Conjunction

   a.   *OR*

$$\text{W} - \text{Aux} - \text{X} - OR - \text{Y} - \text{Aux}_\text{d} - \text{Z} \Rightarrow$$
$$\text{W} - \text{Aux} - \text{X} - OR - \text{Y} - \text{Aux} - \text{Z}$$

   b.   *AND*

$$\text{W} - \begin{bmatrix} \text{GEN} \\ \begin{Bmatrix} \text{PERF} \\ \text{DFPS} \end{Bmatrix} \\ \text{A-TEMP} \end{bmatrix} - \text{X} - AND - \text{Y} - \text{Aux}_\text{d} - \text{Z} \Rightarrow$$

$$W - \begin{bmatrix} GEN \\ \begin{Bmatrix} PERF \\ DFPS \end{Bmatrix} \\ A\text{-}TEMP \end{bmatrix} - X - AND - Y - \begin{bmatrix} NONINDEFPAS \\ TEMP \\ DEFPAS \end{bmatrix} - Z$$

c. *BUT*

$$W - \begin{bmatrix} GEN \\ PERF \end{bmatrix} - X - BUT - Y - Aux_d - Z \Rightarrow$$

$$W - \begin{bmatrix} GEN \\ PERF \end{bmatrix} - X - BUT - Y - \begin{bmatrix} \begin{Bmatrix} GEN \\ PERF \end{Bmatrix} \\ TEMP \end{bmatrix} - Z$$

REL AND COMP COMBINATIONS

We now turn to auxiliary cooccurrences in matrix and constituent sentences where the constituent sentences are relativizations (Data Set #9) and *that*-complements (Data Set #10). We will argue that the interpreted facts provide independent motivation for the auxiliary hypothesis in rule (1) of the Summary of Rules above as reflected in auxiliary agreement rules (2a, b, c), as well as Rules #17 and #18 below. The REL data (Data Set #9) is reducible to the Data Summary #7.

Data Summary #7

GEN REL GEN
GEN REL PERF
DFPS REL GEN
PERF REL GEN
PERF REL DFPS

Thus, every instance of an auxiliary in a matrix sentence in these data is dominated by TEMP and every instance of an auxiliary in an associated relative is also dominated by TEMP. That is, the TEMP category rewrites as GEN or DFPS or PERF. In effect, if either a GEN or DFPS or PERF, then a TEMP, and, if a TEMP, then either GEN, DFPS, or PERF. A cooccurrence hypothesis would be:

Rule #17   REL Auxiliary Agreement

$$W - TEMP - X - Y - Aux_d - Z \Rightarrow$$
$$W - TEMP - X - Y - TEMP - Z$$

It is apparent that the auxiliary hypothesis for BAE given in the Summary of Rules above provides the categories to formulate this cooccurrence statement without requiring that additional structure be postulated. Thus, the auxiliary hypothesis growing out of a consideration of conjoined data is independently motivated by the formulation needed to describe agreement relations between auxiliaries in matrix and constituent sentences where the constituent sentence is a relative.

The COMP data (Data Set #10) reduces to the following:

Data Summary #8

GEN COMP GEN
GEN COMP PERF
GEN COMP DFPS
GEN COMP A-TEMP
GEN COMP PRES

PERF COMP GEN
PERF COMP PERF

A-TEMP COMP GEN

PRES COMP PRES

Once again, making use of the categories available in the auxiliary hypothesis, we obtain the following rules to represent COMP agreement relations:

Rule #18   COMP Auxiliary Agreement

$$W - \begin{bmatrix} \text{GEN} \\ \text{PERF} \\ \text{A-TEMP} \\ \text{PRES} \end{bmatrix} - X - that_c - Y - \text{Aux}_d - Z \Rightarrow$$

$$W - \begin{bmatrix} \text{GEN} \\ \text{PERF} \\ \text{A-TEMP} \\ \text{PRES} \end{bmatrix} - X - that_c - Y - \begin{bmatrix} \left\{ \begin{matrix} \text{NONINDEFPAS} \\ \text{PRES} \end{matrix} \right\} \\ \text{TEMP} \\ \text{GEN} \\ \text{PRES} \end{bmatrix} - Z$$

It is crucial to note the congruence of cooccurrence relations for the conjoining rules and the relativization and complement rules. Almost any other auxiliary hypothesis would have increased the number of symbols required to construct the structural descriptions and changes in these rules.

Thus, not only does this auxiliary hypothesis capture generalizations for the conjoining structures and the REL/COMP structures separately, but it also provides an analysis which suits the needs of both sets of rules. There is then some reason for the auxiliary structure given here: The auxiliary structure contributes to two sets of transformational rule statements which state the cooccurrence relations between conjoined, relative, and *that*-complement sentences and whose formulation is more simple and more general because of that auxiliary structure.

If a test is an operation which is performed on objects with the goal of revealing to the investigator something about the test objects, then the test must represent an hypothesis about the nature of the objects. Because of the tests I have proposed here, I have hypothesized that something importantly true of auxiliary structures is that they cooccur in multi-sentence sequences; that generalizations about them are to be determined from facts about their cooccurrence; that a single hypothesis can account for a great many different kinds of sentence combination facts; that, given the information that the first auxiliary in a string is of a certain type, subsequent auxiliaries are predictable; and so on. On the basis of these considerations, I have argued that Black American English and Standard American English have different deep structures.

A brief comparison of the methodology used here with that used in any standard transformational analysis (cf. Rosenbaum, 1967) should make it clear that they are both one and the same type. More importantly, the use of such methodology has yielded an analysis which has interesting theoretical implications. It leads to the conclusion that BAE and SAE have different deep structures, which in turn bears on the more general theoretical question of how dialect and language differences are to be formally characterized and explained. Indeed, it is *only* by using such methodology in investigations of BAE (and language variation in general) that such issues as the proper characterization of linguistic differences can be resolved.

APPENDIX

Data and Rule Labels

Data Set #1	*OR*
Rule #1	*OR* Auxiliary Agreement
Data Set #2	Auxiliary Data Array
Rule #2	Auxiliary Hypothesis #1
Data Set #3	GEN Cooccurrences with *AND*
Data Summary #1	Summary of Data Set #3
Rule #3	*AND* Auxiliary Agreement (GEN)
Rule #4	Auxiliary Hypothesis #2
Rule #5	*AND* Auxiliary Agreement (GEN) Revised
Data Set #4	PERF Cooccurrences with *AND*
Data Summary #2	Summary of Data Set #4
Rule #6	*AND* Auxiliary Agreement (PERF)
Rule #7	Auxiliary Hypothesis #3
Rule #8	*AND* Auxiliary Agreement (PERF) Revised
Data Set #5	DFPS Cooccurrences with *AND*
Data Summary #3	Summary of Data Set #5
Rule #9	*AND* Auxiliary Agreement (DFPS)
Rule #10	*AND* Auxiliary Agreement (DFPS) Revised
Data Set #6	A-TEMP Cooccurrences with *AND*

Data Summary #4	Summary of Data Set #6
Rule #11	*AND* Auxiliary Agreement (A-TEMP)
Rule #12	Auxiliary Hypothesis #4
Rule #13	*AND* Auxiliary Agreement (A-TEMP) Revised
Data Set #7	GEN Cooccurrences with *BUT*
Data Summary #5	Summary of Data Set #7
Rule #14	*BUT* Auxiliary Agreement (GEN)
Data Set #8	PERF Cooccurrences with *BUT*
Data Summary #6	Summary of Data Set #8
Rule #15	*BUT* Auxiliary Agreement (PERF)
Rule #16	*BUT* Auxiliary Agreement (PERF) Revised
Data Set #9	TEMP Cooccurrences with REL
Data Summary #7	Summary of Data Set #9
Rule #17	REL Auxiliary Agreement
Data Set #10	Cooccurrences with COMP
Data Summary #8	Summary of Data Set #10
Rule #18	COMP Auxiliary Agreement

Data Set #1 *OR*

(1) a. If mother or somebody find out ... = the sentence given by the informant
  b. Mother (find out) } = the presumed source sentences
  c. Somebody find out } for (1) (a)

(2) a. He got in a fight or somethin
  b. He got in a fight
  c. (He got in) somethin

(3) a. I been moppin ... every ... three or four times a week
  b. I been moppin ... three (times a week)
  c. (I been moppin ...) four times a week

(4) a. I was makin noise or somethin
  b. I was makin noise
  c. (I was makin) somethin

(5) a. She be dere in fifteen or twenty minutes
  b. She be dere in fifteen (minutes)
  c. (She be dere in) twenty minutes

Data Set #2 · Auxiliary Data Array

eat + $\emptyset$	= Generic	= GEN
eat + *ED*	= Perfective	= PERF
BEEN + eat + *IN*	= Indefinite past	= INDEFPAS
WAS + eat + *IN*	= Definite past	= DFPS
BE + eat + *IN*	= Atemporal	= A–TEMP
IS + eat + *IN*	= Present	= PRES

Data Set #3   GEN Cooccurrences with *AND*

(6) a. We jus sit dere and talk
     b. We jus sit dere
     c. (We jus) talk

(7) a. I sit dere and looked at him go
     b. I sit dere
     c. (I) looked at him go

(8) a. I bust a egg and I was gitin ready to cook it
     b. I bust a egg
     c. I was gitin ready to cook it

(9) a. I come by dis place and it be dese men in there
     b. I come by dis place
     c. It be dese men in there

Data Set #4   PERF Cooccurrences with *AND*

(10) a. Dese men had a rope and dey wind all four of deirselves up
     b. Dese men had a rope
     c. Dey wind all four of deirselves up

(11) a. He went to camp and my mother told me to write him
     b. He went to camp
     c. My mother told me to write him

(12) a. My father came and I was ready
     b. My father came
     c. I was ready

Data Set #5   DFPS Cooccurrences with *AND*

(13) a. They was talkin and you say
      b. They was talkin
      c. You say

(14) a. Some boys was playin and they betted a lot of money
      b. Some boys was playin
      c. They betted a lot of money

(15) a. I was washin and sleepin
      b. I was washin
      c. (I was) sleepin

Data Set #6   A–TEMP Cooccurrences with *AND*

(16) a. You be talkin to somebody and they was talkin all loud
      b. You be talkin to somebody
      c. They was talkin all loud

(17) a. They be quiet and I won
      b. They be quiet
      c. I won

Data Set #7   GEN Cooccurrences with *BUT*

(18) a. I think his son go to Paul, but I think . . .
      b. I think his son go to Paul
      c. I think . . .

(19) a. I do, but he threw somethin at me
      b. I do
      c. He threw somethin at me

Data Set #8   PERF Cooccurrences with *BUT*

(20) a. We walked across the street but then here come J-six
      b. We walked across the street
      c. Then here come J-six

(21) a. He got it before his birthday but he got it for his birthday
   b. He got it ...
   c. He got it ...

(22) a. I said "dude" to Pee Wee but I was talkin about the girl
   b. I said ...
   c. I was talkin ...

Data Set #9   TEMP Cooccurrences with *REL*

(23) An you *know* cat da us'lly *carry* all de key? GEN:GEN
(24) I *got* a frin name Abraham da *broke* 'is arm. GEN:PERF
(25) He was singin "Luv," a reco'd, da reco'd he *know* call "Luv." DFPS:GEN
(26) I *seen* one boy look like, *look* like his son aroun here. PERF:GEN
(27) An so we saw one, we *saw* a couple of dead bodies da *were* over dere da fell off a cliff. PERF:DFPS

Data Set #10   Cooccurrences with *COMP*

GEN Cooccurrences

(28) She always *tell* everbody she beat me three games. GEN:GEN
(29) An he *say* dey *had* it in de window. GEN:PERF
(30) I *mean* it *was* after nine o'clock. GEN:DFPS
(31) Ey *say* dey *be* countin up you food, man, see how much you ha. GEN:A-TEMP
(32) You *know* da your frien's *are* givin you a bad mark, make you git a bad mark. GEN:PRES

PERF Cooccurrences

(33) An so de man *tol* my muvah she *need* a new starter. PERF:GEN
(34) So he *said* I *did* it n I ain't do it. PERF:PERF

A–TEMP Cooccurrence

(35) Ev'rytime I *come* over to my granmuvah house, she *be* washin. A-TEMP:GEN

PRES Cooccurrence

(36) De man *is signifyin* da da boat *is bein* attack. PRES:PRES

REFERENCES

Chomsky, N. (1965) *Aspects of the Theory of Syntax.* Cambridge, Mass.: M.I.T. Press.

Lakoff, G. (1968) "Instrumental adverbs and the concept of deep structure." *Foundations of Language* 4:4–29.

——, and J. R. Ross (1966) "A criterion for verb phrase constituency," in A. Oettinger (ed.), *Mathematical Linguistics and Automatic Translation.* Cambridge, Mass.: Harvard University Press.

Loflin, M. D. (1970) "On the structure of the verb in Nonstandard Negro English." *Linguistics* 59:14–28.

—— (1969) "Negro Nonstandard and Standard English: Same or different deep structure?" *Orbis* 18:74–91.

Macauley, R. K. S. (1970) "Review of Wolfram's *A Sociolinguistic Description of Detroit Negro Speech.*" *Language* 46:764–773.

Rosenbaum, P. S. (1967) "Phrase structure principles of English complex sentence formation." *Journal of Linguistics* 4:103–118.

Wolfram, W. A. (1969) *A Sociolinguistic Description of Detroit Negro Speech.* Washington, D.C.: Center for Applied Linguistics.

AUTHOR INDEX

SUBJECT INDEX